Modern Principles of
PHYSICAL EDUCATION

PHYSICAL EDUCATION SERIES
EDUCATION AND TRAINING OF TEACHERS

BY JACKSON R. SHARMAN, Ph.D.

PROFESSOR OF HEALTH AND PHYSICAL EDUCATION
HEAD OF THE DEPARTMENT OF HEALTH AND PHYSICAL EDUCATION
UNIVERSITY OF ALABAMA

INTRODUCTION TO PHYSICAL EDUCATION

A PHYSICAL EDUCATION WORKBOOK

THE TEACHING OF PHYSICAL EDUCATION

MODERN PRINCIPLES OF PHYSICAL EDUCATION

MODERN
PRINCIPLES OF
PHYSICAL EDUCATION

JACKSON R. SHARMAN, Ph.D.

PROFESSOR OF HEALTH AND PHYSICAL EDUCATION
HEAD OF THE DEPARTMENT OF HEALTH AND PHYSICAL EDUCATION
UNIVERSITY OF ALABAMA

A. S. BARNES AND COMPANY, INC. · NEW YORK

Printed in the United States of America

DEDICATED TO MY STUDENTS
AT THE
UNIVERSITY OF MICHIGAN

Preface

∾

MANY OF THE professional courses that are ordinarily taken by physical education students deal largely with the techniques of organization, administration, management, and teaching. Practical material of these kinds is valuable and necessary, but all teachers should be familiar at the outset with the philosophy and principles underlying physical education in order that they may gain a general comprehension and unified view of the entire subject.

This book is intended to give upper-division college students and others who might be interested a broad general view of the philosophy on which the present-day program of physical education is based. The principles discussed are thoroughly up-to-date and are based on recent evidence from biology, psychology, sociology, and education. The application of the philosophy proposed will result in a program of physical education suited to conditions that exist in our modern civilization. It must be recognized that there can be no final statement of a philosophy of physical education, because as society changes and people modify their fundamental concepts the accepted aims and values of physical education must change.

The generally accepted democratic philosophy of education has been emphasized throughout this textbook. It seems clearly evident that the majority of American citizens still have faith in a democratic society and intend to maintain that form of social organization. It is appropriate, therefore, that all parts of our program of public education should be designed to prepare on-coming generations for successful living in a democratic society.

In the organization of this book the first two chapters are intended to show how the American program of physical education evolved, and the conflicting viewpoints that still exist. The next five chapters set forth some of the evidence from biology, sociology, psychology, education, and philosophy, on which the principles of physical education are based. The last four chapters apply the principles to the problems of the curriculum, leadership, method, and administration.

The author wishes to make grateful acknowledgment to the many authors and publishers whose publications are quoted.

Acknowledgment is made also of the valuable assistance of MR. WARREN R. GOOD in the preparation of the manuscript.

JACKSON R. SHARMAN.

Ann Arbor
March, 1937

CONTENTS

∽

CHAPTER I

The Background and Province of Physical Education

∾

The function of principles. Principles are essential to successful teaching on a professional level. Teachers who are ignorant of educational principles are tradesmen who, of necessity, must follow fixed, rule-of-thumb procedures. They may have command of, and be expert in the application of certain definite techniques; but they lack the breadth of vision and understanding which is necessary in order that they might modify the program content and the teaching methods as the conditions of society and needs of individual children change. Well-stated principles help to indicate the desired end or destination of the teaching process, and also serve as guide posts along the way; without a knowledge of them it is difficult for a teacher to define the outcomes he wishes to achieve, to select the activities to be used in achieving these outcomes, and to choose the most suitable methods of teaching the activity. It follows, therefore, that every teacher should have command of the principles of physical education and should be familiar with the data from the various fields of human knowledge on which the principles are based.

An understanding of the historical development and contemporary purposes of physical education is of basic importance to a teacher in planning and executing a school program of physical education. One is enabled to formulate a defensible theory of education and statement of guiding principles on the basis of information of this kind when it is combined with data on the biological background of man, the nature of society, the characteristics of the learning process, the school curriculum, the composition of the group of professional leaders, and the approved methods of teaching and administration.

The development of physical education. The development of the school program of physical education in this country has progressed rapidly during the few decades since it was first introduced as a regular part of the curriculum. In large numbers of situations the progress has seemed slow—in some instances, almost reversed—to the individual teachers concerned with the immediate problems in the schools, but in viewing the country as a whole it can readily be seen that great progress has been made along such important lines as legislation, finance, curriculum construction, teacher preparation, facilities, time allotment, and teaching staff.

Many things have contributed to this development; it did not occur merely as the result of chance or through the efforts of enthusiastic promoters. The most basic of these causes include the fundamental changes and conditions that have taken place very rapidly in American society. Some of the significant social influences include the changes in home and family life, the mechanization of industry and agriculture, the urbanization of the population, the growth of metropolitan areas around cities, the passing of the frontier and a modification of the "frontier philosophy," the increase in leisure time for large numbers of people, the improvement in the standards of living, the emphasis on child health, the decline in the birthrate, and the spread of the idea of universal public education for all the children of all the people.

Social changes and developments such as these created new demands on the schools which, in most cases, attempted to meet the challenge by adding new subjects to the school curriculum. Each of these subjects no doubt contains much valuable material and has made worthwhile contributions to the education of children. But this procedure has resulted in a school curriculum divided into compartments, a development which has had the effect of making it difficult, and in some cases almost impossible, for the school program to be of real help to pupils in the solution of problems that confront them in their daily living. The justifiable criticism has been made that the school and the social order are too far apart; that the things children learn in school are useful in only a restricted and limited way, in helping them to understand contemporary social problems. It has been pointed out that children in school do not have adequate opportunities to become familiar with the prejudices, creeds, and problems of an economic, social, religious, and political nature that confront people who are living in the world of real affairs. The school and life must be brought closer together.

As an expediency to meet new demands on the schools, physical education has been included as a subject in the school program in the same compartmentalized manner as other new courses, without any intelligently planned effort to reconstruct the curriculum. This development has tended to establish the idea that physical education is a "special" subject and that teachers of physical education are coaches and special teachers. It has also caused teachers and laymen to think of the aims

[2]

and objectives of physical education as being different from those of education in general.

Other influences besides social changes have helped to shape the American program of physical education. Among these are (1) programs of physical education in foreign countries, (2) the dominant social philosophy of America, (3) the philosophical and psychological theories held by educational leaders, (4) the war spirit at different periods, and (5) movements which have become prominent at different times, such as the playground movement and the widespread interest in camping.

The influence of European programs. Physical education as practiced in some European countries, including particularly gymnastics and sports, has contributed greatly to the content and emphasis of physical education in America. Chief among these influences have been the importations from Germany, Sweden, and England. Physical education in Denmark has attracted considerable attention in this country, but apparently it has not had much influence on our program. Systems of gymnastics and an emphasis on organized class instruction have been the main contributions of the Germans and Swedes. Such sports and games as football and tennis, and an emphasis on recreation and play, have come to us largely by way of England.

The athletic and play activities have made a much stronger appeal to Americans and have been much more popular than gymnastics. Some writers have attributed this to the fact that we have been a nation of pioneers and frontiersmen to whom vigorous competitive sports naturally appealed. It has also been pointed out that the background and traditions of American civilization are English to a considerable extent, and that the majority of our young people have absorbed the spirit and interest in sports from the dominant social and political ideals. Games seem to be clearly more appropriate and appealing to a nation where democracy is emphasized as a political creed, and valued also as a principle in social and economic affairs.

The development of public education. The fundamental social and political philosophy underlying public education in America and the development of our great system of public schools which are open to all the children of all the people have had a significant influence on the development of physical education at different periods in the history of the nation. The attempt to provide free public education for all children, from the nursery school and kindergarten through college, is peculiarly American and is the result largely of the democratic ideal of equality

[3]

of opportunity. The ideals concerning public education which have been ascendent throughout the history of American education were expressed first in Massachusetts and other New England colonies. It was here that the first formal legislation was enacted for the public support and control of education.

In most communities throughout the country, schools were established to provide children with knowledge and skills in the elementary tools of learning. The home, farm, forests, church, and other factors in their environment provided the rest of their education. In most states, the state constitutions recognized education as a function and responsibility of the state; but since the country was sparsely settled and means of transportation and communication were inadequate, the states in most cases delegated the responsibility of education to the individual communities. During the past few decades, since the states have become more thickly settled and society has become more complex, there has been a distinct tendency for responsibility and authority in education to become more highly centralized in the state governments. Concurrently with this development there have been employed state directors of physical education by approximately twenty state departments of education in the larger, more populous, and progressive states. In some states the division of physical education in the state department of education has a staff of several professionally trained educators.

Some of the developments in the history of public education which have been significant in the growth of physical education are (1) the support of education by public taxation, (2) the establishment of the Latin grammar school, (3) the academy, (4) the development of high schools, (5) compulsory education, and (6) the development of an organized philosophy of education.

The beginning of public support for education in America. Public support and control of education in America was first provided by formal legislation in the Massachusetts Bay Colony in 1647. In that year was passed the now famous "old deluder Satan" act. This law made it mandatory on every township containing fifty householders to provide a teacher for the children, and required every town of 100 families to set up a grammar school with a teacher qualified to prepare the youth for admission to the university. Any town which failed to provide schools as required by this act was penalized by being required to pay five pounds (about twenty-five dollars) each year to the school nearest it.

[4]

This legislation was largely the result of the religious interests and convictions of the people of New England. During the early days of this country the church and the state consisted of the same people and the leaders were the same in both. Hence, there was not the clear-cut distinction and differentiation between the two that has since developed and been universally recognized. The citizens of colonial New England placed emphasis on the development of the ability to read and interpret the Bible, and on bringing up children in the faith of their fathers. The Latin grammar schools which were required by the act of 1647 provided a narrow type of education which was suited to the needs, interests, and abilities of a relatively small number of boys. Their main purpose was to prepare boys to understand and speak Latin and to decline Greek nouns and verbs, so as to meet the entrance requirements of Harvard, which was founded in 1636 and was the only institution of collegiate grade in America at the time.

These schools did not meet a widespread need in America and apparently were never popular with the majority of the people. In 1787 and in 1824 laws were passed in Massachusetts which removed the legal requirements for the maintenance of Latin grammar schools in the towns of the state.

Significance of the Latin grammar school. The curriculum of the Latin grammar schools in New England provided for no form of physical education, recreation, or health instruction and supervision. They were motivated largely by the aims of religious training which they attempted to achieve indirectly through an intensive study of Latin and Greek. The philosophy of the Middle Ages, which exalted asceticism and scholasticism, had an important influence in the development of these schools and helped to exclude anything relating to play or the care of the body.

These schools served the purpose, however, of helping to perpetuate the traditions of education and of keeping alive an interest in some form of education. They also helped to establish teaching as an occupation worthy of the efforts of intelligent men and women. Probably the most important contribution made by these schools was the inauguration of public support and control of education which has since become almost universally recognized in this country as a fundamental obligation of a democratic government.

Contributions of the academy to American education. During the period in which the importance of the Latin grammar school was

[5]

declining there was developing another type of school called the academy, which attempted to prepare boys for the affairs of life. Preparation to meet college entrance requirements was not a major aim of these schools. The influence of Benjamin Franklin appears to have been a primary motivating force in the establishment of the academies. He published in 1749 his *Proposals Relating to the Education of the Youth in Pennsylvania*,[1] in which he advocated the establishment of an academy to prepare youth for the duties of active life. He stated that such a school should have a suitable building and a garden, orchard, meadow, and playing fields; these latter so that the boys may be "frequently exercised in running, leaping, wrestling, and swimming." He emphasized that things of the greatest relative worth should be included in the curriculum.

As a result of Franklin's proposal and his efforts, the Philadelphia Public Academy was opened in 1751. The idea underlying the establishment of the Academy promptly became popular in all the Colonies. They increased in number rapidly during a period of approximately seventy-five years and continued to increase during an additional period of thirty to forty years. After the growth of the public high school movement got definitely under way, the expansion of the academies stopped; and by the end of the 19th century they had passed the zenith of their influence.

The academy served the purpose of bringing about revolutionary changes in the curriculum; through the way in which it was financed in many communities it helped to advance the ideal of public control and support of education; it stimulated and developed an interest and appreciation on the part of the masses of the people in education above an elementary level and thereby prepared the way for the development of the high school movement; and it helped to interpret the idea that secondary schools do not exist exclusively to prepare boys and girls for college but also to help them live their everyday lives more successfully.

The development of high schools in America. The rapid spread of democratic ideals in the different states led to a demand that there be provided at public expense and under public control a type of school which would provide higher education for all youth. The academy, which in most cases became formalized and aristocratic with a curriculum influenced largely by the Latin grammar school, could not meet this new demand. There developed a movement, therefore, begin-

---

[1] This document can be found in: Thomas Woody (Editor), *Educational Views of Benjamin Franklin,* pp. 149–82. New York: McGraw-Hill Company, Inc., 1931.

ning with the founding of the English High School in Boston in 1821, for the establishment of a type of secondary school which could meet the needs of an evolving democratic society.

The increase in the number and size of public high schools has been almost phenomenal, especially during the past three decades. During the first fifty years of the movement there was considerable opposition to the development of publicly supported high schools. This opposition came as the result of the inertia which is common to all societies, and from wealthy persons who objected to paying taxes for the support of high schools, and also from some colleges whose faculties did not believe the high schools could prepare persons adequately for college work. This opposition could not stop a movement which was so popular. The Kalamazoo Decision stated that high schools were an integral part of the public school system and could be legally supported by public tax funds. There is at present a well-defined tendency for the financial support of high schools to come from the political units larger than the local district in which a high school is located; the county and the state are in many instances the political units which support high schools.

The early high schools did not attempt to prepare their pupils for entrance to college. In the developments which have taken place in the high schools during the past thirty years, however, practically all high schools have assumed the dual responsibility of preparing pupils either for college or for the more direct activities of life.

The curriculums of very few high schools before 1900 included physical education, but since the publication of the *Cardinal Principles of Secondary Education* [1] in 1918 there has been much curriculum revision, and most progressive high schools now provide instruction in physical education for both boys and girls.

Compulsory education. The first legislation in America to require all children to receive some education was passed in Massachusetts in 1642. The idea of compulsory education did not persist, however, and it was not until 1840, when Rhode Island passed its child-labor law, that mandatory school attendance began to gain favor with the American people. Massachusetts passed the first modern legislation concerning required school attendance in 1852, and by 1885 fourteen states and six territories had legislation making the attendance of children at school compulsory. Since the beginning of the 20th century the enactment of

[1] U. S. Bureau of Education Bulletin, 1918, No. 35. Washington: Government Printing Office.

compulsory school attendance legislation increased rapidly so that by 1918 all states had compulsory school attendance laws.

Before the enactment and general enforcement of these laws only those children remained in school who had the interest, intelligence, ability, and economic background to pursue successfully a narrow and rigid curriculum composed exclusively of the traditional academic and classical subjects. Nearly everyone who did not conform to this pattern was permitted to drop out of school or was expelled.

When compulsory attendance laws began to be enforced the schools found that they had many new, novel, and vexing problems. Children of an extremely wide range of ability, intelligence, and interests were forced to remain in school. The teachers could not evade their new responsibilities by the simple expedient of expelling or crowding out children who offered difficult educational problems. Individuals of sub-normal intelligence, the crippled, blind, deaf, deformed, and incorrigibles all became a permanent part of the school population. This change in the calibre of the student body in schools brought with it a demand that physical education adapt its program of activities and methods to meet the needs, abilities, and interests of large heterogeneous groups of children and youth.

Physical education laws. Various parts of the school curriculum have been prescribed by legislation since the beginning of public education in the country. Curriculum specialists and other interested educators have pointed out repeatedly that an adequate school curriculum cannot be constructed by state legislatures and have recommended that the details concerning the content of the curriculum should be left to the decisions of curriculum commissions and other groups with professional leadership. These recommendations, however, have not prevented the legislatures in nearly all states from enacting laws which require certain definite subjects to be taught.

At least thirty-five states have passed laws requiring physical education to be taught in some grades. In most cases the laws have required this instruction in all elementary and high school grades, but in a few states it is mandatory in the elementary schools only. Three states, North Dakota (1899), Ohio (1904), and Idaho (1913) had physical education laws before 1915, and between 1915 and 1922 a total of twenty-five other states enacted such legislation. The rapid increase in the number of state laws during these years reflects the spirit of military preparedness which was dominant during that period.

[8]

This legislation has had a definite influence on the development of physical education. One significant result of this almost universal requirement was to cause physical education in many states to expand more rapidly than the preparation of the teachers, teaching materials, and facilities would justify. As a result, many educators and other citizens reached the pre-mature conclusion that physical education was a waste of time and had no valuable educational contributions to make. During the past few years, however, professional workers in physical education have been diligently and conscientiously at work in consolidating the gains, strengthening the weak spots in the profession, preparing sound and useful instructional materials, interpreting physical education to the educational profession and the public, securing more adequate facilities, and organizing the data on which to base a justifiable philosophy and acceptable practice for physical education in schools.

The influence of organizations and movements. There have been several movements which have had an appreciable influence on shaping physical education in the United States. Chief among these have been the playground movement, the Young Men's Christian Association, and the widespread interest in camping. The playground movement began in an organized way with the organization in 1906 of the Playground and Recreation Association of America. This organization, now known as the National Recreation Association, with the movement which it has fathered and promoted, has had much influence on physical education through its emphasis on play, wholesome recreation, and the creative use of leisure time.

The Y.M.C.A. has rendered an outstanding service through interpreting and popularizing physical education in hundreds of important communities throughout the nation. This organization also adapted the important systems of gymnastics in a way to make this form of exercise interesting to many Americans. The great interest in camping and outing activities, which has been especially prominent during the past decade, helped to emphasize the recreational and educational aspects of physical education and has served to broaden the scope of responsibilities of physical education teachers.

The increased attendance at professional athletic contests and the influence of the sports pages in newspapers have no doubt been influential factors in shaping the program of physical education in American schools. Outstanding individuals among educators and laymen have also had definite influence on physical education. Theodore Roosevelt, for

[9]

example, did much to stimulate interest in the "vigorous life" and admiration for it.

The influences of wars on physical education. Wars have created important influences on physical education in America and Europe. Both the German and Swedish systems of gymnastics were the direct outgrowth of military reverses in these countries and a desire to develop a unified nationalistic spirit and strong, enthusiastic, and loyal soldiers for the armies. Apparently the current emphasis in Germany on physical education, outings, and recreation, which has brought forth slogans such as *Kraft durch Freude* (strength through joy), has much the same motive.

In the United States the Civil War stimulated much interest in physical education and apparently made immediately possible the Morrill Act which established the land-grant colleges with their required instruction in military tactics. This Act was apparently influential in giving a military slant to physical education for two decades or more. Following the Spanish-American War there was likewise an increased interest in physical education. The World War and the results of the medical examinations of drafted men stimulated again a nationwide interest in physical education, which resulted in a large number of states passing the compulsory physical education laws.

The dominant social philosophy. The fact that compulsory school attendance is universal in this country and that a majority of the states have mandatory physical education laws reflects the democratic ideals which are dominant throughout the nation. Equality of opportunity, including equality of educational opportunity, is one of the foundation stones of a democratic society.

It is clearly evident that a large majority of American citizens believe in a democratic form of society. In general they still have faith in a representative form of government. The democratic philosophy is being more broadly interpreted and more widely applied. At one time the ideals of democracy were applied almost exclusively to political and governmental affairs but more recently large numbers of intelligent citizens have put this philosophy to use in connection with economic and social problems.

Respect for human personality and individuality is one of the peculiar contributions of democracy. As applied to education this means, among other things, that subject matter and methods of organization and instruction must provide opportunities for all children to participate in creative activities, to express themselves, to make conscious choices, and to gain experience in self-direction and self-control.

This social philosophy, which has been dominant in America for a long time, has influenced the school program of physical education in much the same way that it has other parts of educational program. It has helped to emphasize play and freedom in physical education, student leadership, and recreational activities. Formal subject matter and methods are not appropriate in a democratic program of education and, therefore, have not gained wide acceptance outside the large cities that have many citizens who came from foreign countries.

Educational theories. Programs of activities and methods of organization and instruction have been influenced greatly by the psychological and philosophical theories of education that have been current at different periods of time. The conceptions of education as discipline, as preparation for some future time, and as a process of the unfolding of inborn tendencies have been reflected in the practices in physical education. The faculty theory in psychology, the theory of formal discipline, and the various theories concerning the transfer of training have had some influence on methods and content of physical education.

Modern conception of education. At the present time the contemporary educational theories are significant in determining the place and function of physical education in the school program. The conception of education as a process of growth through experience is now accepted by most progressive educators. The statement, adopted from the writings of John Dewey, that education is a process of continuous reconstruction of experience in light of new experiences, is used frequently to describe the modern idea of education. It is held that, as an individual grows and gains in experience he becomes able to carry on better the processes of adjustment.

There are two main types of adjustment; one is the adjustment within one's self which is frequently spoken of as the mental hygiene aspect of adjustment, and the other is the adjustment of the organism to its environment. Both types are necessary for an individual to live happily and be of the most service to society. When a person, through experience, grows in his ability to adjust to society, the process involves not only modifications in his ways of reacting but also changes in the environment. The necessity for adjustment should not under any circumstances be interpreted to mean that education should be used to secure an inflexible, docile, and unquestioning acceptance of society and social institutions as they are. Adjustment and conformity are not the same thing; in fact, they are almost exact opposites. Adjustment stresses activity and change, while conformity calls for the maintenance of things and conditions as they are.

The conception of education as growth does not signify that this growth takes place by additions of compartments or blocks of knowledge or experience. It means that education is a continual process during which accretions to the total experience take place and each new experience becomes assimilated as a composite part of the whole. A suitable analogy might be made between the biological growth of an organism and the growth of experiences; this analogous conception of education is frequently spoken of as the "biological approach" to education.

Principles governing educational aims and processes. In making a choice of the desired outcomes of teaching and of the methods to be used in striving for these outcomes it is helpful to have a statement of principles to use as a guide. The following statements from the Virginia State Curriculum Program are in accord with progressive educational thought and are quoted here as a series of acceptable principles:

I. The school is an agency of society for its perpetuation and re-creation.

A democratic society is a dynamic, stimulating, and cooperative agency created by individual and group action for discovering higher values and more effective ways of attaining them. It is not an end product to be perpetuated in static form through indoctrination of individuals with a fixed system of values.

In function society has evolved many special institutions. Some are primarily protective, conservative, and regulatory, seeking so to control individual and collective behavior as to realize recognized values of the present. Other institutions are primarily creative in that their function is to promote developmental, evolutionary and growth processes in individuals and the social body as a whole. The school has emerged in our society as its chief creative institution. In its processes the school should:

1. Discover and define the ideals of a democratic society.

2. Provide for the continuous re-definition and re-interpretation of the social ideals in light of economic, political, and social changes.

3. Provide experiences for boys and girls which make possible their greatest contribution to the realization of the social ideals. From the social point of view this involves:

a. The definition of understandings, attitudes, appreciations and automatic responses that are necessary for the realization of the social ideals.

[12]

b. The selection from the group culture of materials which will assist most effectively in the realization of the social ideals.

II. *Growth processes in individuals and in society are resultants of continuing interaction between individuals and society.*

Individuals are influenced by changing social groups. They must, on occasion, respond with adjustment to the social group; with acceptance of group ideals; with adoption of approved ways of doing. On other occasions individuals can and do change and control social groups as they do the physical environment. Profound social changes in ideals as a result of social interaction with individuals are easily seen when we consider such cases as "Ye have heard it hath been said, an eye for an eye, and a tooth for a tooth: but I say unto you, . . . love your enemies." Profound social changes in ways of doing are seen in such cases as adoption of the telephone as a means of communication. Just as the present social environment in the United States forces an individual to specialization in occupation with its attendant profound influence on the whole life of the individual, so unique concepts and ways of doing by individuals produce the rapid and profound changes in the social order which are everywhere manifest. Because such interaction is the law of individual and social evolution and growth, society is concerned with individualizing individuals for the creation of new values and with socializing individuals with a view to the conservation and use of existing values.

III. *Individuals differ in interests, abilities, attitudes, appreciations and understandings, habits and skills, and in capacity to learn.*

Since individuals are born with very different endowments they develop at very different rates. In adult life individuals will live on very different levels of intellect, character and skill. The school then must provide differentiated education for a variety of capacities and needs.

IV. *Growth is continuous.*

Education must be a continuous development produced by progressive reorganization of experiences on increasingly higher and more complex levels:

1. The school system should be a series of intimately connected links without a break.

2. There should be a smooth and natural issue from the school into the life of society.

The value of school education is determined by the extent to which it creates a desire for continued growth and supplies the means whereby it may be realized.

[13]

V. All learning comes through experience.

Mere activity does not constitute experience. Experience is both trying or doing and undergoing. When we experience something we act upon it, then we undergo the consequences. Experience as trying or doing involves change, but change is meaningless transition unless it is consciously connected with the resultant consequences. It is only when an activity is continued into the undergoing of experience that the activity has significance for the learner. "It is not experience when a child merely sticks his finger into a flame, it is experience when the movement is connected with the pain which he undergoes in consequence. Being burned is a mere physical change, like the burning of a stick of wood, if it is not perceived as a consequence of some other action" (John Dewey, *Democracy and Education*). When we have had an experience we gain something which may be carried over to enable us to foresee what is likely to happen next, and to gain ability to adjust ourselves to what is coming.

VI. An individual tends to avoid experiences which annoy and to seek experiences which satisfy.

From the very beginning of life an individual gives evidence of a set of desires and aversions which lead him to seek certain experiences and to avoid others. All of the senses respond pleasurably to certain stimuli and unpleasantly to others. A baby with the most limited control over his environment endeavors to satisfy his desires and to avoid his aversions. As rapidly as an individual's control over his environment increases, his efforts are extended to meet stimuli which satisfy his desires and to avoid those which involve his aversions. This has great significance for teachers. It assures us that the teacher who associates school work with punishment is teaching the child to avoid further experiences of that kind. It gives us an understanding of how teachers who have used the memorization of poetry to punish children have developed a thorough going dislike for poetry. In brief, from this principle may be discovered the reason that many things which children are taught to do in school are not continued when school days are over.

Sometimes this principle is interpreted to mean that only easy things will be undertaken in school. This is an unsound conclusion, for very often the highest degree of satisfaction is realized from achieving an extremely difficult task. Observance of this principle in teaching leads almost always to more intensive, intelligent activity on the part of pupils.[1]

The scope of physical education. All of the physical activities in which a person participates contribute to his physical education in

[1] *Procedures for Virginia State Curriculum Program*, pp. 11–13. Richmond: State Board of Education, 1932.

much the same way that all the experiences of an individual, both in school and out, have some educational significance. Ordinarily, however, when we speak of physical education we mean only the vigorous big-muscle activities for which the school plans and provides leadership. Alert teachers of this subject realize that the related experiences, which accompany participation in physical activities, in many cases offer exceptional opportunities for valuable concomitant learnings. Physical education is not entirely a process of muscular and organic development; it serves also as a vehicle for the guidance and education of boys and girls in good and approved ways of behaving and living.

When organized physical education was first introduced in the schools of this country it consisted largely of formal gymnastics with a few games of low organization. At a later date competitive athletics monopolized the program to the extent that many people apparently concluded that a school with a football team had a satisfactory program of physical education. Recently, since its objectives, philosophy, and scientific foundations have been more definitely organized and more clearly understood, better organized programs have been put into operation in a large number of schools. An up-to-date program of physical education provides opportunities for children to receive instruction and to participate in a wide variety of activities including games; gymnastics; marching; stunts; activities on apparatus; tumbling; dancing; water activities; track and field athletics; highly organized athletic sports; combative events such as boxing and wrestling; recreational sports such as handball, squash, badminton, golf, and tennis; winter sports, and outing activities such as hiking, bicycling, canoe trips, and camping.

The foundations of physical education. It is essential that leaders in physical education be thoroughly familiar with its foundations in order to be well qualified to render efficient and effective service as teachers, supervisors, and administrators. The data on which procedures in physical education are based, are drawn from several fields of human knowledge. The principal sources of these data are biology, sociology, psychology, and philosophy; but art and music also make significant contributions, particularly in connection with dancing.

Biology supplies data on the evolutionary background of man; the structure and function of the entire human body, and of its different parts, organs, and systems; how individuals grow and develop; and the illnesses, defects, and handicaps that are peculiar to children. Sociology enables one to know the nature of contemporary society; the social

[15]

changes that have occurred in the past and the ones that will probably occur in the future; and the characteristics of the environment to which pupils must learn to adjust. Psychology attempts to explain how human beings learn; the place of the senses, reflexes, and instincts in learning; and how human character and personality are developed and integrated. The function of philosophy for physical education is to propose a defensible statement of aims and procedures in terms of the data available from the various fields of human knowledge and the desirable outcomes that we accept as being good and worth striving for.

In the remaining chapters of this book will be discussed the principles and foundations of physical education and applications made of them to the problems of teaching, administration, teacher preparation, and curriculum construction.

Summary. A defensible theory of physical education can be based on data concerning the historical development of physical education, the background of man, the nature of society, the characteristics of the learning process, the school curriculum, the composition of the group of professional leaders, and the approved methods of teaching and administration.

In viewing the country as a whole one is able to see that physical education has made rapid progress during the past three decades along important lines such as legislation, finance, curriculum construction, teacher preparation, facilities, time allotment, and teaching staff. This development has been shaped largely by social influences which have been dominant during that period, and by the programs of physical education in foreign countries, the philosophical and psychological theories held by educational leaders, the war spirit at different periods, and movements such as the playground movement and the widespread interest in camping.

QUESTIONS

1. From what sources should data be secured on which to base a defensible theory of physical education?
2. What influences have been particularly significant in shaping the development of physical education in America during the past three decades?
3. What are some of the developments in the history of public education in America that have been especially influential in the growth of physical education?
4. What are some of the ways in which legislation has influenced physical education.

5. The dominant social philosophy in America has influenced the development of physical education in what ways?
6. How have modern educational theories influenced the development of physical education?
7. What should be the scope of an up-to-date school program of physical education?
8. How has the war spirit, which has been dominant at different times in the history of this country, influenced the school program of physical education?
9. What has been the significant contributions to physical education of some of the important movements and organizations in this country?
10. What effect has the movement for universal compulsory education had on physical education?

REFERENCES

Cubberley, Ellwood P. *The History of Education.* Boston: Houghton Mifflin Company, 1920.

Recent Social Trends in the United States. Report of the President's Research Committee on Social Trends. New York: McGraw-Hill Book Company, Inc., 1933.

Rice, Emmett A. *A Brief History of Physical Education.* New York: A. S. Barnes and Company, 1926.

Sharman, Jackson R. *Introduction to Physical Education.* New York: A. S. Barnes and Company, 1934.

CHAPTER II

Different Viewpoints in Physical Education

∾

Conflicting views. In the succeeding chapters the principles under-lying physical education will be discussed. Teachers do not all agree, however, with the principles that have been proposed. Of course, dif-ferences of opinion among theorists and practitioners are not peculiar to physical education. There are many differences in fundamental beliefs among writers, teachers, and administrators in all fields of education. The conflicts that exist among professional workers in physical education are not in the nature of disagreements about relatively unimportant tech-niques of organization and administration but rather in the fundamental conceptions of physical education. It is important that these conflicting views and issues in physical education be recognized and explained in order that the educational objectives of physical education may be used as a guide in choosing the content of the curriculum and the instruc-tional methods to be used. Subject matter and methods have no signifi-cance except as they help in the achievement of the educational objectives.

Sources of conflicting views. There are two general sources that cause issues to arise concerning the principles of physical education. They are (1) changing philosophical and psychological beliefs; and (2) newly discovered facts or facts that have only recently become generally known.

Changes in the point of view of large numbers of people toward play is an illustration of how changes in philosophy cause differences of opinion concerning physical education. The following statements from a bulletin by Robinson [1] illustrate the changes that have taken place in the opinions of the American people concerning play:

YESTERDAY

"All in the college shall be kept at the utmost distance from vice in general, so in particular from softness, and from effeminancy in general.

"We shall therefore insist on their rising early in the morning—this is of vastest importance to both body and mind. On the same principle we pro-hibit play on the strictest terms.

[1] Wm. McKinley Robinson, *Home Play in Rural Areas: A Program Outline for Rural Parent-Teacher Associations.* Washington: National Congress of Parents and Teachers, 1934.

"The students shall rise at five o'clock winter and summer. Their recreation shall be gardening, walking, riding, and bathing without doors; and the carpenter's, tuner's, joiner's, or cabinetmaker's business within doors.

"The students shall be indulged with nothing that the world calls play; let this be observed with strictest nicety; for those who play when they are young will play when they are old."—*Excerpt from the rules of Cokesbury College in* 1788.

TODAY

"Children do not play because they are young; they are young in order that they may play."—*Groos.*

"Give me the direction of the play life of the youth of this generation and I will dictate the world's path tomorrow."—*Daniel Poling.*

"Every little boy has inside of him an aching void which demands interesting and exciting play. And if you don't fill it with something that is interesting and exciting and good for him, he is going to fill it with something that is interesting and exciting and isn't good for him."—*Theodore Roosevelt, Jr.*

"Play is one of the most important spiritual factors in human experience. To bottle up the play life of boys and girls or to pervert it to evil ends is to wrong them at the center of their characters with a hurt that nothing can make up for."—*Harry Emerson Fosdick.*

The puritanical attitude toward play held that anything of a frivolous or playful nature was wrong and should be suppressed. This belief has had a great influence on the thinking of the American people and, combined with the pioneer philosophy, has caused work and hardships to be glorified in the minds of many people. There has been, however, a rapid shift away from this view during the past decade. Large numbers of Americans now believe that play and recreation occupy a most important place in individual and social development. This philosophy of play has not gained universal acceptance and therefore is the source of conflicting views.

The emphasis given by different schools of psychologists to such things as specific learnings and learning in "patterns" or *Gestalten* has caused practically all students of educational psychology and professional education to abandon any faith in the older faculty theory of psychology and the theory of formal discipline. There are, nevertheless, many persons who like to emphasize the disciplinary values of education and who still cling to the older discarded beliefs. Many of these individuals insist that all children should be required to participate in formal gymnastics

[19]

in order that they may be sure to have some experience in doing disagreeable things. Changes such as these in psychological tenets make it relatively easy for differenecs of opinion to exist concerning the fundamentals of physical education.

The facts in regard to reciprocal innervation which were pointed out by Sherrington [1] more than thirty years ago are apparently not yet familiar to all teachers of physical education. Some teachers still teach "static" and "resistive" exercises and believe them to be physiologically wholesome. It has also been only within the past few years that the physiology of respiration has been adequately understood by physical education teachers. Until recently many unjustified claims were made for the beneficial effects of breathing exercises. These statements help one to understand how the ignorance of available facts by some teachers of physical education may be the source of conflicts in fundamental beliefs.

Solution of the problems. There are many problems in physical education which might well engage one's attention. It is probable that some things might be problems in some situations that would not be considered an issue at all in some other situation. An effort has been made in this chapter to point out some of the problems that involve the fundamentals of physical education and are of common interest to teachers throughout the country.

This list of issues has not been determined in any scientific way. It has been prepared from a review of the literature in the field and represents the subjective judgment of the author as to what are the most pertinent issues in physical education. No claim is made that the discussion submitted here in any way solves the problems raised. Each reader must consider the available facts and reach conclusions in light of his own philosophy of life and of education. It is probably true that the nearest approach to the solution of these problems which is practicable at the present time is for a selected group of recognized authorities in the fields of education and physical education to agree on a statement of philosophical principles, bring together the available facts, and then, in light of the accepted philosophy and facts, propose a solution.

Health values of physical activity. It is generally believed that the regular participation in a rational program of physical activity contributes to a healthy state of the human organism. This apparently has

[1] C. S. Sherrington, *The Integrative Action of the Nervous System.* New Haven: Yale University Press, 1906.

always been held to be true by the majority of mankind since the beginning of civilization. It is so commonly accepted as fact that nearly every treatise on personal hygiene by competent medical authorities emphasizes the importance of regular exercise as a health procedure. On the other hand there are those who challenge the health claims that are set forth for exercise. These critics point out that there is a minimum of evidence from laboratory controlled experiments to prove that exercise helps one to be healthy. They insist that clinical observations are valuable in connection with any problem but that data secured under controlled conditions are essential to establish proof of a fact.

There is well supported evidence to prove that exercise develops strength and endurance and that it helps to increase the red bone-marrow.[1] There are no scientifically authenticated data to prove that exercise will build up resistance to infectious diseases. It is commonly believed, however, that when one is in good physical condition he is less likely to contract a disease. There are also some data which seem to indicate that exercise has a beneficial influence on women in regard to menstruation and childbearing.[2] The published results of careful observations cause one to believe that the effect of exercise on body carriage and posture probably has some health significance.

It is believed that there is adequate evidence to justify teachers of physical education in concluding that participation in physical education activities will make a significant contribution toward helping their pupils to be healthy.

Organic development. The problem of the development of the organic systems of the body is related to the question of the health values of exercise. The facts concerning the process of metabolism and the development of cells and tissues give strong support to the hypothesis that the organic systems can be made stronger and more efficient as the result of physical activity. If a person has well developed and smoothly functioning bodily organs and is free from disease he is a healthy individual. There is only a limited amount of evidence from the results of controlled experiments which shows directly and specifically the developmental effects of exercise. There is such a large mass of data, however,

[1] Arthur H. Steinhaus, "Why Exercise," *Journal of Health and Physical Education,* V (May, 1934), 5.

[2] Margaret Bell and Eloise Parsons, "Dysmenorrhoea in College Women," *Medical Women's Journal,* XXXVIII (February, 1931), 31–35.

Carl Schrader (translator), "The Influence of Physical Education Activities upon Constitution, Child-Bearing and Menstruation of Women," *Journal of Health and Physical Education,* I (November, 1930), 47.

from the field of physiology which supports this belief that practically no well informed persons doubt it.

A reserve of energy and endurance accrues to the person with an organic development beyond that which normally takes place as the result of maturation. This enables such an individual to live a more interesting and dynamic life. The available evidence indicates, however, that the organic development which comes through physical activity must be achieved throughout the years when children are growing and maturing. This emphasizes the necessity of providing ample opportunities for all children to participate in vigorous activity from early childhood until physiological maturity is reached.

Good body mechanics. There is much difference of opinion in regard to the values and standards of good posture and also as to the best methods to be used in teaching good body mechanics. Some teachers are enthusiastic about the possibilities of postural training through physical education while others claim that many of the abnormalities of bodily carriage are in reality deformities and no amount of exercise can correct them. Carnett [1] from his long experience in the field of medicine concludes that poor posture causes many ailments that can be relieved by even a partial improvement in posture. Klein [2] from his study carried on in the schools of Chelsea, Mass., believes that an instructional program which stresses good posture can secure improvement in large numbers of children. Rogers,[3] however, reaches the conclusion from his studies that bodily carriage is largely the result of the anatomical structure of each individual which he inherited from his ancestors. He also points out that in some city school systems which have emphasized orthopedic work for a long period of time the pupils apparently have poorer posture each year they remain in school. Deaver [4] has shown that there is no significant relationship between posture and other factors such as health, intelligence, motor ability, vital capacity, and strength. The report on Body Mechanics, from the White House Conference on Child Health and Protection, states there are no rigid and definite stand-

[1] John B. Carnett, "Extracts from Discussion," *Body Mechanics, Education and Practice,* p. 48. Report of the Subcommittee on Orthopedics and Body Mechanics. White House Conference on Child Health and Protection. New York: The Century Company, 1932.

[2] Armin Klein, "What Price Posture Training," *Journal of Health and Physical Education,* III (December, 1932), 14–15, 54–55.

[3] James Frederick Rogers, "The Long and Short of the Carriage Business," *Journal of Health and Physical Education,* III (December, 1932), 11–13, 58–59.

[4] G. G. Deaver, "Posture and Its Relation to Mental and Physical Health," *Research Quarterly,* IV (March, 1933), 24–29.

[22]

ards that should be prescribed for evaluating the posture of all individuals. It is clear that the evidence concerning posture is not conclusive.

It seems, therefore, that teachers of physical education should be cautious and conservative in regard to the desirable postural outcomes that they claim can be secured through physical education. In light of what is known concerning body mechanics it appears that all teachers of physical education at all school levels should give a small amount of class time to direct instruction in bodily carriage so that all pupils will have some experience in the "feel" and appearance of good posture. In teaching all activities an effort should be made to encourage all pupils to carry themselves in an erect and mechanically efficient way.

Character development. A hackneyed and threadbare witticism directed at coaches of unsuccessful athletic teams is that although they are failures as coaches they are great builders of character. Instructors of academic subjects in high schools and colleges also frequently speak in sarcastic and sneering terms of the character-building efforts of physical education teachers. These statements illustrate the fact that large numbers of people do not appreciate, and attach very little importance to, the opportunities that exist in physical education for the development of desirable character traits. The persons who doubt the character-building values of physical education frequently point out that much of the leadership in physical education and athletics lacks specialized training which would qualify these teachers and coaches to make intelligent and worthwhile contributions toward the development of character. It is also claimed that the instruction in physical education is all organized on the basis of winning the largest possible number of games or on some other basis that is not conducive to character development.

There are, however, large numbers of educators and well informed laymen who have deep convictions concerning the excellent opportunities that exist in physical education for the development of desirable character traits. These advocates of physical education state that one's character is the sum total of his habits and attitudes as expressed in behavior. It is also claimed that habit formation is largely dependent on satisfactions which are associated with reactions, and that responses which are tied up with emotional expression tend to become established as attitudes. They point out that there are innumerable situations in connection with physical education in which satisfaction and emotional expression can be associated with desirable or good ways of behaving. Thus, the experiences gained in connection with physical education activ-

[23]

ities are particularly important and valuable in building character. It is claimed that these experiences should be emphasized.

Physical education has other advantages in the development of character. The type of situations that exist in physical education make it relatively easy to observe objectively the character outcomes in the behavior of the pupils. There is also a dynamic urge or drive to behavior back of most reactions in physical education; the motivation is natural and innate which causes the experiences of the pupils to be completely meaningful. Physical education is rich in situations in which pupils must make ethical choices and carry on activities which are based on these choices. This provides much valuable experience that is similar to the experiences that the pupils will have throughout life. Another condition in physical education is that it provides excellent opportunities for direct instruction in character as well as for the use of the indirect or incidental method and combinations of these methods.

There have been several excellent studies made on the subject of character education. But the evidence concerning objectives, methods, and outcomes is far from complete. From what is known, however, it seems that teachers of physical education should consider seriously their responsibilities and opportunities for shaping the characters of their pupils. It is believed that one is fully justified in assuming that physical education is one of the most important and vital phases of the educational program for the development and integration of desirable character traits.

Physical education as recreation. Many professional workers in the field of recreation apparently spend a large part of their time in assuring people that a complete recreation program includes many things in addition to physical recreations. It does, of course, but experienced recreation leaders realize that the "core" of practically all municipal recreation programs is made up of physical recreations. For, while considerable numbers are interested in one or more such forms of recreational activity as music, art, dramatics, literature, and handicrafts, the vast majority of the whole population are interested in physical recreations either as participants or as spectators. Nearly all young people are glad to take advantage of any available opportunities to participate in games, dancing, and other forms of physical recreation.

Mental hygiene authorities state that physical recreation is not only of value to the physical organism, but is of even more importance in mental hygiene. The opportunities which are provided for relaxation and forgetfulness and freedom from one's actual or imagined worries is

[24]

of much significance in the maintenance of sound mental health. The experiences involving successful achievement, cooperation with a social group, and the sense of belonging and being accepted and recognized are of much value in the integration of well-balanced personalities.

Then, there are those who agree that physical recreations are eminently worthwhile but say that such activities have no relation to physical education. They claim that physical education is primarily an exercise procedure, is engaged in teaching activities to classes of pupils in gymnasiums, and has nothing to do with the recreational life of boys and girls. They contend that the needs of their pupils, so far as physical recreations are concerned, are adequately met by schools which provide intramural athletics and other recreational opportunities. This group fails to recognize the fact that the only pupils who seek the opportunity to participate in intramural athletics are the ones who have enough knowledge and skill to take part in the activities with a reasonable degree of success. Required physical education classes in all schools are the only practicable way in which the masses of children can be helped to develop the minimum knowledge and skills essential for participation in organized physical recreation. The activities which are taught in physical education classes should be of a kind that will prepare the pupils to take part successfully in intramural athletics and other recreation programs. Teachers of physical education should recognize their responsibility to develop enough skill on the part of all their pupils to enable them to play with satisfaction at least a few recreational games and sports.

Required participation in physical education. The question of required physical education at the different school levels is the source of much argument and differences of opinion among workers in the field of physical education. The preponderance of opinion seems to be in favor of requiring participation in physical education of all children through high school. On the college level the sentiment does not seem to be so definite, but apparently the majority of college teachers of physical education favor at least two years of required work in physical education for all college students. Outstanding committee reports and yearbooks indicate a sympathetic attitude toward compulsory participation in physical education. Whether or not physical education should be required of all pupils depends largely on the objectives that are accepted for education. It is true, of course, for any phase of education that the subject matter and methods used are determined largely by the dominant objectives.

Persons who advocate universal compulsory physical education assume that all can take part in physical education with profit to themselves and to society. If this is to be done a much broader curriculum offering must be provided in physical education than has ever been provided. This will necessitate much more complete facilities and staff, which will cost a great deal more money than is now being spent for physical education. Unless the public is willing to pay for a broader curriculum in physical education so as to provide for the great range of needs, abilities, capacities, and interests which exist in the population of school age, and also to provide adequate facilities and staff for conducting such a curriculum, there should be some limitation placed on the number of pupils permitted to take physical education.

Levels of achievement. Where physical education is required, there is frequently considerable difference of opinion as to the nature and content of the requirement. Some teachers advocate the establishment of definite levels of achievement as goals to be achieved in the elementary school, high school, or college rather than the requirement of participation for a certain number of hours, semesters, or years. The sentiment in favor of requiring the achievement of certain definite goals is particularly strong among college instructors, but some teachers believe such a plan would be desirable at all school levels.

A requirement of this kind might be carried out in a college for example, by setting levels of achievement in swimming, team games, dancing, and recreational sports. A student who could pass the prescribed tests when he entered as a freshman would not be required to attend any classes in physical education while in college. Students who could not pass one or more of the tests would be required to attend instructional classes in these activities until they reached the minimum required achievement. Under the present form of college organization the faculties of some institutions would probably not be willing to prevent a student from graduating if he failed to reach a minimum achievement in physical education. It does seem feasible, however, in even the most conservative colleges to require regular attendance at physical education classes throughout the entire four years of the college course of all students who have not met the minimum requirements in physical education. A large number of leaders in the field of physical education believe that a similar plan would be desirable for boys and girls in senior high schools.

The teachers who emphasize the values of the regular exercise gained

[26]

through physical education usually are most definitely opposed to an achievement requirement in high schools and colleges. This group insists that all students should be required to exercise regularly in order to secure the hygienic benefits thereof. The ones who see physical education more largely as an educational and recreational procedure are more likely to favor a requirement based on levels of achievement.

Differentiation in curriculum. Most educators give lip service to the ideal of providing a curriculum to meet the individual needs of pupils. In actual practice, however, very little is done about it except in a few of the better and more progressive schools. Apparently even less effort is made to provide a differentiated curriculum to fit the needs and abilities of individual pupils in physical education than in the more traditional academic subjects. In New York the state department of education seems to have met with a reasonable degree of success in stimulating teachers to attempt a form of individualized instruction based on the use of the Rogers Test. While this is the only large-scale attempt that has been made to adapt a physical education program to the individual needs of the pupils, there have been several notable adaptations in some of the high schools of Detroit and in other cities; but the instances are not by any means numerous enough to typify general practice.

One of the methods that has been used successfully in adapting instruction in physical education to the individual needs of pupils is to teach a common "core" of activities to all the pupils in a class. These "core" activities should be such that all the pupils can do them satisfactorily and enjoy them. In addition to this common offering there should be a number of particular and specialized activities that the pupils of varying needs and abilities should practice as individuals or as small groups.

The problem of providing a differentiated physical education curriculum in small high schools is particularly difficult to solve. The following procedures either singly or in combination are believed to be of value in the solution of this problem: (1) Set definite achievement standards in a limited number of activities. These standards should be scientifically determined for accurately classified groups of pupils. The work of Neilson and Cozens [1] should be valuable in this connection. (2) Arrange for expert guidance and instruction from the state depart-

---

[1] N. P. Neilson and Frederick W. Cozens, *Achievement Scales in Physical Education Activities for Boys and Girls in Elementary and Junior High Schools.* New York: A. S. Barnes and Company, 1934.

ment of education or some other source of expert help. This assistance might be given regularly by means of correspondence or radio, although it is especially important in this case that the instruction be carefully and efficiently organized. (3) Provide short periods of intensive instruction by specialists who go from school to school.

Unified educational experiences. The organization of the subject matter in physical education for purposes of instruction is a matter about which there is a lack of agreement among teachers of physical education. Some insist that physical education should be taught always as a separate and distinct subject; that it is desirable to have specialized teachers of physical education at all school levels beginning not later than the fourth grade. The development of motor skills and neuro-muscular coordinations is believed by them to be the most important outcome of instruction in physical education.

Others are very much in favor of making instruction in physical education as largely as possible a part of broader educational experiences such as are provided in "projects" and "big units." For instance, a fourth grade is studying about the American Indians. If physical education is to contribute to the project it may provide instruction and leadership in games, dances, and outing activities that were peculiar to the American aborigines. Many of the younger and more progressive teachers believe that when instruction is organized in this way the hygienic values of exercise are secured and that greatly enriched educational experiences are simultaneously provided.

It does not seem possible under present forms of school organization to organize all parts of the physical education program as an integral part of a scheme to provide larger unified educational experiences for pupils. The teachers, however, should understand the values and advantages that can be gained by helping children to have comprehensive experiences that are rich in meanings and interests.

Teaching ideals in connection with physical education. Another problem about which there is much disagreement has to do with the responsibility of physical education teachers for the teaching of ideals. Many of these teachers insist that their main job is to improve the skills and playing ability of their pupils. They believe that if they take time to help their pupils form desirable ideals, there will be a loss in the efficiency of learning motor skills.

Those who believe definite efforts should be made to teach ideals and attitudes are convinced that the efforts of physical education teachers should not be confined to the development of motor skills. Many of them point out that a reasonable emphasis on the practice of desirable ideals and attitudes would be justified even if it did limit somewhat the development of skills. But the opinion of many experienced teachers and the results of studies such as that by Clevett [1] indicate that such traits as honesty and fair play can be developed successfully through the same experiences from which a maximum development of playing skills are secured. In light of the available evidence, there is no justification for failing to seek every available opportunity in physical education to teach pupils to behave in desirable social and moral ways.

Academic credit for physical education. The question of credit for physical education toward high school graduation and college entrance has been debated by many teachers and administrators. At present the practice of giving credit for physical education is not very widespread. In several states one Carnegie unit of credit is allowed for physical education in high schools that have an approved program. Sixteen units are usually required for high school graduation and frequently only fifteen units are required for college entrance. Allowing one unit credit for physical education, therefore, is not likely to create any serious administrative problems.

Those who believe it is undesirable to give credit for physical education say the content of the program is so intrinsically interesting and makes such a natural appeal that pupils should be encouraged to participate in physical education for the satisfactions that accrue from the participation itself. These teachers claim that artificial and extrinsic motives in the form of credit detract from the educational values of interesting and valuable activities. They point out that all other phases of education are handicapped and made partially sterile through the domination of a system of units and credits, and suggest that pupils in many cases become more concerned with accumulating credits than with gaining rich and meaningful experiences.

Other teachers insist, however, that it is useless for physical education to attempt to stand alone without credit in the educational program. The fact that practically all administrators, teachers, pupils, and laymen evaluate the worth of our educational offering in terms of credit makes it difficult for physical education to command professional respect from many people unless the school organization allows credit for it. It is

[1] Melvin A. Clevett, "An Experiment in Physical Education Activities Related to the Teaching of Honesty and Motor Skills," *Research Quarterly*, III (March, 1932), 121–27.

[29]

probable that the present system of units and credits in American education will in time be discarded, but there is no evidence that this will take
place immediately. It seems, therefore, that physical education should be
relieved of the discrimination now made against it in the administration
of schools, and that, as long as American educational practice is based on
credit and units, physical education should be accredited in the same way
as other valuable subjects of instruction.

The place of inter-institutional athletics. The field of athletics
has probably created as many problems in physical education as all other
parts of the physical education program together. One of these problems,
that usually must be considered in planning an instructional program, is
what place inter-institutional athletics should occupy in the school
program.

One view is that competitive athletics are in reality displays of showmanship and that they cannot be run primarily as educational activities.
These people agree, of course, that all experiences of an individual have
some educational significance, but they insist that school and college faculties and administrators do not want athletics to be conducted so as to emphasize the education of the pupils who participate. They point out that
dramatic productions in many institutions are not under the direction of
the department of dramatics or of English, but are coached by outside
professionals brought in for that specific purpose. In a similar way, they
say, it is justifiable to have competitive athletics conducted primarily as
exhibitions, organized and taught by persons without the academic and
professional qualifications that are usually required of regular faculty
members. Many physical education teachers who hold to this point of
view think their colleagues are assuming unnecessary worry and concern
by attempting to justify athletics as part of the physical education program and to inject educational principles into athletics. These teachers
recommend that they concern themselves with the general program of
physical education designed for the education and recreation of the student body as a whole, and that athletics be permitted undisturbed to
become specialized showmanship.

Apparently most people in physical education do not agree with this
view. Most think of athletics as an integral part of the physical education
program, a part to be conducted in a way that will emphasize its educational aspects. An analogy often used has been that of a pyramid: the
base is compared with the opportunity for all pupils to participate in
physical education activities; like the narrowing series of layers, a smaller

number should participate in different elective activities including various parts of an intramural athletic program; the peak of the pyramid is compared with the inter-institutional program of competitive athletics in which a small group of highly selected and unusually skillful pupils should take part.

These teachers also state that it shows a lack of professional aggressiveness to refuse to wrestle with the educational problems that are raised by the program of athletics. They believe that physical education teachers should face these problems, try to diagnose and analyze them, and attempt to bring about their successful solution.

The scope of physical education. Not only do school people differ concerning the place of competitive athletics in physical education but there is much difference of opinion in regard to other activities. Some teachers believe that dancing is a specialized field and is not properly a part of the physical education program. Others say that plays and games are more truly part of a recreation program than of physical education. Some of the older teachers contend that physical education should be concerned only with the definitely organized exercises that are participated in by individuals or groups for the purpose of achieving some definite physiological purpose. Usually these exercises are in the nature of formal gymnastics and apparatus exercises.

The more modern and widely accepted ideas concerning physical education conceive of it as including all the vigorous activities of a person that involve the big muscles of the body. This includes, of course, many activities that are part of one's work and other experiences in life. All of these contribute to one's physical education. They are clearly, however, not a part of the school program of physical education. This program includes activities such as sports, games, athletics, water activities, rhythms, gymnastics, stunts, combative events, and outing activities. Teachers of physical education are primarily concerned with providing numerous and wholesome opportunities for boys and girls to receive instruction and participate in these activities.

Summary. There are two general sources that cause issues to arise concerning principles of physical education. They are (1) changing philosophical and psychological beliefs; and (2) newly discovered facts or facts that have only recently become generally known.

Some of the problems in physical education about which there is much disagreement include (1) the health values of physical activity, (2) the possibilities of organic development through physical education, (3) the values of good posture, (4) character development, (5) physical education as recreation, (6) required participation in physical education, (7) required levels of achievement, (8) the differentiation of the curriculum, (9) unit instruction in physical education, (10) teaching ideals through physical education, (11) credit for physical education, (12) the place of inter-institutional athletics, and (13) the scope of physical education.

QUESTIONS

1. What are the two general sources that cause issues to arise concerning the principles of physical education?
2. In what ways have the viewpoints of large numbers of people changed toward play?
3. What is the avaliable evidence concerning the health values of physical activity?
4. How can physical exercise contribute to the development of the organic systems of the body?
5. What contribution can physical education make to good body mechanics?
6. What contributions to character development should be expected from physical education?
7. What significance has physical education in the preparation of pupils for the wholesome use of leisure time?
8. What different viewpoints have been expressed in regard to required participation in physical education?
9. What procedures might be used to provide a differentiated physical education curriculum to meet the individual differences of pupils?
10. What should be the relation of interinstitutional athletics to physical education in general?

REFERENCES

Body Mechanics, Education and Practice. Report of the Subcommittee on Orthopedics and Body Mechanics. White House Conference on Child Health and Protection. New York: The Century Company, 1932.

Leonard, Fred Eugene. *A Guide to the History of Physical Education.* Philadelphia: Lea and Febiger, 1927.

Rice, Emmett A. *A Brief History of Physical Education.* New York: A. S. Barnes and Company, 1926.

Sharman, Jackson R. *Introduction to Physical Education.* New York: A. S. Barnes and Company, 1934.

Steinhaus, Arthur H. "Why Exercise," *Journal of Health and Physical Education,* V (May, 1934), 5.

CHAPTER III

Biological Foundations of Physical Education

∾

Child development. In a study of the fundamental bases of physical education and of its influence on child development one must be familiar with the facts concerning physical growth, mental growth, behavior, nutrition, the influence of environment, the effect of heredity, and the significance of various social factors. The principles concerning mental and personality growth, behavior, and the influence of society were discussed in the preceding chapter. In this chapter emphasis will be given to the fundamental principles of physical education which are mainly biological in nature.

This will include the application to the problems of physical education of the facts and principles concerning (1) the development of man's body, (2) the effect of heredity, (3) the development of the human skeleton, (4) muscular development, (5) the relation of mental and physical development, (6) the ages of development, (7) the functioning of the nervous system, (8) general motor ability, (9) the relation of energy to life, (10) respiration, (11) types of body-build, and (12) the defects of children.

The development of man's body. The available evidence, such as that provided by remains, fossils, and impressions in rocks, indicates that there are several well defined periods or eras through which animal life has passed in its development from one-celled animals to conscious, intelligent man. A summary of what is known will help one to have some notion about man's phylogenetic, or ancestral, heritage. This knowledge should serve to some extent as a guide in planning and teaching physical education.

There are reasons for believing that during the earliest ages, covering approximately one third of the time since the appearance of life on this planet, myriad swarms of one-celled plants and animals existed in the waters of the earth. Following this period the dominant forms of life were animals without a spinal column known as invertebrates. This group included such animals as shell-fish, shrimps, sponges, and starfish. Out of these invertebrates developed fish-like forms of animals such as the primitive shark with a cartilaginous skeleton, and then many forms

[33]

of fishes. With the development of fish we have a beginning of the backbone, skeleton, jaws, fins, and internal glands. The next higher order of animals that occupied the world were the amphibians which included animals such as the salamander, frog, toad, and newt. These animals lived both on land and in water, and had true legs for locomotion. They were also the first animals to use lungs for breathing.

While the dominance of the amphibians was waning there were developing the reptiles which were the dominant animal form during the next geologic era. We see reproductions of giant reptiles portrayed often in advertisements and in moving pictures. The reptiles breathed air exclusively, developed a more highly organized nervous system, better sense organs, four legs with claws for capturing food, and an improved circulatory system. From one of the types of reptiles the birds developed. There developed from another type of reptile some animals known as pro-mammals which provided another step upward in the development of four legs, a nervous system, sense organs, teeth, and a temperature regulatory mechanism. From these came the mammals with a great development of the nervous system, frontal areas of the brain, skillful use of forelegs, and upright posture, culminating in man.

Application to physical education. It may be observed that each animal type at each successive period of time has contributed something toward making the body of man what it is today. In viewing these facts it is seen that the internal glands and the organs of locomotion which developed later into leg and foot were present in fish and therefore are among the oldest organs in the biological development of man. The nerves and nerve centers which control the big muscles of the trunk are likewise seen to be the oldest and most fundamental part of the nervous system. In considering facts such as these one is led to believe that physical education should be taught in such a way as to provide opportunities for the exercise and development of these racially old organs and systems.

It would seem, for example, that a strong and healthy nervous system can be built better when the older and more original nerve mechanisms are well developed. It is believed that this part of the nervous system is concerned with the control of the muscles of the trunk and that the best way it can be developed is through vigorous exercise of these muscles. Some writers have advanced the theory that the great increase in recent years of nervous and mental diseases has been due, among other things, to the fact that most modern people live a sedentary life beginning at a rather early age and do not secure a fundamental development of the nervous system through vigorous physical activity. Whether or not all these beliefs are valid, there seems to be ample evidence from what is known of man's biological background to give some indication of the kind of activities that should be included in the physical education program and of the way in which they should be taught.

The effect of heredity. The general development of the human race or of mankind provides a common heritage that is the same for all people. The traits and characteristics which make up each individual as a distinct personality are inherited, however, from one's immediate ancestors. The inheritance that contributes to making the bodies and personalities of persons is usually spoken of as of two kinds—the biological inheritance and the social inheritance. The biological inheritance includes the traits and characteristics which are passed on from parents to children through the genes which are component parts of the chromosomes. The chromosomes are rodlike bodies which form in the nucleus of the germ cells during the process of cell division after fertilization of the egg cell has taken place. The social inheritance is the accumulated experience of past and present generations of human beings which is passed on to the younger members of society through some form of education. This education is gained by on-coming generations not exclusively through school experiences but also through experiences in the home, the church, the playground, the theater, and a large number of other social institutions. These two kinds of inheritance probably have equally important parts in influencing the all-round growth and integration of a person.

Since time immemorial there have been arguments concerning whether heredity or environment is more important in the development of an individual. The potentialities of a person are determined by the germ plasm, and more particularly by the genes in the chromosomes. Within the limits imposed by our biological inheritance there are, in most individuals, almost unlimited possibilities for growth and development. Very few people ever approach the limits of growth in mental and physical achievements of which they are capable.

The environmental factors to which a child is exposed at home and at school have much influence on the rate and limit of his development. Factors such as food, clothing, shelter, disease, play, exercise, and security are of fundamental importance in maintaining growth and happiness of children. It seems accurate to state, therefore, that every person is the result of his biological inheritance, his social inheritance, and the influ-

[35]

ence of environmental factors since the time of the fertilization of the egg cell by the sperm cell.

A number of the specific facts from the study of heredity are of direct interest to teachers of physical education. A discussion of three of these follows.

1. Most authorities agree that acquired characteristics cannot be passed on biologically to the offspring. This fact is illustrated by the observation that the feet of Chinese babies are normal even though the feet of Chinese women have been bound through succeeding generations for centuries. There are large numbers of other examples which may be drawn from daily experience and from scientific studies. It will be seen, therefore, that muscular development, skill in the high jump, or other acquired traits cannot be passed on from parents to children.

2. In general, diseases are not inherited. Many persons are of the opinion that tuberculosis and cancer can be inherited. The best available evidence indicates that a person may inherit weak organs which might predispose him to some disease, but that the actual disease itself cannot be inherited. Even congenital syphilis probably represents an early infection of the embryo, rather than transmission through the germ plasm. Knowledge of this fact should cause teachers to study the history of each pupil and to make certain of a complete medical examination for every child who might have inherited a tendency for certain diseases.

3. The studies of Davenport indicate that body stature is determined by the length of the head and neck, the trunk, the thigh, and the lower leg. These four segments of the body may grow at separate rates entirely independently of each other. The relative lengths of different segments are different in each individual. These data cause one to realize the fallacy in attempting to secure a uniform symmetrical development of each pupil or to bring about any uniform ratio between the length of the different segments of the body.

The development of the human skeleton. In man, as in all vertebrates, the skeleton is internal and is composed largely of bones with the necessary cartilages and ligaments. In the invertebrates, such as the turtle or lobster, the skeleton is in most instances on the outside of the body. An internal skeleton such as that of man makes it possible for an organism to grow and adapt to its environment through change in the organism itself as well as through modification of the environment. A skeleton of this type is a fundamental essential for an active, growing, experiencing animal. The skeleton in man, containing more than two hundred bones, serves to support the body in an upright position, provides the foundation for attachments of the muscles, and gives protection to vital organs such as that provided to the brain by the skull and to the heart and lungs by the ribs. The marrow of bones is also the source of new blood corpuscles. Bone is formed of connective tissue, in and around which has been precipitated such mineral salts as lime, sodium, potassium, and magnesium. The lime salt which is most abundant is tricalcium phosphate. It comprises at least half the weight of bones and gives them their qualities of hardness and rigidity. It takes more than two tons of force to crush a cubic inch of compact bone. The skeleton in cooperation with the muscles provides the means by which the body moves about. This characteristic which enables the organism to gain many new experiences and develop adaptive abilities has been of much significance throughout the entire period of the development of the human race. The skeleton and muscles working together through the use of the joints provide applications of all three kinds of levers in securing efficient mechanical use of the body.

According to the available evidence it seems that growth energy is inherent mainly in the skeletal tissue. Hence it is essential that a routine of living be maintained which will not handicap the growth of the skeleton. This tissue is of fundamental importance in general growth. When a baby is born his head, trunk, and vital organs are relatively large. The legs and arms are much shorter in proportion to the rest of the body than in the case of adults. As a child grows older these proportions between the trunk and the arm and legs change. Especially just preceding and during the age of adolescence is bodily growth accelerated. During these years boys and girls frequently increase in height very rapidly. In many cases this rapid growth places a physiological strain on the entire organism which results in an individual's appearing lazy and clumsy. The skeletal system of the body (particularly the arms and legs) grow faster than the circulatory system and other organic systems. This causes some individuals to have a body size approximating that of an adult but with a total organic development more nearly like that of a child. Teachers of physical education and athletic coaches should be unusually cautious not to stimulate or permit these rapidly growing children to participate in unduly strenuous and prolonged physical activities. Danger in this connection is more likely to exist in connection with competitive athletics and more specifically in interscholastic athletics. Boys and girls should be at least seventeen years old before they compete extensively in highly organized competitive athletics and even then every precaution should be taken to prevent organic strain, over-fatigue, or other injury.

[37]

The effect of physical activity on the skeleton. In the human embryo most of the skeleton consists of cartilage. Ossification of the bones begins before birth and is not completed until an individual reaches physiological maturity. Growth and ossification of bones is actively in progress in each normal properly nourished individual until the age of about seventeen or eighteen. There is some evidence to indicate that bones are rebuilt and remodeled during the process of growth according to the lines of stress bearing upon the bone.[1] It seems reasonable to believe, therefore, that physical education can play an important part in determining the inner structure of bones and also the relative position of the bones in the skeleton. As a consequence the entire form, posture, and carriage of the body may be very definitely influenced.[2]

Bone tissue, like muscle or any other kind of tissue, if not used tends to stop growing and may not mature normally. Each kind of cell has a characteristic metabolism. Bone cells, for example, have a different metabolism from that of the liver or of muscles. All cells use oxygen, hydrogen, carbon, and nitrogen, but cells of different kinds use them in different proportions. This means that if the development of the structure of bones is to be enhanced the metalobism of the bone cells must be stimulated through activity. These facts indicate, among other things, that it is particularly important for bones to be used by means of vigorous exercise during the age of adolescence when the bones are growing so rapidly.

Muscular development. Many uninformed persons apparently believe that physical education is primarily concerned with muscular development as an end in itself. Teachers of physical education should realize that motor learning is an important aspect of the general education of a person.

At birth the muscles comprise about one-fourth of the total body weight and by the time physiological maturity is achieved they constitute almost one-half of the body weight. The muscles grow most rapidly between the ages of fourteen and sixteen. During the period from birth to maturity muscles grow a great deal in strength and size but decrease steadily in elasticity. That is, as a person matures, his muscles become stronger but less elastic. When a muscle increases in size and strength as the result of exercise it is because the muscle fibers become larger.

[1] See Jesse Feiring Williams, *A Textbook of Anatomy and Physiology,* p. 90. Philadelphia: W. B. Saunders Company, 1932 (4th ed.).

[2] For a more extended discussion see Eugen Matthias, *The Deeper Meaning of Physical Education,* pp. 7–10. New York: A. S. Barnes and Company, 1929.

No new muscle fibers are formed. The large muscle groups develop and become coordinated earlier in life than do the finer muscles. A child can walk and run, for example, before he can talk, thread a needle, bat a ball, or do a running high jump.

The symmetry of muscular development should likewise be given attention. If some muscles of the body fail to keep pace in their development with the muscular system in general a detailed medical examination should be sought to determine the cause for the failure of the muscles to maintain a balanced development. Such a condition might indicate a predisposition to disease.[1]

The relation of mental and physical development. The studies which have been made on the relation of mental and physical development have not found definite enough relationships to justify the prediction of mental development on the basis of physical development in an individual or group, even if complete data concerning physical development were available. Most of the studies have used averages of different age groups and have determined the statistical correlations between mental and physical traits. The physical traits which have been correlated with mental development include such anthropometric measurements as height, weight, and head size; ossification of wrist bones; stage of dentition; and age of puberty. In nearly all instances there has been found a small positive correlation between mental and physical development but the correlations are not large enough to be significant, except possibly with the lower types of the feebleminded. The most that can be said from these results is that further substantiation is given to the general principle that good traits tend to go together.

It has been suggested that studies in this field cannot be made successfully by using the statistical method of correlation or by taking the average of the physical characteristics of a large number of individuals. Probably a method that offers opportunities for securing sound data involves a large number of studies of the growth of normal individual cases. It might be possible to generalize from the data secured in this way as to the probable growth curves of other individuals.

Constancy of development. The studies of constancy of development have contributed some facts that apparently are of immediate interest. These facts include a demonstration of the constancy of growth in

[1] For a discussion of this point see the Report of White House Conference on Child Health and Protection, *Growth and Development of the Child: Part IV, Appraisement of the Child*, p. 248. New York: The Century Company, 1932.

individual physical and mental characteristics for the majority of individuals. This means that a child who is short for his age will probably be short as an adult and that no great reversal in the relative rate of growth in either mental or physical traits is likely to occur during the period of adolescence. Each segment of the body, such as the head, the trunk, the arms, and the legs, has a separate rate of growth, but the composite growth of the different segments results in a constancy of growth in height and weight in the majority of cases. The ossification of the wrist bones and the eruption of teeth do not proceed with as much constancy as growth in height and weight. Neither is there uniformity in the development of intelligence as measured by intelligence tests. One is justified in concluding, however, that development is approximately constant for any physical or mental trait.

Unsynchronized development. Another interesting observation is that different parts of the body grow at different times and at different rates. Some illustrations of this fact follow. The arms and legs may grow rapidly during a given period, while at the same time the circulatory and respiratory systems are growing very little. Several teeth may erupt during the time that the ossification of bones is taking place slowly. The larger skeletal muscles may develop rapidly during a period when the finer coordinations between the eyes and smaller muscles are maturing slowly.

In view of these facts it has been proposed that studies of the relation between physical and mental development could be made more profitable by means of a composite of physical measurements instead of by individual measurements. The proponents of this point of view show that this was the theory used in the development of mental tests. It is claimed that if the fluctuations in the development of the different parts of the body could be smoothed out by averaging a large number of measurements it would be possible to secure a clearer measure of physical development. This in turn would make it easier to find any true relationship between mental and physical development.[1]

An illustration of a possible unsynchronized maturation in the human body is the development of the nervous system. It has already been stated that the length of body segments, age of puberty, height, weight, dentition, and ossification of bones may develop at different rates. It is

[1] For a discussion of this point see the Report of the Committee on Growth and Development of White House Conference on Child Health and Protection, *Growth and Development of the Child: Part IV, Appraisement of the Child,* p. 208. New York: The Century Company, 1932.

likewise true that the nervous system may develop at a rate different from that of other body parts and characteristics. It seems probable that the uncorrelated development of the different parts of the body may be related to the fact that each type of cell has a peculiar metabolism of its own.

These facts concerning the uneven development of the body during the years of immaturity should guide physical education teachers in the selection of activities and choice of methods. Every precaution should be taken to avoid stimulating children, by means of the social pressure of the group or by other means, to attempt to reach levels of motor achievement that are likely to require excessive effort or endurance. Thoughtful teachers and coaches are often convinced that some boys who are called "quitters" or "yellow" have not yet achieved the organic development essential for sustained, determined, and protracted effort. A high school boy, for example, may be a "quitter" and lack "fight" in running the mile but may prove to be an indefatigable worker and very successful at throwing the javelin or some other event that does not require great endurance.

Age of development. The uneven and unsynchronized development of the human body is accompanied by irregularity of development in intelligence, personality, knowledge, and educational achievement. Educators have adopted titles to describe the different types of development. These titles include chronological, anatomical, physiological, mental, educational, emotional, and other kinds of "ages."

The chronological age is simply the calendar age in terms of years, months, and days. The anatomical age is expressed in terms of the maturity of parts of the body. It is usually expressed in terms of the ossification of the bones, particularly of the small bones in the wrist. Anatomical age is also sometimes determined by the stage of dentition. Physiological age is indicated by the signs of puberty. This is usually determined in boys by the amount and color of the pubic hair, and in girls by the onset of menstruation. Mental age is determined through the use of intelligence tests which seek to measure the ability of a person to adjust his environment and to solve a group of standardized problems. The educational age is used to express the ability of children to achieve certain established norms in the customary school subjects such as reading and spelling. Not very much progress has been made in the effort to develop measures of emotional and personality maturity.

In most cases the relative development which has been achieved is expressed in the form of a quotient. These quotients are obtained by using the age of development reached as a numerator of a fraction and the chronological age as the denominator. A quotient of 1.00, or of 100 as it is usually expressed in giving these quotients, means that the individual is normal or average in the characteristic being measured. If, for example, a boy is exactly 144 months old and has a mental age of 15 years or 180 months, his intelligence quotient would be $\frac{180}{144}$, which is 1.25 and is usually given as 125. This would mean that this boy was considerably above the average in intelligence. Other kinds of quotients are obtained by similar procedures.

Knowledge of the different "ages" and quotients is helpful to teachers in guiding the educational program of children. Conscientious teachers should give careful consideration to the contribution that an understanding of each makes to an intelligent analysis of the needs of each child. No one of these "ages" or quotients, however, furnishes an adequate basis on which to build a sound program of physical education.

The functioning of the nervous system. It is generally agreed that all behavior has a neural basis. The complexity of the nervous system makes possible the superior adjustment and behavior of man. The human nervous system consists of three component parts known as receptors, connectors, and effectors. The first of these parts of the nervous system includes a large number of receptors or sense organs with their sensory or afferent nerves. These receptors are sensitive to stimuli from without and within the body. The effectors include the muscles and glands with their motor or efferent nerves. Between the receptors and effectors are the connectors which are groups of connecting neurones that serve to integrate and combine the stimuli received by the receptors with the responses that are made by the effectors. It should be understood that the nervous system functions as one complete unit and not as three separate segments or units. The receptors, connectors, and effectors are not independent units in any sense. The workings of the nervous system have sometimes been compared with those of a large telephone exchange with the connectors in the central nervous system serving as "central" or the telephone exchange. Such an analogy may help one to visualize the nervous system but it describes very inadequately the elaborate and efficient patterns of connections and nerve ramifications.

There are usually recognized three levels of nerve action. The first of these takes place in the spinal cord and includes reflexes and other forms of direct automatic response to a stimulus. The second level of nerve action takes place in the midbrain and includes responses which are more complicated but do not involve consciousness. The third or highest level of response depends on consciousness and involves the cortex of the cerebral areas of the brain. It is on this level that experiences make permanent impressions which can be used at later times in making decisions and solving problems. The use of all three of these levels increases greatly the number and complexity of the reactions which can be made.

Sensations. The sense organs or receptors with their different nerves serve the purpose of receiving stimuli and transmitting them in the form of nervous energy to the spinal cord or brain. Some of the sense organs may be classified as external and receive stimuli from outside the body. There are many other sense organs which receive sensations from the internal organs of the body. The senses which enable one to have experiences and receive sensations include (1) the sense of sight which is dependent on the functioning of the eyes; (2) the sense of smell which involves patches of olfactory mucous membrane located on the turbinate bones in the upper part of the nose; (3) the sense of hearing which involves the ears; (4) the sense of taste which depends on taste buds situated in the papillae located on the tongue and palate to determine salt, sour, bitter, and sweet; (5) the sense of equilibrium which involves principally the semicircular canals of the inner ear but also involves sensations received from the muscles and joints which enables one to tell from sensations, without the use of the eyes, the position and movements of the body; (6) the sense of feeling which depends primarily on the skin to receive stimuli of touch, cold, warmth, and pain; (7) the systemic sense which enables one to receive internal sensations from the different organic systems of the body such as the digestive, respiratory, and circulatory systems; and (8) the kinesthetic, or motor, senses which make it possible for an individual to receive sensations from the muscles and tendons. These sensations are important in the contraction of voluntary muscles and in securing good muscular coordination. They are particularly important in the development of motor skills.

Although sensations originate in sense organs located in different parts of the body they are centralized and combined into patterns by the central nervous systems. One's knowledge concerning a football, for example, is gained through a combination of sensations of sight, touch, and smell. Our experience in connection with a tempting beefsteak is

[43]

made up of visual, olfactory, gustatory, and kinesthetic sensations. The combining and grouping of sensations in this way so as to bring about meaningful experiences is one of the very important functions of the cortical areas of the brain.

Visual and motor sensations. All forms of sensation are important in physical education, although the ones received through the kinesthetic and visual senses are probably of more immediate and direct significance. The visual sensations are received through the eyes and the optic nerves. The exact details of the process of how light waves which strike the eye are transformed into nerve impulses are not clearly understood. One theory holds that the vibrations of the light waves stimulate in a mechanical way the nerve endings in the retina of the eyeball. Another theory holds that the process, which takes place in the rods and cones of the retina, is photochemical in nature.

The kinesthetic sensations originate in sensory spindles which are buried in the muscles and tendons. These spindles are composed of small groups of muscle or tendon fibers approximately 1 to 4 millimeters long and $\frac{1}{5}$ to $\frac{1}{4}$ millimeter wide. Nerve fibers are wrapped around each group of muscle or tendon fibers and terminate inside the spindle. These spindles are stimulated mechanically by the contractions of the muscles and the pulling of the tendons as the muscles and tendons are used during motor activity. The impulses are carried to the brain, thereby enabling one to be conscious of the movement of any part of the body. The kinesthetic sensations received in this way play a fundamental part in developing the well coordinated motor skills which are necessary to play well such games as golf, tennis, and football and to participate skillfully in other physical education activities.

Reactions. All stimuli that affect receptors elicit some form of response. These responses may be muscular and glandular reactions or they may be more definitely mental reactions that involve cortical neurones and which are only indirectly concerned with muscular or glandular activity. In physical education we are, as a rule, more directly interested in reactions of the muscular and glandular systems. The glands which are of the most importance are the endocrine glands, frequently called the ductless glands or the glands of internal secretion. They include the thyroid, adrenal, and pituitary glands, and others. These reactions are of much significance and are closely associated with emotional responses. Responses of the muscular system are usually associated with bodily movement and the responses of the glandular system are usually concerned with emotional reactions such as fear, rage, sadness, joy, and terror.

Nearly all behavior above the level of a direct response to an immediate stimulus involves a combination of the activity of several different effectors. Even a relatively simple motor movement includes a number of muscular coordinations and also the brain. In emotional responses, most of the effectors of the body are usually concerned.

The large supply of sensory and motor nerves and the complexity and richness of the connecting or coordinating nerve units are important characteristics of man which enable him to make a tremendously large number and variety of responses. An unusually large number of nerves is supplied for the movements of the arms and hands. This large supply of nerves constitutes an enlargement of the spinal cord which is located between the shoulders. It seems probable that this exceptional nervous equipment for receiving sensations and making motor responses with the hands and arms may account for the apparent preference of boys and girls for games which involve the use of the hands and arms.

Reciprocal innervation. The ability of the nervous system to execute efficiently the process known as reciprocal innervation is of much importance in physical education. It is this cooperative activity of the nervous system that permits a group of muscles to contract smoothly and efficiently by causing the antagonistic muscles to be inhibited in their action. For example, when the biceps contract to bend the arm the triceps relax so as to permit the movement to be carried out smoothly. When a person is just beginning to learn a motor skill, such as serving in tennis, or dancing, he frequently appears awkward and tense. This is due to the fact that he has not developed satisfactorily the necessary coordinations between the different muscle groups concerned.

The relaxation of antagonistic muscles is the natural way for muscles to react, and any artificial and formalized exercises which fail to recognize this principle are not physiologically wholesome. So-called static exercises in which both a flexor and the antagonistic extensor muscles are held in contraction at the same time should not be recommended. Such exercises form the basis of many commercial "systems of physical culture."

Muscle tone. When a person is normally healthy, all the muscles of the body are in a constant state of slight contraction. This is believed to be caused by slight stimuli which are constantly received through the nerves. The moderate tension on muscles makes it possible for them

[45]

to react to stimuli much more quickly and effectively than would be possible if recovery from complete relaxation had to be accomplished. The muscles have a "running start," so to speak, and are therefore able to react promptly with the minimum expenditure of energy. This is important in all kinds of muscles but it is particularly important in the involuntary visceral and cardiac muscles. The very existence of life itself depends on the smooth and efficient functioning of these muscles.

It is generally believed that the muscle tone of all the muscles of the body is much the same. If the skeletal muscles, including the large muscles of the trunk, are soft and flabby and in poor tone it is quite likely that the visceral and cardiac muscles are likewise in a poor condition. It seems, therefore, that the maintenance of good muscular tonus is not only essential for good body mechanics but that the efficient functioning of the more fundamental organic systems is likewise dependent on the tone of the muscles of the body.

General motor ability. In light of the available evidence it is apparently inaccurate to state that there is such a thing as general motor ability. It seems that most motor skills are specific and are not closely related to others. The facts on this point are particularly definite in regard to finer coordinations and movements involving the smaller muscles. Many students of the problem of motor ability have proposed the hypothesis that there must be certain fundamental basic motor capacities underlying the more complex activities in which people ordinarily take part. A number of studies have been made in the effort to find and describe these basic motor capacities that were supposed to exist. Carefully controlled tests have been made of such traits as speed of hand movements, eye-hand pursuit movements, ear-hand motor rhythm coordinations, postural steadiness and stability, and of speed in serial discrimination of stimuli presented by the eye and ear. The weight of evidence from these studies is opposed to the hypothesis of basic capacities. Some individuals made high scores on several of the tests but these scores were judged to indicate that those individuals had a wide variety of specific skills.

There are some data to indicate that the specificity of the finer motor skills exists in young children and therefore is probably not the result of previous training. Some investigations have also been made to determine whether skill in industrial operations could be predicted from the scores made on the Stanford Motor Skills Unit. The results showed that there was no relationship between the scores on this test and efficiency in typewriting or knitting mill work. It seems, therefore, that successful performance in motor activities involving the finer coordinations depends more on the methods used than on the fundamental motor capacities of the individuals. This means that much emphasis should be given to the techniques of training and practice. It means also that teachers should give much attention to analyzing motor skills in order that the finer coordinations may be clearly understood.

Basic capacities in physical education. There are some indications that certain basic motor capacities underlie the larger and more general neuro-muscular coordinations which are used in physical education. There is not ample evidence to enable one to predict the motor skill at one age from the skill at an earlier age. It seems, however, that with the available measurement instruments the probable success in physical education activities can be predicted for boys with a reasonable degree of accuracy and somewhat less accurately for girls. Brace's scale of motor ability tests, Cozens' tests of general athletic ability in college men, McCloy's tests of athletic power, Rogers' physical capacity tests, and MacCurdy's tests of motor capacity are some of the more successful efforts to devise such tests.[1] All of these tests include activities that involve the large muscles of the body. They provide the means by which pupils may be classified for physical education and also make it practical to provide programs of physical education suited to the individual needs of pupils.

Relation of age, sex, and nutrition to motor skills. The relation of age, sex, and nutrition to motor ability is of much importance to physical education teachers in the choice of activities and methods. A large number of studies have shown that there is a definite relationship between chronological age and motor ability. The investigations which have been reported show that as children become older they gain in motor control. There are not available for the same individual, however, data over a period of years which would enable one to plot individual

[1] David K. Brace, *Measuring Motor Ability.* New York: A. S. Barnes and Company, 1927.

Frederick Warren Cozens, *The Measurement of General Athletic Ability in College Men.* Eugene: University of Oregon, Physical Education Series, Vol. 1, No. 3, 1929.

Charles Harold McCloy, *The Measurement of Athletic Power.* New York: A. S. Barnes and Company, 1932.

Frederick Rand Rogers, *Tests and Measurement Programs in the Redirection of Physical Education.* New York: Teachers' College, Columbia University, 1927.

Howard Leigh MacCurdy, *A Test for Measuring the Physical Capacity of Secondary School Boys.* New York: Teachers' College, Columbia University, 1933.

[47]

growth curves of motor control. Even though there is a rather well established relationship between chronological age and motor skills, there is nevertheless a wide range of skill in any event among any group of normal individuals of any given age. It is especially important that this normal distribution of skill be recognized by teachers when they are using norms or averages such as, for example, the Philadelphia Age Aim Charts or the Los Angeles Achievement Expectancy Tables.

There are apparent no significant sex differences in motor ability before about five years of age. As children become older the differences between the sexes become more evident and specific. Boys seem to be superior in most types of physical achievement but there is some evidence to show that girls excel in steadiness and in some complex movements.

Reports by Gesell[1] and the results of other studies indicate that there seems to be very little relationship between malnutrition and motor ability. Children with rickets seem to do about as well on motor tests as do children without rickets. Even though the limited data do not indicate that malnutrition is a significant factor in the development of motor skills, general observations and common sense lead one to believe that if one hopes to have good general health and to do well in physical activities he should be adequately nourished. It is recommended, therefore, that teachers of physical education emphasize to their pupils the importance of eating nourishing well-balanced meals if they hope to make progress in the development of motor skills.

The relation of energy to life. Every form of activity, whether it be playing football, solving a problem in geometry, thinking about the last holiday, or wishing for another vacation period, causes some expenditure of energy. The greatest expenditure of energy comes, however, as the result of vigorous activity of the voluntary muscles. All energy is supplied to the human organism in the form of nourishment. All food, both vegetable and animal, is either directly or indirectly the result of the process of photosynthesis. This is the process whereby the green chlorophyll material in plants absorbs energy from the sunlight and synthesizes carbon dioxide and water to form carbohydrates. During the process oxygen is given off. These carbohydrates can in turn be used to nourish either plants or animals. All energy, therefore, may be accurately described as being obtained from the sun. If we burn wood,

[1] Arnold Gesell, *Infancy and Human Growth.* New York: The Macmillan Company, 1928.

coal, or oil, we are merely releasing, by the process of oxidation, latent energy which has been stored in these substances during the past.

Life processes which necessitate an expenditure of energy result in the breaking up of cell protoplasm for the release of energy. This involves the oxidation of protoplasmic materials, with the concomitant giving off of body wastes which are removed from the body by means of the excretory system. The oxygen needed for this process is secured through breathing. In order to rebuild the depleted cells, food must be eaten, digsted, absorbed into the blood, and carried by the circulation to the cells of the body that need it. When the food reaches these cells it is assimilated and built into living protoplasm. The process of tearing down cells is called katabolism and the process of building up cells is known as anabolism. The two taken together are known as metabolism. The total metabolic process is almost synonymous with life itself. Since foods of all kinds are dependent on the chlorophyll of plants for securing their latent energy it may readily be seen that the process of photosynthesis is of fundamental importance in biology and that all life depends on it.

Factors that influence energy requirements. There are a number of factors which influence the energy requirements of children and which in that way affect the rate of metabolism. These include the external temperature, the amount of food consumed, the carbohydrate and fat consistency of the diet, the presence of fatigue, the adequacy of sleep, the results of training, the efficiency of the muscles in doing work, and the emotional status of an individual.

A number of studies have demonstrated that the metabolism of a person is increased by lowering the external temperature to which he is exposed. The work of Lusk [1] and of others shows that the amount of food of each class which is consumed is a significant factor in determining the amount of energy produced by the body. It has also been shown that a diet high in carbohydrates seems to result in greater muscular efficiency than a diet rich in fats. [2] The results of several well conducted studies indicate that as fatigue progresses the amount of oxygen consumed increases. It is known that sleep slows down the metabolic rate. Training has the effect of increasing muscular efficiency and also the efficiency of the respiratory, circulatory, and nutritive processes.

[1] Graham Lusk, *Elements of the Science of Nutrition.* Philadelphia: W. B. Saunders Company, 1928 (4th ed.).

[2] August Krogh and Johannes Lindhard, "The Relative Value of Fat and Carbohydrates as Sources of Muscular Energy," *Biochemical Journal,* XIV (July, 1920), 290.

Muscular efficiency is measured in terms of percentage. This percentage is obtained by using as a divisor the increase in metabolism (over and above the basal metabolism) which resulted from the doing of the work, and taking as a dividend the amount of work done. The quotient found by this process of division indicates the percentage of muscular efficiency. Both the amount of work done and the increase in metabolism are expressed in calories. A calorie is defined as the amount of heat required to raise the temperature of one kilogram of water by one degree Centigrade. As the efficiency of muscles increases the amount of work which can be done by a given amount of energy becomes larger.

Mental, emotional, and nervous activity require the expenditure of energy and increase metabolism. Most of the data available on this point have been collected from studies of adults, but the results are no doubt applicable also to children.

Function builds structure. The facts and authoritative opinion concerning metabolism indicate that when cells are broken down they are rebuilt more strongly so that they have more endurance and can withstand more strain. This is an illustration of the generally accepted principle that function builds structure. In light of this principle it is apparent that physical education plays an important part in bodily development, including particularly the organic systems. A person will grow naturally and achieve a certain size without much exercise, as the result of his biological inheritance. This sedentary development will probably progress reasonably well, but physical education provides the means of developing in each individual a reserve of energy and endurance beyond that which would normally accrue as the result of maturation. Vigorous physical activity, such as is usually included in programs of physical education, requires the release of a great deal of energy by the entire body. The release of this energy necessitates the oxidation of cell protoplasm and the consequent rebuilding of the cells. This results in increased and accelerated development of the organic systems of the body. In order for physical exercise to be of the most value in organic development, it must be participated in regularly by boys and girls throughout the years in which bodily growth is taking place. From a biological point of view, exercise by adults helps to maintain the normal functioning of the nutritive processes and helps one to "keep fit," but it is not clear that much organic development can take place after a person reaches physiological maturity.

A person, who has developed the organic systems of his body to the

[50]

extent that he has a reserve of energy and endurance, beyond that required for sedentary living, is better equipped for living well. Such an individual is better able to meet the crises of life and to get a maximum of satisfaction and pleasure out of the experiences which he has in life. He has the energy to participate in interesting, adventurous, and challenging activities and to live on a higher level.

Respiration. As has already been pointed out, the oxygen used in the processes of metabolism is secured through the activity of the respiratory system. Breathing is brought about in a mechanical way by the actions of the muscles attached to the ribs and by the action of the diaphragm, which is a muscle that divides the trunk into the thoracic and abdominal cavities. In the process of breathing the muscles attached to the ribs raise them, and at the same time the dome-shaped diaphragm becomes flatter by contracting. The downward action of the diaphragm and the raising of the ribs and shoulders increases the volume of the thorax and creates a partial vacuum. This results in the atmospheric pressure, causing air to rush into the lungs. The lungs are elastic and follow the chest wall. The larger the thorax is made, the greater is the amount of air that enters the lungs. In ordinary breathing about one pint of air is inhaled; but when a definite effort is made to raise the ribs and shoulders and to depress the diaphragm, as much as three quarts of air may sometimes be inhaled. Exhalation results from lowering the ribs and raising the diaphragm. Through the acts of inhaling and exhaling, the lungs are enabled to carry on an exchange of gases in the blood that circulates through them. The blood gives off carbon dioxide and takes on oxygen from air in the lungs. It is the oxygen secured in this way which makes it possible for oxidation to take place in the cells of the body and release the energy which is necessary for the activities of life.

The nerve center which controls the action of the diaphragm and of the intercostal muscles in breathing is known as the respiratory center and is located in the lower part of the brain, called the medulla. Breathing is controlled automatically by this nerve center. This makes it unnecessary for one to give conscious attention to the breathing function. When the body needs more oxygen, one automatically begins to breathe deeper and faster and continues to do so until the normal balance between oxygen and carbon dioxide in the blood is restored.

The facts about the respiratory function indicate that the blood cannot be super-charged with oxygen by means of deep breathing. If one participates in deep-breathing exercises, it will result merely in a reduced rate of breathing until the percentage of oxygen in the blood returns to normal. There is some evidence to show that the breathing of pure oxygen will hasten recovery from fatigue after strenuous exercise. There are not adequate data to justify one in believing that the breathing of pure oxygen before a period of vigorous exertion will increase one's endurance or cause competing athletes to improve their previous records. This fact, apparently, is not understood by all coaches.

The published report of a study by Karpovich [1] indicates that the breathing of pure oxygen by athletes would have some beneficial effect for a few seconds if each athlete breathed the oxygen immediately preceding his competitive efforts. The results of this one study, however, do not furnish adequate proof that this would always be true in the majority of cases.

It is seen, therefore, in the light of the established facts that breathing exercises as a routine part of the physical education program, and the administration of oxygen to athletes, should not be advocated.

Differences in males and females. Up until the age of puberty the differences between boys and girls are not great enough to be particularly significant so far as physical education is concerned. Usually boys and girls play together in the same groups quite agreeably and successfully until they reach about eleven years of age. After the sex differences begin to manifest themselves, boys and girls show different interests and the anatomical differences become more pronounced.

Boys are stronger than girls. This is particularly true in regard to the muscles of the shoulder girdle. The hips of girls are broader, the legs are relatively shorter, and the thigh bones join the pelvis more obliquely than in boys. The center of gravity of the female body is lower than that of the male. In most cases the muscular strength of girls and women is less in relation to the total body weight than that of boys and men. These facts indicate that girls and women should not be expected to excel in activities which emphasize speed in running or that require support of the body by the arms.

Body types. Since the beginning of civilization men have apparently been interested in the differences of body build and have attempted to assign some significance to different types. Patterson [2] has selected

[1] Peter V. Karpovich, "The Effect of Oxygen Inhalation on Swimming Performance," *Research Quarterly,* V (May, 1934), 24–30.

[2] Donald G. Patterson, *Physique and Intellect,* p. 231. New York: The Century Company, 1930.

and tabulated in the following table details of certain features of physical types which have been described by different writers from Hippocrates to the present. It is interesting to observe the approximate uniformity of classes and terminology that have been used by all these writers.

TABLE I

CLASSIFICATION OF BODY TYPES

Authority	Type		
	1	2	3
Hippocrates	Habitus Apoplecticus		Habitus phthisicus
Walker (1852)	Nutritive beauty	Locomotive beauty	Mental beauty
Carus (1853)	Phlegmatic (region of digestive organs prominent)	Athletic (bones and muscles strongly developed)	Asthenic (narrow chest, long body skeleton and muscles poorly developed)
Viola and later Naccarati	Macrosplanchnic type	Normosplanchnic type	Microsplanchic type
Pende	Hypervegetative type		Hypovegetative type
Sigaud	Digestive type	Muscular type	Respiratory cerebral type
Davenport	Fleshy	Muscular	Slender biotype
Kretschmer	Pyknic type	Athletic type	Asthenic type

The classification of body types that appears most often in the literature in this field is the one proposed by Kretschmer.[1] He found from his studies that three ever-recurring principal types are found among men and women. These types were designated as asthenic, athletic, and

[1] Ernst Kretschmer, *Physique and Character.* New York: Harcourt and Brace, 1925.

pyknic. He found also various small groups which did not conform to any of these three "typical" types. These were grouped as a special dysplastic type.

The asthenic group includes the lean, narrowly built persons. The athletic type have a strong skeleton and musculature, average height, relatively broad shoulders, prominent chest, and tapering trunk. The persons of middle height, broad rounded figure, broad face, and short heavy neck are classed as pyknic. In the dysplastic type Kretschmer classified the figures with some abnormality.

There have been efforts from time to time to place persons with different types of body-build in homogeneous groups for participation in athletic activities. It has often been said, for example, that the pyknic type is best suited for football, the athletic type for running, and the asthenic type for high jumping. Others have attempted to show that the pyknic type is best suited for playing in the line on a football team and that the athletic type is best suited for backfield positions. Efforts at this kind of classification have not been very helpful, because some of the most famous sprinters have been short and stocky while others have been long and lean. Some great backfield stars in football have been short and broad and others, equally great, have been tall and relatively slender. Glowacki [1] in her study of women students at the Univrsity of Michigan found no relationship between body type and choice of recreational activities. In this group of women she found that the athletic type ranked first with the highest health ratings. The mixed type was second, the asthenic third, the pyknic fourth, and the dysplastic type was last.

It does not seem practical, in light of the facts, to recommend any particular kind of physical activities to boys and girls on the basis of their type of body build. Other things seem to be the determining factors in the achievement of success in athletics. The available data indicate that the asthenic type might show a somewhat more marked susceptibility to certain diseases of the respiratory and circulatory systems. It would be wise, therefore, for teachers of physical education to take particular care that the necessary preventive and protective procedures are followed in regard to this group.

Physical defects in children. Studies made in the past few years seem to show that the presence of physical defects in children is not as

[1] Felice Marie Glowacki, Constitutional Body Types as Related to Recreation and Health Ratings, pp. 38–39. Unpublished master's thesis, University of Michigan, 1934.

closely related to mental and personality deficiencies and to retardation in school as was formerly thought. It is agreed by all physicians and teachers, however, that it is highly desirable for all remediable defects and unhygienic modes of living to be corrected. This is necessary in order that each child may be free to grow, learn, and enjoy life to the extent of his capacity.

A number of studies have reported on the prevalence of physical defects among children and adults. The most comprehensive work on this problem was done in connection with the examination of drafted men during the World War. The statistical reports of these examinations show that about one-fourth of the young men between the ages of 21 and 31 were rejected on account of physical defects, and that almost half of this age-group had one or more defects that were serious enough to handicap the individuals. In some of the states that had large immigrant populations, more than two-thirds of the young men had serious physical defects and almost one-half of them were rejected. There have been published, also, several studies purporting to show that at least two-thirds of the school children in the nation are physically defective. Keene has summarized a number of these studies.[1]

A knowledge of the prevalence of defects in children or familiarity with the statistics which have been accumulated from the examination of large numbers of children does not enable one to plan a program of physical education suited to the needs of a particular individual child. These data on the condition of the masses of children do serve the purpose, however, of impressing teachers with the importance of an accurate examination to determine whether each child is handicapped by the presence of one or more defects. The results of an individual examination of each child should guide teachers in planning and teaching individualized programs of physical education.

Summary. The biological principles of physical education are important in helping teachers guide the development of children. Some of these principles are derived from what is known of (1) the evolutionary development of man; (2) the biological and social heredity of man; (3) the development and nature of the human skeleton; (4) the effect of physical activity on the skeleton; (5) the development of the muscular system; (6) the relation of mental and physical development; (7) the rate of development of different parts of the body and of different traits

[1] Charles H. Keene, *The Physical Welfare of the School Child*, p. 9. Boston: Houghton Mifflin Company, 1929.

and characteristics; (8) the functioning of the nervous system; and (9) the functioning of the respiratory system.

It is also important for teachers to know the nature and function of muscle tone. The data bearing on the question of general motor ability and of basic capacities in physical education are significant. The facts on the relation of age, sex, and nutrition to motor skills should be known to teachers of physical education. Knowledge of the processes of metabolism and of the expenditure of energy is of much importance. The anatomical and emotional characteristics of males and females are significant in the choice of activities and instructional methods. Apparently body types are not closely related to the choice of physical recreations. There are many data which show the prevalence of defects among children. These data are important for emphasizing the importance of adequate examinations to determine the status of each child. In planning a program, however, it is essential that the needs of each individual child be considered.

QUESTIONS

1. What applications of the facts bearing on the evolutionary development of man may be made to the teaching of physical education?
2. What are some of the specific facts concerning heredity which are of direct interest to physical education teachers?
3. What characteristics of the skeleton are significant from the standpoint of physical education?
4. What effect does physical activity have on the skeleton?
5. What are some of the data that have a bearing on the efforts of some teachers to bring about symmetrical bodily development in their pupils?
6. What is the significance of reciprocal innervation to teachers of physical education?
7. Why should teachers of physical education be conversant with the data on muscle tonus?
8. What bearing have the facts concerning metabolism on the teaching of physical education?
9. If you were a swimming coach what are some of the facts concerning the respiratory system that should be of particular interest to you?
10. What differences in males and females are significant for teachers of physical education?

REFERENCES

Gesell, Arnold. *Infancy and Human Growth.* New York: The Macmillan Company, 1928.

Keene, Charles H. *The Physical Welfare of the School Child*. Boston: Houghton Mifflin Company, 1929.

Matthias, Eugen. *The Deeper Meaning of Physical Education*. New York: A. S. Barnes and Company, 1929.

Report of the Committee on Growth and Development of the White House Conference on Child Health and Protection, *Growth and Development of the Child*. *Part IV, Appraisement of the Child*. New York: The Century Company, 1932.

Williams, Jesse Feiring. *A Textbook of Anatomy and Physiology*. Philadelphia: W. B. Saunders Company, 1932. (4th ed.)

CHAPTER IV

The Sociological Foundations of Physical Education

Relation of physical education to society. The characteristics of contemporary society, the dominant ideals of the nation, the established social institutions, and the accepted social and educational philosophy have significant influences on the objectives, subject matter, and methods of physical education. One may be inclined to conclude as the result of superficial consideration that only recreation and social institutions for the promotion and protection of health have any relationship to physical education. Such a conclusion, however, is not sound because all phases of modern society are so closely interrelated that any changes in society may result in unplanned and frequently unforseen social problems. Several examples of such interrelation follow.

1. Developments in industry affect employment.
2. Changes in types of adult work influence the programs and curricula of the schools.
3. Changes in international policies by the government affect domestic politics.
4. Changes in immigration policies affect population trends and demand for agricultural and manufactured products.
5. Changes in the demand by the masses of the people for increased social services affect taxation and governmental policies.
6. Developments in communication and transportation tend to standardize the ways of living of the rural and urban people, and have much influence on the forms of recreation participated in by large numbers of people.
7. Changes in consumption habits affect the amount of leisure time of the people and the demand for facilities and opportunities for spending leisure time.

Society makes man what he is; every thought, habit, ideal, or material comfort which accrues to anyone is the result of the experiences and cultural background that are made possible by society. Intelligence, character, personality, and skills are likewise made possible by association with others. The culture in which a child grows up provides the influences that shape and mould his personality. These facts emphasize the importance of teachers being concerned with the background, goals, and contemporary characteristics of American culture. The success of a teacher's efforts to direct and guide the integration of the personalities of his pupils is determined largely by the cultural influences with which they are associated.

Physical education is a definite and integral part of the programs of the social institutions that are concerned with education, recreation, and physical and mental health. The past experiences in physical education of the human race form a large and significant part of the social heritage which is passed on from one generation to another, and contribute definitely toward helping people live happily and freely. The information which is included in the remaining pages of this chapter shows the necessity of including physical education as part of all school programs, and sets forth some of the sociological principles on which it should be based.

The need for physical education. Ordinarily we do not interfere with vital processes unless something goes wrong with them. If a person's digestion, respiration, or locomotion is functioning smoothly and efficiently we do not ordinarily perform a surgical operation on him or require him to take medicine. This guiding principle applies equally well to a social organism. If the children in a savage society receive adequate education, through their daily experiences as members of the tribe, to enable them to adjust successfully to their environment, no schools are established by the adult savages for the education of the children. Likewise, if the individuals in a highly organized and complex industrial society could find adequate opportunities for creative activity and intelligent self-expression through their work and could participate in satisfying, enjoyable, and developmental recreations during their leisure time, the members of society would not provide and finance much organized physical education. It is when the ordinary everyday experiences of people prove to be clearly inadequate to prepare them for successful adjustment in their society that organized education becomes necessary. In extremely simple societies practically no education through organized schools is necessary. But as society becomes more complex and civilization more advanced, it becomes increasingly important and essential to prepare each individual for successful living in his environment, and to transmit accurately from generation to generation the accumulated social heritage of the race.

The characteristics of American society are such that most individuals

[59]

ordinarily cannot participate extensively in play activities or express themselves through other forms of wholesome recreation. In nearly all communities, therefore, a comprehensive program of physical education is needed to meet the developmental, recreational, and educational needs of the children and youth.

The social learnings of men. The adjustment activities of man are determined to some extent by the structure of the human organism, by reflexes, and by instincts. The details of bodily structure that appear to be most significant are (1) the way the nervous system is organized, (2) the structure of the throat and head which makes possible the human voice, and (3) the hand with its opposed thumb which makes possible fine manipulations and accurate movements.

Reflexes are important in most of the vital processes of living and reproduction. The knee jerk is the reflex most often used as an illustration, but this kind of reaction is fundamental in digestion, respiration, vision, and most other essential physiological processes of the body. Instincts are believed by some psychologists to be inborn or innate motives to behavior. It seems clear, however, in the light of recent developments in psychology that most of the things we ordinarily call instincts are the result of our social inheritance.

The ability to learn is man's great and important means of adjustment. The structure of the body, the reflexes, and instincts are significant; but none of these things is comparable in importance with the ability of man to modify his ways of reacting and behaving as the result of experiences. Human beings learn most of the things that are useful to them in life from their association with other people. If each individual were to depend exclusively on his own trial-and-error learnings, no one would ever be very intelligent and progress of civilization would be impossible.

Mankind for many centuries has passed on from generation to generation the accumulated learnings of the race. During the earlier periods of man's history this transmission of experience took place largely by word of mouth but during more recent centuries carvings, writings, and printing have been used with greatly accelerated effectiveness for this purpose. It remains for each generation to decide what shall be passed on by means of organized education to the oncoming generation. It seems to be clearly evident that the experiences which should be perpetuated should be the ones that will help the younger generation to adjust most successfully as individuals and as a group. The knowledge, traditions, loyalties, reverences, and ideals which seem to be most valuable should be taught. And prejudices, biased pre-judgments, hatreds, and intolerances should be eliminated through education.

Our social inheritance can be changed, directed, and controlled. Thereby hangs, not a tale, but a fundamental and far-reaching significant fact. Teachers have the opportunity and the responsibility of making each generation more intelligent, happier, and better in every way than the preceding generation. Physical education can and should make its contribution toward carrying on and improving the social inheritance, especially in regard to recreation, health, and sportsmanship.

Socialization of the individual through physical education. All normal human beings naturally seek the company of others. This trait developed in the human race during the centuries when mankind was in keen competition with the forces of nature and the ravages of wild animals in order to survive. Individual men found it necessary to cooperate so that their combined strength might be used for the safety and advantage of all.

Association with other people makes it possible for human beings to gain experiences, have ideas, think, and be intelligent. Out of the organized need and values of association and cooperation, man has developed and emphasized worthy traits such as altruism, loyalty, sympathy, and gregariousness, A person who possesses such characteristics to a marked degree is usually said to be well socialized. He is able to "play ball" with his social group; he can see the justice and advantages of social cooperation, and he recognizes the unfairness and short-sightedness of selfishness.

Many thoughtful teachers of physical education have pointed out the large numbers of opportunities that exist in play and physical recreation for providing social experiences for boys and girls. Every conscientious teacher should recognize these opportunities and seek to use them to promote the socialization of his pupils and to increase their ability to adapt and adjust to their social environment.

The socializing influences of physical education are particularly valuable in the education of boys and girls. Take as an illustration the case of the son of the ash-man who lives across the railroad tracks and who consistently breaks through the line on the football team and throws for a loss the son of the banker, who lives in the big house on the hill. Consider the situation where the daughter of the tenant farmer is the best player on the girls' basketball team; or the instance in which the daughter of the Italian fruit dealer is the best dancer in the dancing class. When boys and girls have experiences such as these they are almost sure to develop a more democratic and tolerant attitude toward all classes of society. Lessons of this kind are valuable not only to members of the particular groups concerned, but also to the whole student body.

Socialization of the group through physical education. The socialization of the individuals who make up a group contributes to the socialization of the group and to the development of a community or collective spirit. Opportunities of associating with other people help all to see that their hopes, aspirations, fears, and joys are much the same and tend to create a kinship of shared interests. When these common interests become definitely established and integrated they cause the group to be a compact unit; not merely a number of separate individuals located in proximity to each other. The unified spirit which dominates such a group is called by sociologists the social mind.

It seems to be generally agreed by students of social problems that physical education can make definite contributions toward the socialization of a group. The opportunities that it provides for the close association of people in interesting activities and for the building of a community of interest through efforts, successes, and failures in physical activities are two of its significant features. Sports, in particular, are valuable in developing mutual respect and interest among different social groups and classes. In nearly all instances the best players are chosen for the team and the best runners and jumpers win their events, regardless of their social status. These facts which may easily be observed help to develop a group consciousness and spirit.

The institutions of society. There have developed out of human experience, covering a period of centuries, a large number of institutions that serve to make social living function with a reasonable degree of security, decency, and satisfaction. Outstanding in importance among these institutions of society are the family, government, education, recreation, vocations, religion, and morals.

Institutions change to meet changing social conditions, but there is a great social inertia which prevents institutions from changing as rapidly as some aspects of society change. Many people seem greatly to regret that such is the case, and to chafe and fret because they cannot remake social institutions quickly whenever it appears to be expedient to do so. A large number of sociologists, however, believe it is good and desirable that complete changes in social institutions must take place slowly. They

[62]

point out that the accumulated, organized experiences of the race should not be dissipated recklessly. The achievements that have been made in regard to family, government, education, religion, and other social institutions have been accomplished as the result of much labor, suffering, and sacrifice over long periods of time. It would seem to be the height of folly, then, for the members of a social group to permit any relatively ignorant or selfish persons to undermine or destroy the institutions of society that were established with such great difficulty. Society should change or abolish its institutions only after deliberate consideration and trial of the proposed substitute in restricted situations.

During some periods, changes in society take place much more rapidly than in other periods of the same length. It has been pointed out repeatedly that social changes have taken place more rapidly in America during the past two decades than during any period of similar length in the history of the country. It is highly desirable that teachers of physical education be familiar with the basic social institutions and keep themselves informed of the current changes that are taking place in society.

The place of physical education in education. A social emphasis in education is clearly evident to any critical student and observer of current educational problems. This emphasis has been present throughout the past century but it has become particularly dominant during the past two decades; it has fluctuated in intensity from time to time, being especially strong about the time of the World War and probably weakest during the period of materialism and artificial prosperity immediately before the debacle of 1929. In regard to the school curriculum it is evident that contemporary social developments have placed the social studies in a position of foremost importance.

The philosophy of education which has accompanied and been a part of this democratic social emphasis has stressed the idea that education is a process of growth and adjustment through experiences. Self-directed pupil activity and practice in making conscious intelligent choices and decisions have been emphasized. The enthusiastic proponents of this philosophy of education have brought forth and popularized a large number of expressions or slogans around which have been organized many school procedures that are meaningful to large numbers of teachers. Among the more widely used of these expressions are the following: *the education of the whole child, the child-centered school, learning by doing, the activity school and curriculum, purposeful activity, activity*

[63]

leading to further activity, and *freedom of expression.* Phrases of this kind have no doubt helped many teachers to understand more clearly the essential features and practical applications of a modern educational philosophy, but to others they have apparently been slogans that were repeated in a parrot-like manner.

Physical education is particularly well adapted to the application of the social and philosophical democratic principles that are accepted and emphasized in progressive education. Freedom of choice and self-direction, participation in complete unified experiences, pupil initiative and leadership, and participation in intrinsically interesting activities can all be provided naturally and easily through physical education. These facts indicate that every program of organized education for children should provide liberally for all children to participate in physical education.

Education and recreation. Recreation is a fundamental human need which is necessary for everyone in order to insure morale and to make possible the health and growth of personality. There are different kinds of activities that serve as recreation. Many things, such, for example, as gardening, fishing, handicrafts, music, and dancing, are work for some people and recreation for others. The activities most often included in organized programs of recreation are music, art, literature, dramatics, handicrafts, parties, and other forms of social recreation, and such physical recreations as athletics, games, water activities, outings, and winter sports. The physical recreations are usually the core of a recreation program because they make a more widespread appeal. Nearly all normal young people welcome an opportunity to take part in athletics, play, and outings, but only a limited number of people, apparently, are enthusiastic about each of the other forms of recreational activity.

This condition represents a deficiency in the education and cultural development of the American people. Nearly everyone should be educated for leisure in such a way that he or she can live gracefully and fully throughout his life. We should strive to bring all to the point where their lives are not divided into compartments of play, labor, recreation, and education, but where they become masters of the art of living and seek enthusiastically to bring the practice of this art to a high state of excellence. "A master in the art of living draws no sharp distinction between his work and his play, his labor and his leisure, his mind and his body, his education and his recreation. He hardly knows which is which. He simply pursues his vision of excellence through whatever he is doing and leaves others to determine whether he is working or playing. To himself he always seems to be doing both. Enough for him that he does it well." [1]

An adequate program of education should provide experiences for students which will enable them to gain skills, interests, and appreciations in a wide range of physical, artistic, literary, musical, dramatic, and other kinds of activities. Such an education would help prepare the majority of people for living interestingly and taking an active part in creative activities. The following quotation indicates the fundamentals of an education for leisure.

An education which trained young people for work, but not for play, for labor but not for leisure, for toil but not for recreation, was a half-done job. The traditional method . . . of loading young people with knowledge, mostly in the form of book learning, and then turning them loose on the world with the *creative* part of them undeveloped, with no aptitudes, with no skill, no interests for the occupation of their leisure, was a procedure humanly inadequate and socially dangerous. [2]

The importance of recreation. The mechanization of industry and of agriculture has removed most of the opportunities that people formerly had for creative expression through their work, and has, in connection with other social changes, contributed to a great increase in the amount of leisure time available to nearly all Americans. The time was when a man who made a wagon, a chair, or a pair of shoes began with the raw materials, performed all the operations, and completed the article with a minimum amount of help from any one else. Such practices allowed each workman to take a keen personal interest and to express himself through his work. He felt a satisfaction in completing each article.

With nearly all industry organized on a mass production basis, almost every workman performs one task in a routine way that requires practically no training or skill. The published statements of Henry Ford enable us to take the automobile industry as an illustration. Several years ago he wrote that he employed many thousand men and that there were 7882 different types of jobs in his factory. Of these jobs 949 were classified as heavy work requiring strong able-bodied men, 3338 required men of ordinary physical development and strength; and the remaining

---

[1] Lawrence Pearsall Jacks, *Education through Recreation*, p. 37. New York: Harper and Brothers, 1932.
[2] *Ibid., loc. cit.*

3595 jobs required very little physical exertion and could be satisfactorily filled by the slightest, weakest sort of men.

The length of time required to become proficient in the various occupations was about as follows:

43 per cent of all the jobs require not over one day of training

36 per cent require from one day to one week

6 per cent require from one to two weeks

14 per cent require from one month to one year

1 per cent require from one to six years. The last jobs require great skill—as in tool making and die sinking.[1]

The necessity for routinization of activity is explained in the following quotation:

We expect the men to do what they are told. The organization is so highly specialized and one part is so dependent upon another that we could not for a moment consider allowing men to have their own way. Without the most rigid discipline we would have the utmost confusion. I think it should not be otherwise in industry. The men are there to get the greatest possible amount of work done and to receive the highest possible pay. If each man were permitted to act in his own way, production would suffer and therefore pay would suffer. Anyone who does not like to work in our way may always leave. The company's conduct toward the men is meant to be exact and impartial. It is naturally to the interest both of the foremen and of the department heads that the releases from their departments should be few.[2]

These facts clearly demonstrate the necessity of all classes of people receiving the kind of education that will equip them to participate during their leisure time in activities which will permit freedom, relaxation, and creative self-expression.

Education for leisure. There is an abundance of data to show that large numbers of Americans have more leisure time than they have ever had before and that this condition will continue to exist indefinitely. This is true of employed persons and is greatly increased, of course, during periods of economic depression when large numbers of people are out of employment. The existence of this large amount of leisure time for such large numbers of employed people indicates that America has arrived at one stage in a Utopia that man has been seeking and hoping

[1] Henry Ford, *My Life and Work*, p. 110. Garden City, New York: Garden City Publishing Co., Inc., 1922.

[2] *Ibid.*, p. 111.

[66]

for since the beginning of the race. Mankind has been engaged in an intense struggle for existence throughout all time, until recently, when the improvements of methods in agriculture and industry have made possible a reasonable degree of security and more leisure from the drudgery of securing the means of a bare existence.

This greatly increased amount of leisure time offers opportunities that may cause either good or bad results. It is true in regard to leisure, as in nearly all other things, that the opposite of that which is good is worse. The history of nations and civilizations shows that when people have had an abundance of leisure, there has been a tendency for them to go to excess in dissipation and vice. Drunkenness, gambling, and looseness of standards in relations between the sexes have been common. There is a danger that the increase of leisure in America will result in degradation and retrogression of society, but it also offers the opportunity for the development of a much higher culture and civilization than we have ever known in this country. The schools and colleges must catch the spirit and vision of the new leisure in order that a new point of view and better understanding of modern life may be developed among the masses of the people.

Physical education has a real and distinct challenge to take a leading part in the education of the masses of the people so that they may profit most from the increased leisure which has come to them. The specific contributions which physical education can make are (1) to help the majority of people develop enough skill in definite recreational activities to enable them to participate successfully and with satisfaction in these activities during their leisure time, and (2) to strive to develop in most people a love for and favorable attitudes and appreciations toward vigorous physical recreations which will serve to motivate participation in this form of recreation.

Physical education and health. The data on the vitality of the American people indicate that much can be done through education to prolong the period of vigorous and active life, to reduce the amount of sickness, and to increase the endurance, energy, and enthusiasm of large numbers of people. Such accomplishments would enable many individuals to live at a much higher level, get more pleasure out of life, and be of more service to society and to mankind in general.

Physical education can do much to stimulate an interest on the part of young people in a buoyant, healthy, vigorous type of personality. The rules and foundations of hygienic living can be effectively taught in

[67]

connection with many play and athletic activities; and boys and girls can be motivated to live healthfully and cleanly.

The scientifically recorded data in physiology and many accurately recorded clinical observations over a long period indicate that the generally accepted principle, "function builds structure," applies to the exercise of the organic bodily systems through physical activity. It seems to be true beyond serious question that if normal children and youth participate in vigorous physical exercise the bodily organs and systems will be made stronger and more efficient.

Specialists in the field of mental hygiene claim also that good bodily development and control are among the foundations of good mental health. The experiences of success, satisfaction, relaxation, and pleasure which can be secured easily through physical education likewise are said to be valuable from the standpoint of mental hygiene.

Physical education and family life. The family developed historically out of the need for caring for human offspring, and it is around children that the family is integrated. It is the most fundamental and important social group and provides the closest, most meaningful form of contacts and experiences. It is no doubt true that during most of the time covered by recorded history the family has been a more important social institution than it is at present. During previous centuries the family provided most of the education, religious instruction and guidance, character development, recreation, and vocational occupation that young people received. In recent years other agencies, such as schools, churches, playgrounds, community centers, commercial entertainments, and factories, have been provided by society to meet many of these needs.

Regardless of these changes, however, the family is still the most important social institution and provides the best basis for relationship between the sexes and the best means for rearing children. Social statistics show that the percentage of divorces and of suicides is much greater in childless families than in families with children. Since the family is a basic institution in our social order, it should have some significance in determining the objectives, program, and procedures of physical education. Probably the health of children and recreation in the home are the two points of contact at which physical education can make the most direct contributions to family life in America.

The right to be well born should be guaranteed to every child. The marriage of people with similar dominant defects contributes greatly to the increase and perpetuation of such terrible handicaps as feebleminded-

[68]

ness; insanity, physical deformities, moral delinquencies, epilepsy, and personality weaknesses. If individuals who possess outstanding hereditary handicaps could be prevented from propagating their kind, the defects could be almost eliminated in a few generations. It is likewise true that parents would have much finer, stronger, and more intelligent children and society would be greatly improved if every young man and woman in choosing a mate would avoid seriously defective individuals, and refuse also to marry anyone with weaknesses similar to those possessed by him or herself.

The effect on children of the venereal diseases of their parents is another thing which dooms many individuals to a life of suffering, inferiority, and inefficiency. It has been reported, for example, that gonorrheal infection of mothers causes at least 80 per cent of all blindness which dates from time of birth. This is brought about by the infection getting in the eyes of babies during the process of being born. It has also been stated on good authority that syphilis causes a large percentage of locomotor ataxia, epilepsy, feeblemindedness, and idiocy.

Physical education teachers probably can do much to stimulate a great interest and build wholesome ideals concerning the development and maintenance of a beautiful and smoothly functioning body. A keen sense of "keeping fit" and an enthusiasm for living a vigorous and dynamic life are other valuable results which might be secured. It seems to be true beyond serious question that by these and other means physical education can emphasize naturally and wholesomely eugenic marriages and sound social hygiene practices.

A normal and natural interest in observing the laws of healthful living and "training rules" is one of the valuable outcomes which should be expected from physical education. Most young people are interested in playing well and participating successfully in athletic events, and are often eager to live in a way that appears to contribute to success in these activities. In this way physical education provides a strong, effective, and desirable motivation for health practices. A spirit of play, recreation, and good sportsmanship, and skills useful in home recreation are other possible contributions of physical education to successful and happy family life.

Physical education and religion. In most communities it is agreed that religious worship, teaching, and interpretation is almost exclusively the responsibility of the organized churches. A large number of churches and other religious organizations use some phases of physical

[69]

education as part of their programs (1) to build and maintain morale on the part of young people, (2) to supplement other efforts to hold aloft high ideals, (3) to build an appreciation of ethical principles, (4) to inculcate a spirit of loyalty for the organization, and (5) to provide a program of wholesome physical recreation for the young people in their membership.

The leaders in these organizations realize, no doubt, that physical education provides interesting activities which can be used to secure such objectives, but that participation in these activities will not, in and of itself, automatically bring about such results. The quality of the outcomes depends almost entirely on the quality of the leadership. Well qualified teachers who have clearly defined objectives in mind can use physical education as a means of bringing about desirable changes in children, but relatively ignorant, unskilled leaders who lack vision and high ideals may cause boys and girls to learn ways of reacting or behaving that are highly objectionable.

Other social institutions. Among the many other social institutions that have much influence on the present program and the development of physical education are the press, the theater, moving pictures, radio, scouting, boys' clubs, camps, Y.M.C.A., Y.W.C.A., labor unions, and women's clubs. In the nation as a whole and in almost innumerable local situations one or more of these institutions has direct and indirect influences on physical education. The successful teacher or administrator must make a societal analysis of the community and state in which he is working, and determine as accurately as possible the influences that these various institutions have had on physical education in the past and the probable influence that they will have in the future.

In most communities all of these agencies are friendly to physical education in a general way. It is obligatory on the part of teachers, however, to explain and interpret to them the objectives, content, and methods of the school program. In this way the professional leaders in physical education can use and direct the influences of these institutions to good ends. Otherwise they may make demands of the leaders and attempt to shape the program in a way that will not be conducive to the best interests of the pupils. An illustration of the bad effects of unguided influences is the common practice of newspapers insisting that high school athletics be conducted in a showmanlike way with great emphasis on winning championships. Although this practice is generally recognized by educators as being objectionable there are no cases on record where any real, well planned, intelligent effort has been made to interpret to editors and reporters the ideals and educational policies of a comprehensive program of physical education.

National ideals. It is true, no doubt, that America does not have as large a number of integrating cultural ideals as some of the older nations of the world but there are some dominant ideals which are common among the majority of the people in all social classes in all sections of the country. These national ideals have been very important in determining the objectives and form of our educational program and in shaping the program of physical education.

The spirit of aggressiveness which has created the "go-getter" type of personality is one of the ideals which has influenced education and physical education. It apparently has been responsible for the intense spirit with which many Americans participate in sports, and has caused large numbers to emphasize the idea of playing *against* other people instead of playing *with* them. The current social philosophy stresses cooperation in all aspects of life; if physical education is to make the maximum contribution toward the preparation of individuals for successful living in a cooperative democratic society we must emphasize team-play, cooperation, and unselfishness in all our sports and games. Many educators believe that the way in which athletic sports have been conducted has helped to aggravate and strengthen the tense spirit with which large numbers of our citizens work, eat, move, play, and do most of the things in life. The newer, more relaxed, graceful, and wholesome spirit is more appropriate to present social conditions and ideals, and physical education should be conducted in a way to contribute to the development of this spirit.

Other important ideals which are dominant throughout the country relate to self-government, liberty, freedom, and equality of opportunity. Each of these is significant from the standpoint of physical education.

Self-government. The democratic ideal holds that the power of government rests with the people and is delegated by them to their elected representatives. In theory, a republican form of government in a democratic society is expected to look after the interests of the population as a whole so as to secure fair play and equality of opportunity for all. This principle has found widespread application in the thinking of the American people, not only in regard to politics, but also with reference to education, economics, industry, and social problems in general.

This attitude toward education has had the fortunate result of causing

[71]

the majority of citizens to take a great deal of interest in public education and to retain a high degree of local school control in most communities throughout the country. This, in turn, has caused the people to make an effort to provide free schooling for all children.

The application of the democratic principle is reflected in even the simple routine procedures of class organization and management. The election of team captains and squad leaders, the prevalence of group discussions of the best form and methods of performing activities, and the provision of opportunities for all children to participate are examples of how this ideal of self-government influences the school techniques. Since we are living in a democratic society it is highly appropriate that all educational activities be of such a nature as to prepare children better for life in that form of society. We still have much progress to make, however, before all of our schools have a curriculum, a form of organization, and instructional methods that are well suited to a truly democratic form of education.

Practical experiences which prepare children for the duties of citizenship are common in physical education. Electing leaders, respecting officials, recognizing the justice of penalties, realizing the importance of rules in any successful game or group undertaking, and playing together for the good of the team or group, are illustrations of the activities in physical education which help to make good citizens.

Equality of opportunity. Equality of educational opportunity is the principle on which the American program of public education is based. When we speak of "equality of educational opportunity" it is not meant that every child should have the same education. It means that each child in America should have the opportunity to develop his particular talents to the point which will enable him to get the most satisfaction out of life and to be a good member of society. The person whose interests and abilities qualify him to be a good tradesman or mechanic should be provided with a type of education to meet his needs as well as that provided for an individual interested in entering a profession or business. The ideal that it is the responsibility of the state to provide equal educational opportunities for all the children of all the people is recognized in the constitution of the United States and is accepted by a large majority of American citizens.

There are some individuals and a few organized groups who are still opposed to this principle. They state that every man should pay for the education of his own children, that "every tub should stand on its own bottom," and that the amount of money possessed by a child's parents should determine the amount and quality of his education. There are a few other persons who believe that the public should provide free education for all children through the elementary school, but that beginning with the junior high school a child's educational opportunity should depend on his parent's ability to pay the full cost of his education. The persons who hold these reactionary views are interested in keeping our economic and social structure exactly as it is. They are opposed to change. They are a very small minority numerically in American society, but in some communities they exert considerable influence in shaping the educational policies.

The majority of American parents demand more of their public schools than that they serve as an institutionalized type of nursemaid to care for children and teach them the rudiments of reading, writing, and arithmetic. Our public schools are expected to help boys and girls to really live. To live so that the individuality and personality of each child may grow and develop to the utmost.

It is expected that all children be helped to live so that they will be physically and mentally fit to meet enthusiastically and joyfully the probems of life.

They must be prepared to spend the rapidly increasing amount of leisure time through the wholesome use and appreciation of good music, good art, good literature, good drama, and good games.

American youth must be provided with the knowledge and attitudes which will help them to maintain the best traditions and loyalties of the American home.

They must be given guidance in the choice of a life work and in some cases be prepared for a definite vocation.

The opportunities and responsibilities of citizenship must be made plain to both boys and girls.

Above all else, parents expect the public schools to shape the thinking and conduct of children so that they will behave at all times in a way which is recognized as being good and desirable. In other words, the public schools are expected to strengthen and improve the character of the pupils.

Physical education contributes definitely toward the achievement of the outcomes which parents expect from the public schools. Participation in wholesome vigorous play is conducive to growth and development, and to normal functioning of the organic systems of the body. This effect is an important contribution of physical education. Its possibilities for the stimulation and guidances of social traits and abilities are probably of more significance.

The place of the school in physical education. The school is the agency that society has set up to carry the major responsibility for organized education. Schooling and education, however, are not necessarily the same thing; education is much broader than schooling and involves all of the experiences of an individual from birth to death. The organized experiences that are provided by schools for children play a very important part in their education, particularly in passing on to each generation the social inheritance of the race.

The school, of course, should not assume the responsibility for doing anything for the education of children that some other agency of society can do better. Such a large number of responsibilities have been placed on the schools which formerly belonged to the home, the church, the farm, and other social institutions, that it seems imperative for the schools to avoid seeking new responsibilities that can be adequately carried by some other agency. School authorities should realize that there are a large number of other institutions actively engaged in some form of physical education. Among these are playgrounds, parks, Boy Scouts, Girl Scouts, Camp Fire Girls, Y.M.C.A., Y.W.C.A., churches, community centers, settlements, and camps. Large numbers of boys and girls participate in physical education activities as part of the programs of these organizations. Many others have opportunities to exercise through play and work in many different kinds of situations.

The school program of physical education can make certain distinct and peculiar contributions that cannot ordinarily be gained through other types of experiences. Some of the important characteristics of physical education in schools follow:

1. Experience and activities in schools are better organized, selected, and graded.

2. School experiences are usually presented and managed by the teachers in a way to secure the most effective and efficient learning.

3. The school program and organization makes it possible to organize experiences and activities so as to leave no gaps.

4. In schools it is easier to make efficient use of time by having each activity repeated often enough to guarantee learning, yet not enough to be a needless waste of time and effort.

5. School experiences can be arranged so as to shorten trial-and-error, thus

[74]

enabling the pupils to learn in a short time what otherwise might take several years.

Summary. The objectives, subject matter and methods of physical Λ education are influenced greatly by the characteristics of contemporary society, the dominant ideals of the nation, the established social institutions, and the accepted social and educational philosophy. A review of sociological data indicates clearly the need for physical education in a modern program of education.

It is generally agreed by students of social problems that physical education can make definite contributions toward the socialization of individuals and groups. Since a social emphasis is prominent in education at the present time it can be easily seen that physical education is an important part of modern democratic education.

The widespread recognition of the fact that recreation is a fundamental human need has tended to place increased emphasis on the recreational aspects of physical education and on the opportunities that it offers for the worthy use of leisure time. Mental and physical health can also be advanced through participation in physical education. The health of children and recreation in the home are probably two of the most important contributions that physical education can make to successful family life in America.

A large number of churches and other religious organizations use some phases of physical education as part of their programs. Many other social institutions, such as the press, theater, moving pictures, camps, Y.M.C.A., and labor unions, also have significant influences on the program of physical education. National ideals such as the spirit of aggressiveness, liberty, freedom, self-government, and equality of opportunity have been influential in shaping the physical education program in the United States.

QUESTIONS

1. What characteristics of contemporary society have been particularly influential in shaping the physical education program during the past few years?
2. Of what significance to physical education are the social learnings of man?
3. In what ways can physical education be used particularly well for the socialization of individuals and of groups?
4. What social institutions are of outstanding importance to physical education?

5. In what way is physical education particularly well adapted to the practical application of the social and philosophical principles that are accepted by modern education?

6. Of what importance to physical education are the social developments and changes which have caused greatly increased attention to be given recreation during the past few years?

7. What contributions to the health of pupils may be expected from physical education?

8. What contributions to successful family life in America should be expected from physical education?

9. In what ways have American national ideals influenced the school program of physical education?

10. What particular contributions can the school make to physical education that cannot be made by playgrounds, camps, and other social institutions?

REFERENCES

Finney, Ross L. *A Sociological Philosophy of Education*. New York: The Macmillan Company, 1929.

Jacks, Lawrence Pearsall. *Education through Recreation*. New York: Harper and Brothers, 1932.

Peters, Charles Clinton. *Foundations of Educational Sociology*. New York: The Macmillan Company, 1930.

Williams, Jesse Feiring. *The Principles of Physical Education*. Philadelphia: W. B. Saunders Company, 1932. (Revised)

CHAPTER V

Functions of Physical Education In a Democratic Society

ॐ

Nature of American civilization. An overwhelming majority of American citizens want to maintain in this country a democratic form of society and government. The results of all elections and the consensus of the expressions of people in all walks of life substantiate this statement. It is true that there is a considerable minority that would prefer a socialistic, communistic, or some other form of social organization, but this group is small in relation to the total population.

We now use the term *democracy* to mean a form of governmental organization in which the people elect the officials who make and enforce the laws, the right and power of government reposing in the people and being delegated by them to elected officers. The democratic philosophy emphasizes the importance of human personality, teaches that individuals must be treated as persons and not as things which form cogs in the social machine, and stresses the ideal that society and government should be organized in a way that will result in the common good.

Characteristics of current society. The dominant social ideals advocated by pioneer thinkers in America have changed greatly in the last few years. Society has always been in a process of change and the ideals of the people have likewise been constantly in a state of flux. It is frequently difficult to recognize contemporary changes which are taking place in society. The fixedness and persistence of people's points of view and ways of behaving create a social inertia which make it difficult to deliberately bring about planned changes in society. It seems, however, that the ideal of rugged individualism—of selfishness, of lack of consideration for others, of brutal competition—which has held sway for many years is being supplanted by a spirit of sportsmanship, social cooperation, and unselfishness.

It is essential that teachers of physical education understand these changing ideals and that their work be planned and taught in a way that will help to strengthen this new spirit. The ideal of teamwork, of unselfish subordination of personal interests for the good of the team, and of intelligent cooperation should be emphasized.

[77]

Other social changes which have some significance in connection with the teaching of physical education include: (1) the development of means of transportation and communication which make more necessary a cooperative society rather than an individualistic and competitive society; (2) changes in business and industry which have transferred commercial production from the home to factories and have routinized all manufacturing processes to the extent that many workmen are merely automatons who find no opportunity for self-expression in their work; (3) the greatly increased amount of leisure time which has come to nearly everyone, which places on education an increased responsibility to prepare all pupils more adequately for the happy and successful use of leisure time; (4) changes in family and home life in America which have tended to remove recreational activities from the home and to restrict the social and recreational interests of large numbers of people; (5) the health conditions, particularly among people of middle age, which indicate that there are important opportunities for physical education to make a contribution to race vitality; (6) an apparent increase in mental disease during the past ten years; (7) a wide development of scientific attitudes, with the result that many teachers and other citizens question the objectives and procedures in physical education; and (8) changes in the sources from which numbers of people get authoritative guides to living. These trends have resulted in changed functions of the church, the home, and other social institutions, and have added to the responsibilities of education in all its phases.

Social-economic goals for America. The procedures of teaching physical education are influenced by the kind of society and civilization in which the program is functioning. These procedures are also determined to a considerable extent by the kind of society that American people would *like* to have.

It is commonly assumed that the preamble of the Constitution of the United States stated in a general way the kind of society the people of this country wanted 150 years ago. This document stated that justice, domestic tranquility, general welfare, and liberty were desired by all people.[1] There is no reason to believe these things are not still desired by the majority of American citizens. The economic, industrial, and

---

[1] The preamble of the Constitution follows: "We the People of the United States, in order to form a more perfect Union, establish Justice, insure domestic Tranquility, provide for the common defence, promote the general Welfare, and secure the Blessings of Liberty to Ourselves and our Posterity, do ordain and establish this CONSTITUTION for the United States of America."

social changes that have taken place since the adoption of the Constitution have served to obscure these goals and ideals and to cause many selfish and ignorant people to ignore them and seek to belittle them. It has seemed desirable, therefore, to many of the leading educators of the nation that a re-statement of our national goals be made in terms of present-day needs. In conformity with this sentiment the National Education Association at its 1931 meeting passed a resolution authorizing the appointment of a committee to propose to the Association a statement of desirable social-economic goals for America. The committee has proposed such a statement and is continuing with its work in order to "indicate the materials and methods which the schools of the nation should use to attain these goals."

The desired goals. It is believed that the ten goals which have been proposed are ones which will result in the highest degree of good to the largest number of Americans. The names and brief discussions of these goals follow.[1]

1. *Hereditary strength.* The biological inheritance of people determines very largely the enjoyment and satisfactions that they may secure from many of the experiences of life. The available evidence indicates that rapid and fundamental changes are taking place in the hereditary strength of the American population. Many students of the problem of population believe that the quality of the biological inheritance of each succeeding generation is degenerating. It seems to be true that in an intelligent society it is practical to bring influences to bear on mating and the control of human reproduction which will raise the hereditary strength of the population.

2. *Physical security.* To be "well born" is highly desirable but a good inheritance will not result in the greatest individual and social good if the growth and development of one's body and personality are hindered by detrimental influences. The influences which might interfere with a person's physical security include the entire absence of, or inadequate, medical and public health service; lack of law enforcement; careless and unintelligent driving of automobiles; poor nourishment; and thousands of other factors over which any one individual has little if any control.

3. *Participation in an evolving culture.* If an individual is to have experiences which will enable him to develop a wholesome and well

---

[1] For a detailed discussion of these goals see "What Are Desirable Social-Economic Goals for America?" *Journal of the National Education Association,* XXIII (January, 1934), 6–12.

[79]

integrated personality he must have the ability to participate successfully in the life of the society in which he is living. The development
of this ability is dependent to a considerable extent on the contacts that
an individual has with other people in many different kinds of situations.
The school is only one of the institutions of society which should supply
the opportunities for these contacts. The home, the church, the playground, the theater, the workshop and many other social institutions
have such responsibilities along with the school.

4. *An active, flexible personality.* One of the important goals in a
democracy is to develop individuals who have the ability to exercise self-
direction, to guide their actions by intelligent choices and decisions rather
than to act on the basis of impulse, to adapt to changing social conditions,
and to find means of self-expression through cooperative activities that
will result in good for the social group. In order to contribute to the
development of individuals who possess these abilities physical education
must provide situations in which boys and girls will have opportunities
for the development of personal initiative, discriminating judgment and
choice, flexibility of thought and conduct, individual differences, and
cooperativeness.

5. *Suitable occupation.* A democratic society should seek to provide
every individual with a congenial occupation. It is believed that pur-
suing a life work for which one is not suited results in much unhappi-
ness and conflicts of personality. Important aspects of this responsibility
of society are the guidance of youth in the choice of an occupation, the
training of individuals for the occupation of their choice, and the placement and advancement of each worker in the field of work for which
he has been prepared.

6. *Economic security.* Probably the greatest handicap to human happiness and the growth of wholesome personalities is the lack of economic
security. A democratic society should make it possible for all to earn the
necessities and comforts which are required for living a happy and creative life. This will include such fundamental essentials as comfortable
and healthful homes, adequate nutrition for all members of every family,
recreational skills and facilities, opportunities for participation in hobbies
and other cultural and creative activities, and protection from the devastat-
ing effects of unemployment, illness, and old-age disability.

7. *Mental security.* Protection from untruths by a commercialized
press, screen, and radio should be one of the services rendered by organized democratic society to its members. Even though the radio broad-

[80]

casting facilities, the newspapers, and moving pictures are owned by private corporations, they have a responsibility to the public which makes it possible for them to exist and make profits. Society should hold these concerns to a strict accounting of their responsibility and should protect the citizens from the efforts of selfish interests to control the thoughts and opinions of the population for the purpose of making money.

8. *Equality of opportunity.* This nation was founded on the principle that all people should have equal rights and opportunities and that there should be special privilege for none. The Declaration of Independence stated: "We hold these truths to be self-evident, that all men are created equal, that they are endowed by their Creator with certain unalienable rights, that among these are Life, Liberty and the pursuit of Happiness."

Modern educators do not interpret this statement to mean that all individuals are equal in intelligence, ability, or achievement but that they are entitled to equality of rights and opportunities. It likewise means that every individual must assume responsibility for the public good, up to the level of his ability.

9. *Freedom.* Most of us when we think of freedom think of political freedom from a tyrant. There are other kinds of freedom, however, which in many respects are more important in the development of human personality and happiness. Among these are freedom of self-expression, freedom to make one's own judgments and decisions, to choose one's own mate, to choose an occupation, to decide on a place of residence, to make political decisions, and to decide one's religious beliefs.

A democratic society should guarantee to every individual the greatest amount of freedom that is possible without infringing on the rights of others and that is compatible with such public interests as decency, health, safety, and quiet.

10. *Fair play.* The fundamental principles of sportsmanship should permeate all the dealings between members of a democratic society. This should be true in government, business, family life, recreation, and all other relationships of people. The way physical education is taught has much influence on the development of attitudes of fair play in boys and girls. If teachers encourage their pupils to evade the rules of games, to be cunning, to take questionable advantage of technicalities, and to participate in other unfair practices it is probable that poor attitudes will be formed which will carry over into other situations in life. Physical education should be taught in such a way as to contribute to the achievement of the practice of fair play in all human relationships.

[81]

Purpose of universal education. The principle of universal education is widely accepted and adhered to among nearly all classes of American society. It is based on two fundamental assumptions: (1) that the state has an inherent right to perpetuate and improve itself, and (2) that every individual in a democracy has the right to an educational opportunity which will enable him to live a full, successful, and abundant life.

The first of these assumptions is predicated on the belief that society provides education, not to let one group of individuals have an easier time in life than another group, but as a protection to the state. The second assumption is based on the democratic ideal which emphasizes the sacredness of human personality and freedom of self-expression.

A comprehensive program of public education should make it possible for all boys and girls in school to participate in physical education. It offers many opportunities for the stimulation of individual growth and for the preparation of pupils as citizens in a democratic society.

Values of universal education. The general acceptance of the idea of free schooling for all children at public expense was secured only after many years of intensive effort. The greatest battles for free public schools were fought in most states during the fifty years preceding 1875, but in many communities even now the historic arguments of former days are used against the public schools.[1]

The values of universal public education have been grouped as economic, social, and political. The economic values include increasing the wants of the masses of the people which would result in greater buying, providing vocational training which would make for greater efficiency in business and industry, and the development of a more intelligent and discriminating buying public. The social values include such things as the preparation of people for the use of leisure time, the establishment of common ideals, the improvement of standards of conduct, the development of criteria for distinguishing between beauty and ugliness, and the educational guidance of children who might otherwise attempt during their childhood to compete in the industrial world. Politically the main value of universal education is to provide a literate population that can participate more intelligently as voters in a democracy.

American faith in education. It is clearly evident to any accurate observer that the masses of American people have faith in education.

---

[1] These arguments have been summarized in *Evaluating the Public Schools*, pp. 7–9. Washington: National Education Association, 1934.

Millions of parents believe that education can help their children to a finer and higher life. Large numbers of mothers and fathers have made tremendous sacrifices in order that their children may have the key to opportunity which they believe education provides. Most of them believe that there may be achieved through education a fairer and better civilization, that their children can achieve greater security and peace, and that the next generations can be led to a greater intellectual and spiritual level of living.

The widespread faith in education places a great responsibility on teachers and school administrators. Physical education, along with the rest of the educational program, must definitely and conscientiously try to help all pupils to "realize from experience that the successful and pleasant life is the good, simple, honest, and self-sacrificing life which is to be obtained only by using all of one's abilities to distinguish between selfishness and social welfare, between the good and bad, between truth and falsehood, between beauty and ugliness." [1]

General goals of public education. The people have established and maintain free public schools in all the states. Some of these schools are much better than others, but all of them are supported by citizens who believe that the schools will achieve good results. Physical education and all other parts of the school program are expected to contribute to the achievements of the desired goals. These goals must be clearly recognized and understood if progress is to be made toward their achievement. Statements of the general goals of public education have recently been adopted by the Michigan Education Planning Commission. [2] It is believed that these are goals which education, including physical education, may well seek to achieve. They follow.

ONE. *To cultivate a deep regard for democracy and an intelligent appreciation of democratic institutions.*

This goal implies that effective democratic institutions constitute the best means for insuring justice and liberty; for maintaining the equality of political, social, and economic opportunities; for fostering growth and progress; and for furthering truth and honesty.

TWO. *To develop those qualities of character which are of special significance in a democracy.*

[1] Alexander G. Ruthven, "Experiencing Education," *Problems and Progress at the University of Michigan,* p. 7. University of Michigan Official Publication, Vol. XXXV, No. 16 (January 27, 1934).

[2] This is a commission of officials representing influential organizations of agriculture, business, education, industry, labor, as well as certain state organizations of women. The Commission was named by the State Superintendent of Public Instruction.

This goal implies that citizens in a democracy must possess certain qualities of character that are not required in other forms of society. This preparation requires the development of a personality that will find expression in responsible self-direction, self-control, and self-appraisal in both individual and cooperative behavior. This implies emphasis (*a*) on understanding and appreciation instead of blind obedience; (b) on fair and honest dealings instead of exploitation; (*c*) on investigation instead of thoughtless acceptance; (*d*) on openmindedness instead of prejudice; and (*e*) on the promotion of the common good instead of selfish advancement of the individual.

THREE. *To develop the willingness and the ability to cooperate effectively in a democratic society.*

Democracy succeeds in proportion to the capacity of the people to solve their problems through voluntary self-directed cooperation. This goal requires a system of education, in organization, materials, and method of instruction, which will provide in the school an environment that will most nearly approximate an ideal democratic society. In such a school pupils and students may participate actively in the life of the school, molding it to their needs and aspirations and adjusting themselves to it.

FOUR. *To develop the ability to use the most effective and reliable methods in searching for truth.*

In a democracy, new generations should be prepared to discover new truths and to revise their practices accordingly. The training proposed in this goal will furnish necessary preparation for the cooperative discovery and solution of the problems created by the complexity and interdependence of our social, political, and economic relationships. It will also increase the power of citizens to cooperate successfully in creating the best conditions of living for all.

FIVE. *To develop the effective use of the fundamental knowledge and skills required by all.*

This goal demands effective training in the arts of reading, writing, spelling, language, and arithmetic. Such arts are essential tools of common understanding and communication.

SIX. *To insure an abundant social and individual life in accordance with each individual's capacity and ambition.*

This goal involves provision for proper and adequate training in problems of health, in desirable home membership, and in the worthy and constructive use of leisure time. It also calls for the general and specific vocational training required for economic sufficiency.

SEVEN. *To provide training in the specialized and professional services which are requisite for society.*

Society must have the services of persons specially equipped in the preservation and further development of the knowledge, skills, and techniques vital to the advancement of society as a whole. This goal recognizes that the valuable and useful accumulation described as "the social inheritance" must be preserved and transmitted from generation to generation. Through research and experimentation this inheritance should be increased.

EIGHT. *To provide for the enrichment of adult life.*

This goal is receiving attention because our increased leisure demands provision for continued education for adults, and the changing social and economic conditions require the provision for retraining for both the vocational and the avocational aspects of life.

NINE. *To plan for the continuous appraisal and readjustment of the educational program to fit changing conditions.*

When scientific discoveries and inventions force us to set aside old ways of living, the schools should provide new activities which give definite practice in making adjustments to new situations in order that society may be modified through the process of orderly change rather than through revolution. This goal is important in a democracy because social and economic conditions change and education must also change accordingly in order to make its contribution at each stage of social progress.

The functions of physical education. Among the institutions of society the school has definite functions to perform. In a similar way physical education has certain responsibilities in the educational program. It is necessary for teachers of physical education to recognize the specific things that their field of education should contribute toward helping the school render the maximum service in a democratic society. Some statements which set forth the functions of physical education in a democratic society follow.

1. *Physical education should seek to provide for the masses of the people in a democracy a common background of games, sports, dances, and outing activities.* In this way physical education can contribute to the development of a desirable uniformity in common ideals and attitudes among all classes of society throughout the nation. These ideals and attitudes should relate to social and moral behavior, to the responsibility of individuals as citizens of the state, and to the support of practices which are accepted as being good.

Physical education, though it is only one agency of education, just as education is only one of the agencies of society which can be used to develop an integrated citizenry, offers some of the best opportunities for the social unification of the population in a democracy. A desirable similarity in appreciations, loyalties, traditions, imageries, reverence, and ideals should be sought through education, and the experiences that boys and

[85]

girls have in physical education should help to develop this similarity. Social unification may thereby be helped.

2. *Physical education should seek to develop some sport into an American institution through which the people may gain a practical idealism.* In order to serve this purpose the spirit of some game must be developed and must secure almost universal recognition. The development of rules will not be sufficient. This spirit must be one of respect for a high standard of behavior. The game must set a high ideal and provide for putting this ideal into actual practice. It must provide the dramatization of things which are good and fine—honor, courage, strength, and courtesy. It must set a model of conduct for our American civilization.

The players who take part in this game must have objective experiences, such as a game provides, which embody ideals of unblemished behavior. Americans use a large number of expressions, which are taken from games, to express ideals. Among these are "the New Deal," "play ball," "hit the line hard," "play the game," "right off the bat," "that's a knock-out," "from the word go," "block him out," and "tackle hard." It is possible that one of our present group games which has the advantage of age and some tradition may be revised in spirit and serve to develop such idealism in American society. It seems more probable, however, that the long and difficult task of popularizing a new game and the ideals that go with it, must be accomplished in order to develop an American sport into an important moral institution.

3. *Physical education should teach to all boys and girls some of the physical activities which constitute part of the cultural heritage of the race.* Among these activities are dancing, running, climbing, jumping, striking, and vaulting over obstacles such as ditches and hedges; throwing objects such as the javelin, discus, and weights; and the activities such as jousting, which are usually associated with knighthood and chivalry. Participation in activities of this kind provides opportunities for children to live, in a way, some of the past experiences of mankind. Pupils in school read about the place that these activities played in the lives of their ancestors, and it is probably sound educational procedure to provide opportunities for them to have experiences in practicing these activities.

Many teachers believe that the practice of physical activities which are old in the history of the race helps children to have a clearer understanding of the cultures and civilizations through which the human race has passed. It also seems probable, too, that an appreciation of modern

[86]

civilization can be developed in this way and that boys and girls can be helped to appreciate their privileges and responsibilities as members of the social, political, cultural, and economic groups to which they belong.

4. *Physical education should prepare each individual to live more happily during the period of childhood and youth and also during adulthood.* In order to prepare individuals to live happily physical education must help them to do better the everyday commonplace things that they do in their daily living. Reading newspapers, for example, is something that nearly everyone does every day. A large part of the space in newspapers is given to accounts of sports and games. In order to read this section of a newspaper intelligently a person must know much about these activities. There are a large number of things, which most people do often, that physical education should help individuals to do better. In this connection it seems highly probable that modern physical educators could learn much of value by studying the purposes and practices of the German *Turnvereine* and attempting to adapt some of the techniques used by them to the solution of modern American problems. Apparently they contributed much to building a spirit of nationalism in Germany. It may be that some of their procedures could be used to get Americans to consider more seriously and intelligently our political, social, and economic problems.

The program of physical education must include provisions for adult education as well as education for school children. In order to help either children or adults to live happily, Briggs [1] says, three problems must be solved: (1) we must know just exactly how most people spend their time, (2) we must determine the relative desirability of the different activities participated in by most people, and (3) we must determine how the pupils can be taught to do well the desirable things which will be most likely to contribute to happy living.

5. *Physical education should provide every boy and girl with experiences, in sports such as football, basketball, baseball, and golf, which will help them to develop an understanding and appreciation of the sports and of the place they occupy in the everyday lives of American citizens.* Some of the highly organized American games and sports are of much interest to a large proportion of the population. It is believed that every well educated citizen should know enough about these games to understand how they are played and to appreciate the difference between

[1] Thomas H. Briggs, *Secondary Education*, p. 258. New York: The Macmillan Company, 1933.

good and poor playing skill. These things are necessary in order that a person may read intelligently newspapers and magazines because a large part of these publications is given to reports and discussions of athletics. It is also necessary that one be intelligent in regard to sports in order that he may spend part of his leisure time as an understanding spectator and as an agreeable associate or companion to others who are interested in sports. An understanding of the significance of many expressions borrowed from the language of games, such as "good cricket," is dependent on a knowledge of the games from which the expressions come.

We cannot depend on sentiment and emotionalism to provide educative experiences for all school boys and girls in the major American sports. We must definitely plan our teaching so as to develop a knowledge and appreciation of the fine points of the games. Some of the methods by which they may be done are (1) the use of motion pictures, (2) explanations at school assemblies, (3) explanations by officials or by well qualified announcers during interruptions of games, (4) promotion of an extensive intramural program, (5) definite teaching toward this end in the required physical education classes, (6) the preparation and distribution of a "primer in football" and similar manuals of appreciation for other sports, and (7) provision of games during the regular school hours with all pupils attending and officials lecturing on the fine points of the game.

6. *Physical education should seek to develop in boys and girls broad and varied interests which will be likely to lead on to other desirable activities and interests.* A person who has many broad and varied experiences can see and appreciate many more meanings in each experience than can the individual who has had only a limited number of narrow experiences. Every one interprets each new experience in terms of his past experiences. A person is likely to be interested chiefly in the activities which he understands and which have considerable meaning to him. Physical education, therefore, should emphasize team games, recreational sports, and outing activities because it seems that these activities provide a wide range of experiences which are rich in meanings to boys and girls. The interests stimulated by these natural play activities are likely to lead on to further activity and thereby contribute to ever-widening circles of interests which are held in common with many other people.

7. *Physical education should provide at each school level opportunities*

[88]

for participation by all pupils in physical activities suited to the innate tendencies and acquired interests and abilities of each child. In conformity with the democratic principle of equality of opportunity it is essential that opportunities be provided for universal participation in the school program of physical education. If each child is to take part in physical education with benefit to himself, it is necessary that his inborn motor, emotional, and mental characteristics be considered in planning his program of activities. It is equally important that his interests and the level of achievement he has reached be recognized.

To provide physical education for only certain groups of children in school or to provide only one general program which all pupils are expected to follow is contrary to the democratic ideals which emphasize the importance of individuality and the development of human personality. The individual differences of each child should be taken into consideration in planning the school program of physical education.

8. *Physical education should help boys and girls to recognize and consider intelligently the opportunities for a life vocation that exist in physical education, recreation, camping, and related fields.* One of the important functions that the public schools in a democracy should serve is to help boys and girls choose a life work in which they will be happy and render the best service to society. One of the outstanding characteristics peculiar to the American form of society and government is that every individual has an excellent chance to rise above the social and economic class into which he was born. This is one of the main differences between a democratic society such as we have in the United States and the societies which exist in some of the older nations of the world. It is important, therefore, that every reasonable effort be made to help all boys and girls find the vocation for which they are best suited.

Physical education has the responsibility of providing the data and information concerning the nature of and opportunities in physical education and related fields as a life vocation which will enable boys and girls to evaluate it intelligently.

9. *Physical education should teach boys and girls how to play games and to participate in other physical activities that are suitable and enjoyable as leisure-time recreations.* The greatly increased amount of leisure time which is available to most people emphasizes the responsibility of the schools to prepare the masses of the people to spend their free time in socially desirable activities. Leisure should not be considered an absence of activity but as a kind of activity which is meaningful, interesting,

[89]

and purposive to the participants. Traditionally, we have glorified work and frowned on recreation and play. "Dying in harness" has been one of the praised attributes of the American business man, but it should be the source of humiliation and shame rather than of boasting. Only dumb animals who have cruel inhuman masters ever "die in harness."

Aside from physical recreations, there are many types of activities such as music, art, literature, dramatics, and handicrafts which can be used advantageously during leisure time. All boys and girls should have preparation in some of these so that they may be used as recreational interests. But everyone should also have the skills and interest which will enable him to spend a part of his leisure time in such physical recreations as golf, tennis, handball, swimming, fishing, hunting, and horseback riding. It is the responsibility of the physical education program in schools to provide the instruction which will prepare all individuals to participate successfully in wholesome physical recreations of this kind.

Summary. The majority of American citizens believe in a democratic form of society and government. There have been a large number of significant changes in American society during the last two decades. These changes with their attendant changes in the functions of the schools are of much importance to teachers of physical education.

The school is a social institution that has definite functions to perform. In a like manner physical education as part of the school program should assume the responsibility for definite and specific functions. These functions include (1) providing a common background of physical recreations for the masses of the people; (2) developing some sport into an American institution; (3) teaching to all boys and girls some of the activities which constitute part of the cultural heritage of the race; (4) helping to prepare children to live more satisfactorily as children and as adults; (5) providing every boy and girl with knowledge and understanding of the highly organized popular American sports; (6) teaching to all pupils in school recreational games that can be played with other congenial persons; (7) providing leadership in vigorous physical activities suited to the needs and abilities of the pupils; and (8) guiding boys and girls in the consideration of physical education as a vocation.

QUESTIONS

1. What changes in the social ideals of pioneer American thinkers have taken place in the last few years?

2. What social changes have occurred during the past decade that are particularly significant to physical education?

3. What are the desirable social goals for America that have been proposed by the National Education Association?

4. What is the principle and purpose of universal education?

5. What are the general goals of public education which were proposed by the Michigan Education Planning Commission?

6. What values should be expected from providing the masses of the people a common background of games, sports, dances, and outing activities?

7. What desirable educational results should accrue from teaching all boys and girls some of the physical activities which constitute part of the cultural heritage of the race?

8. What are some of the ways in which physical education can help individuals to live more happily during the period of childhood and youth and also during adulthood?

9. In what ways may physical education help to develop broad and varied interests other than those in physical activities?

10. What contribution should physical education make toward preparing pupils to spend their leisure happily?

REFERENCES

Adams, James Truslow. *The Epic of America.* Boston: Little, Brown and Company, 1931.

Briggs, Thomas H. *Secondary Education.* New York: The Macmillan Company, 1933.

Sharman, Jackson R. *Introduction to Physical Education.* New York: A. S. Barnes and Company, 1934.

Williams, Jessie Feiring. *The Principles of Physical Education.* Philadelphia: W. B. Saunders Company, 1932.

CHAPTER VI

Psychological Foundations of Physical Education

~

Functions of psychology in teaching. Human beings are able, because of the nature of the human organism, to use past experiences in solving new problems and also to create ideas, ideals, and more concrete things by anticipating the future. In order that pupils may make the most efficient and effective use of individual, group, and race experiences in meeting novel situations it is necessary that they and their teachers know and be able to apply productive and effectual methods of learning. The data underlying these methods are included in the science of psychology which deals with how human beings think, feel, and act.

There are several specialized fields of psychology each of which is concerned primarily with particular types of problems. Among these are: (1) genetic psychology, which includes the studies which have been made of social development, intelligence, and emotional responses of adults and children at different age levels; (2) abnormal psychology, which includes the study of mental abnormalities; (3) social psychology, which includes a study of the effect on behavior of such institutions of society as religion, recreation, the family, customs, traditions, and government; (4) comparative psychology, which includes a study of the behavior of lower animals, higher animals, and primitive man, and a comparison of these forms of behavior with that of civilized man, thereby helping us to understand how the human mind develops; and (5) educational psychology which includes the facts and principles from the entire field of psychology that are particularly applicable and helpful in learning and teaching.

A knowledge of educational psychology helps one to know how children learn and behave. When a normal child is born he has many potentialities for development, and it depends very largely on the experiences which he has at home and at school whether these potentialities will develop along wholesome and sound lines or along undesirable and anti-social lines. It should be emphasized that heredity does not make a human personality but provides only the potentialities, and it is largely one's environment, education, and the sum total of his experiences that determine how he really develops. Heredity and environment, nature and nurture, combine to make each individual what he is; no person is the result of only one of these factors.

The topics in educational psychology which are most important in teaching physical education relate to (1) the original nature of man, (2) the physical basis of behavior, (3) the motivation of behavior, (4) the learning process, (5) the principles of learning, and (6) transfer of training.

Original nature. Education is concerned primarily with changing or modifying the ways in which individuals behave or react to stimuli. It is assumed that the changes secured are good and desirable and in most cases they no doubt contribute in a desirable way to intellectual and personality development. Human beings have many relatively universal ways of reacting, which are largely the result of the kind of body man has inherited from his ancestors and more specifically of the peculiar nature of the human nervous system. The innate or inborn characteristics of man have been grouped by psychologists as (1) reflexes, (2) instincts, (3) emotions, and (4) capacities.[1]

There is no clearly defined line of demarcation between these different kinds of tendencies-to-react but it has been found convenient to group these traits in some such manner for discussion. These natural and inherited patterns of behavior are handed down from generation to generation as part of the endowment of the species. They apparently are inherited in the same way that the shape of one's body, the color of the hair and eyes, and the texture and pigmentation of the skin are inherited. From earliest infancy they help the human organism to make adjustments to its environment and to gain experiences that contribute to growth and development. Crying, nursing, and random movements are some of the inborn ways of reacting that are possessed by infants. It is on these biologically inherited tendencies-to-behavior that learning and growth are built. These traits can be modified by experience and, therefore, they depart slightly from the original pattern with successive performances, being shaped and modified by experience and practice. When a person becomes older and gains a broader and more meaningful range of experiences his ways of reacting and behaving become less original and reduce his dependency on innate urges.

Reflexes. Reflexes are certain simple involuntary reactions which

[1] Rudolf Pintner, *Educational Psychology*, p. 6. New York: Henry Holt and Company, 1929.

occur in different parts of the body and follow regularly a given stimulus without any premeditation. Examples of reflexes are the knee-jerk, the eye wink, sneezing and vomiting, the pupillary reflex, and in infants the grasping reflex and sucking. Some reflexes could probably be modified with much effort and training, but it would be unwise to change the reaction patterns of most reflexes. Persistent efforts along these lines would probably prove detrimental to one's health and interfere with the normal growth of personality. The reflexes and their possible modification are not of great importance to education but the other types of innate tendencies are important and significant in the education of boys and girls.

Instincts. Psychologists are not unanimous in their beliefs concerning the existence of traits or characteristics that can be definitely called instincts. It is generally agreed, however, that there are many tendencies that are common to all human beings, which are present at birth, and which appear regularly in all individuals without any previous opportunities to learn the responses involved. Traits of this kind are said to be innate, unlearned, and instinctive.

The original tendencies of man, which are usually described as instincts, play a very important part in determining individual behavior and the form of social organization under which human beings live. The desire for social approval, the fear of ridicule and disapproval, the urge to excel and dominate, and the desire to manipulate things are examples of native tendencies which have much influence in determining our behavior and in shaping the entire pattern of our lives. The urge to excel, for example, if directed intelligently in a favorable environment, may cause a person to go above and beyond what would ordinarily be expected in worthwhile achievements. But if this innate tendency were to find expression along undesirable and antisocial lines the evil results might exclude any possible good. The native characteristic of man which causes him to get satisfaction from living with others has been a fundamental influence in guiding the development of our social order and in determining the nature of our educational program.. If man gained most pleasure and satisfaction from a solitary way of living instead of being a social animal, as he is, the kind of society in which we live and the educational program that we have would be entirely different.

Emotions. The emotions are native and original ways of reacting that are closely akin to reflexes and instincts but they possess some differences that are important. Instincts and reflexes find expression in many ways but most often through activities which involve the voluntary skeletal muscles. Emotional reactions involve mostly the viscera, the endocrine glands, and the autonomic nervous system. An emotion is a response that results from a general stirring-up of the different organic systems of the body. Changes in the processes of circulation, respiration, digestion, and glandular secretions are some of the reactions which make up the complex series of responses that compose an emotion.

There are a large number of emotional responses of which the human organism is capable and many proposals have been made by psychologists for the classification of emotions into groups. Watson has stated that *fear, rage,* and *love* are the three primary emotions. Every human being has many other emotions which have grown out of the primary emotions and have been shaped by the experiences of each individual. Every emotion is a vague, general, diffused kind of reaction and it is difficult to isolate and analyze emotions for purposes of description and discussion.

Physiology of emotions. In order for one to gain an understanding of the emotions and emotionalized behavior it is desirable that he know some of the more important facts concerning the physiology underlying them.

The nervous system and the glandular system are believed to play the most important parts in the origin and expression of the emotions. The *autonomic nervous system* is the part of general nervous system of the body that supplies nerves to the internal organs such as those of digestion, circulation, respiration, and the endocrine glands. The autonomic nervous system is connected to the central nervous system, and the stimuli which it carries to the different organs serve to control and integrate the activity of these organs. One of the important functions that is served by the cranial, sympathetic, and sacral nerves which compose the autonomic nervous system is to transmit and reflect in different parts of the body changes which take place in other parts. This enables the body to prepare quickly for fights, flights, and other emergencies by increasing the flow into the blood of secretions from the ductless glands, controlling respiration, stopping the process of digestion, modifying the blood pressure, and making other necessary physiological adjustments.

The integrated action of the autonomic nervous system and the glandular system is especially important in emotional expression. The glands of internal secretion include the adrenal, thyroid, thymus, pituitary, and pineal glands, and the ovaries, testes, and pancreas in part. The liver also at times has been classified as a gland of internal secretion, although the glycogen given off by the liver is not a true internal secretion. Apparently the secretion of the cortex of the adrenal gland is more significant in the stimulation and expression of the emotions than that of the other endocrine glands. The substance secreted by these glands is also important in the regulation of many other bodily processes. When a human being is under great emotional stress the adrenal glands increase greatly the quantity of their secretions that are poured into the blood stream. This substance apparently serves to cause a rise in blood-pressure, to increase the heart action, the number of white cells in the blood, and the capacity of the red corpuscles of the blood to absorb oxygen.

Nearly all parts of the body are involved in emotional experiences; particularly the viscera, ductless glands, the involuntary muscles, the nervous system and the muscular system which makes expression possible. Apparently the activities of the viscera and the consciousness of emotional experience interact on each other. This means that activities of the viscera may cause the feelings of emotion, and that emotions may also influence greatly the visceral processes. These phenomena may be thought of as functioning in a circular manner, with each phase complementing and stimulating the other.

Educational significance of emotions. Physical education teachers, probably more than teachers of other subjects, should be concerned with the influence of emotions on educational experiences because it seems to be clearly evident that physical education situations are more completely charged with emotional stimuli than other parts of the school program. Psychologists agree that it is highly desirable for all individuals to have adequate opportunities for the wholesome expression of the emotions and other natural urges. It is almost universally accepted as being true that the continued repression of emotional expression will result in the development of undesirable traits of character and types of emotional instability. In guiding the experiences of children emphasis should be placed on the things *to do,* rather than on things *not to do.*

In order that children may be able to adjust and live successfully in a complex society it is necessary that some native tendencies be checked and redirected. It is essential that everyone develop many good habits of social behavior, emotional control, and self-reliance. The technique of "sitting-on-lid" which is employed by some teachers is an unintelligent procedure and in many cases may cause emotional urges to find expression along undesirable and harmful lines. Physical education teachers should seek to organize and conduct their program in a way to provide the maximum of freedom and opportunities for emotional expression. Formal, teacher-dominated methods are clearly out of place in a school that seeks the maximum development of individuality and personality on the part of all pupils.

Modification of original nature. From the standpoint of education the most important and significant thing about the emotions is that their form of expression can be modified as the result of experience. It is probably true that the original tendencies of man, including his emotions, can be more easily and successfully modified than those of any of the lower animals. One of the things which makes this possible is the flexible nature of the human nervous system that contributes to the capacity to retain impressions and profit by past experiences. The possibilities of change and modification are greatest at the time of birth and become progressively smaller as a person becomes older, but apparently there are possibilities of change throughout life.

The work that Watson [1] has done on conditioning the fundamental reactions of babies, the experiments of Pavlov and his students on the conditioned reflex in the dog, and similar reports by other qualified observers show how original nature may be conditioned and modified by associating emotional reactions with situations that under ordinary circumstances do not arouse any emotions.

The role of maturation in behavior. It has been pointed out repeatedly by psychologists that many traits and characteristics of human beings, as well as of other animals, emerge in orderly genetic sequence and are not dependent to any appreciable degree on training and experience. The available data indicate that organic maturation plays a very important part in shaping the behavior of children. When we use the term "maturation" we mean the natural growth and development of traits, characteristics, reactions, and abilities which take place almost independently of any opportunities to learn. There is a large amount of well-authenticated data to support this maturation hypothesis which is particularly significant in connection with the teaching of physical education. One of the important lessons which it teaches is that it is a fallacy to attempt to teach complicated physical activities to young children before their fundamental motor reactions have matured enough to enable them to learn complex skills. Studies made on chickens, birds, and other

[1] John B. Watson and R. Rayner, "Conditioned Emotional Reactions," *Journal of Experimental Psychology*, III (February, 1920), 1–14.

animals, as well as those on human beings, lend support to the hypothesis that certain fundamental reactions come as the result of maturation.

Gesell has brought together much of the evidence on this problem from clinical, experimental, and normative observations. - A summary of his material which has been drawn from five different sources is given here.[1]

1. The development of prehension, or grasping, a pellet 8 millimeters in diameter, throughout the first year of life showed significant progressive changes in behavior pattern. The evidence indicated that maturation, not experience and training, accounted for the changes in the reactions.

2. A study of the development of prehension in a pair of identical infant twins contributed much interesting data in regard to the development of behavior patterns and gives additional support to the maturation hypothesis. Controlled observations were made of prehensory reactions to cubes and pellets of these twins, who were premature and retarded. When they were 28 weeks old they did not notice the pellet, but they did note a cube. At the age of 38 weeks they reacted to the pellet in an almost identical manner, and at 40 weeks the twins again reacted to the pellet in a remarkably similar way. They were given the same examination again under the same conditions at the age of 42 weeks and it was found that great improvement in reacting had been made by both twins and that their reactions were almost identical. The results of this study indicate that maturation was responsible for the observed changes in the prehension patterns.

The results of other tests carried on with these twins at the age of 44 weeks with a test-performance box, and at 48 weeks with a pellet and bottle test lend additional support to this theory.

3. Observations of the limitations of training on identical twins are other sources of data which help to show the influence of maturation on behavior patterns. A study using an experimental method was conducted by Gesell to determine the relative influence of training and maturation. He called his procedure the method of "co-twin control." In this experiment the twin that was trained was designated as T, and the one that was used as a control was known as C.

Beginning at the age of 46 weeks Twin T was given systematic training in stair climbing and cube behavior for 20 minutes daily for a period of 6 weeks. When the twins were one year old, which was at the end of the six weeks training period, Twin T was a relatively expert stair climber, and the untrained Co-twin C was unable to climb the stairs, even with assistance. But after one more week at the age of 53 weeks the entirely untrained Co-twin C could climb the staircase without any assistance.

[1] Arnold Gesell, *The Guidance of Mental Growth in Infant and Child,* pp. 274-92. New York: The Macmillan Company, 1935.

Similar results were secured in the part of the experiment having to do with cube behavior.

4. Extrinsic factors such as malnutrition, restricted exercise and function of parts of the body, and deviations from normal environmental influences such as an abnormally long or short gestation period, do not appear to have much influence on the maturation of a human being. Development of reactions and behavior seems to be relatively normal and stable in spite of influences which apparently should seriously handicap growth.

5. Gesell states that emotional behavior follows a process of progressive maturation in much the same way as grasping and stair-climbing ability. The primary emotions, such as fear, are subject to maturation from within as well as to changes brought about by conditioning influences and experiences. The available evidence emphasizes the importance of maturation.

The physical basis of behavior. It has been pointed out repeatedly that each experience of an individual involves the entire organism, and that any upset of the equilibrium between an organism and its environment results in adaptative behavior until the state of equilibrium is restored. Emphasis has also been placed on the fact that each experience of an organism results in some permanent change. The important physical characteristics of human beings which make possible human behavior include the nervous system, the sense organs, the endocrine glands, and the skeletal and muscular systems. One of the widely accepted theories which has been advanced in explanation of the learning process is discussed in the following paragraphs. It should be emphasized that this explanation is only one of many that have been proposed, but it seems to be the one that is most generally accepted.

A description of the nervous system usually includes a discussion of (1) the receiving mechanism, (2) the connecting mechanism, and (3) the reacting mechanism. These three parts of the nervous system make it possible for a complete circuit to be formed between the place of stimulation and the muscles or other organs of reaction. Stimuli are received by the sense organs, and one generally accepted theory holds that an impulse is released or generated by the action of stimuli on the receptors. According to this theory an impulse travels along a nerve to the central nervous system by some chemical or electrical process.

The nerves that carry impulses to the central nervous system are called afferent nerves and the nerves that carry impulses from the central nervous system to the effectors are called efferent nerves. The points of contact between nerve cells are called synapses.

[99]

The receptors have been classified by Perrin and Klein as follows: [1]

A. The somatic receptors:
  1. Exteroceptors.
    a. Distance receptors.
      (1) Organ of vision—the eye.
      (2) Organ of audition—the outer ear, middle ear, vestibule and cochlea of inner ear.
      (3) Organ of smell (also an interoceptor)—olfactory epithelium of nose.
    b. Contact receptors—the cutaneous sense organs.
      (1) Organs of touch and pressure.
      (2) Organs of heat.
      (3) Organs of cold.
      (4) Organs of pain (in addition to interoceptors for visceral pain).
  2. Proprioceptors.
    a. Organs of position and equilibrium—semicircular canals, saccule and utricle of the internal ear.
    b. Organs of kinesthetic functions.
      (1) Organs in muscles.
      (2) Organs in tendons.
      (3) Organs in joints, or on articular surfaces.
B. The visceral receptors:
  1. Interoceptors.
    a. Receptors of the digestive system.
      (1) Organs of smell (listed above).
      (2) Organs of taste—taste buds on tongue and pharynx.
      (3) Organs or sensory cells of hunger—in stomach.
      (4) Organs or sensory cells of thirst—in mucous membrane of pharynx.
      (5) Organs or sensory cells of nausea—in stomach.
    b. Receptors of circulatory system.
    c. Receptors of respiratory system.
    d. Receptors of reproductive system.

The central nervous system. The cerebrospinal nervous system is particularly important in learning. The autonomic nervous system plays an important part in emotional expression and is indirectly involved in learning. One theory of learning claims that there is *synaptic resistance* to nerve impulses at each synapse in the central nervous system and that

---

[1] F. A. C. Perrin and D. B. Klein, *Psychology,* pp. 22–23. New York: Henry Holt and Company, 1926.

[100]

each time this resistance is broken down through the exercise of a reaction the resistance becomes permanently weaker and the path of the impulse through the synapse becomes more definitely established. It is believed that in this way habits and other kinds of reactions are formed. Many experiments which have been carefully conducted have provided data which cause many qualified students to question this theory of learning. The exact nature of the neurological processes involved in learning are unknown but it has been supposed that learning involves changes in the nervous system and that the synapses play a significant part in these changes.

The central nervous system serves the function of receiving impulses from the receptors of the body, correlating and coordinating these impulses, and directing them over appropriate efferent paths to the reacting mechanisms. This is a very important process, because without it the large number of stimuli which are constantly stimulating the human organism would result in many confused and conflicting reactions. A widely accepted theory of this function sets forth that stimuli as such do not bring about reactions but that situations which are composed of a combination of stimuli are the cause of human behavior. Each of the impulses that make up a situation reaches the central nervous system over a different afferent path. It is necessary that these impulses be arranged in a definite pattern in order that they may prove effective in causing activity. It is assumed that these patterns are organized and coordinated in the correlation centers of the brain. The thalamus, which is part of that portion of the stem underneath the cerebrum, is believed to be one of the most important of these correlation centers. It is not known exactly how this process is carried on but it is clear that a selection of impulses is made and that they are sent out from the central nervous system over appropriate efferent nerves to effectors which cause observable behavior. It has also been definitely demonstrated that this process can be made more efficient through training.

The effectors. The effectors are usually grouped in two classes as (1) the somatic and (2) the visceral. The somatic effectors include the skeletal muscles, and the visceral include the smooth muscles and the glands. The smooth or involuntary muscles are the ones that are involved in the functioning of the organic systems of the body such as those of digestion, circulation, and elimination. The secretion of glands is determined to a great extent by stimuli. The secretion of the duct glands such as the salivary, gastric, intestinal, pancreatic, and sebaceous are important in the fundamental physiological processes of the body, but function only indirectly in learning. Since the secretion of the ductless glands such as the thyroid, parathyroids, pituitary, thymus, adrenals, the pancreatic islands of Langerhans, pineal gland, testes, and ovaries, are closely associated with the emotions it is believed that they are of great significance in many learning situations.

The motivation of behavior. Motivation is a term frequently used to describe the drives or urges from within a person that cause behavior. A large number of terms and expressions may have been used by psychologists to describe these inner incentives, impulses, wants, purposes, and interests. Apparently most of these expressions are used to denote the same thing. One widely accepted theory which seeks to explain the foundations of motivation seems to be based largely on the teachings of dynamic and Gestalt psychology. This theory insists that all activities of a human organism originate in its wants and impulses, and that stimuli from the environment play a very insignificant part in causing behavior. Thorndike, on the other hand, states that drives are the result of physiological readiness of the situation-response mechanism, and that when a situation stimulates the organism the connections which are in a state of readiness react promptly and with greater facility. Dewey emphasizes interest and insists that it is the most powerful motivating force.

Motives are usually divided into two general classes as (1) innate and (2) acquired. The innate motives are largely physiological in nature and acquired motives are predominantly social, although it seems to be true that in most motives there is a physiological factor. The following classification should prove helpful to teachers in understanding the nature of motives:

1. Motives aroused primarily by organic conditions, needs, or cravings, such as hunger, sex, thirst, and sleep.

2. Instinctive and prepotent tendencies, such as self-assertion, fighting, and manipulation.

3. Emotions and feelings of satisfyingness and annoyance (closely related to 1 and 2).

4. Unconscious forces.

5. Habits, attitudes, ideals, interests, sentiments, purposes, and mind sets.[1]

The use of motives. Interesting activities that have meaning to

[1] Charles E. Benson, James E. Lough, Charles E. Skinner, and Paul V. West, *Psychology for Teachers,* p. 105. Boston: Ginn and Company, 1933 (revised).

pupils do not ordinarily have to be motivated by artificial means. The difficulty in motivation usually comes in trying to get children to learn things that are too difficult, valueless, or meaningless to them. Most pupils apply themselves zestfully to the solution of problems and the learning of activities which are properly introduced and which appear to the learners as being of some worth. The motives that are used by some teachers frequently do much more harm to pupils than good. It is essential, therefore, that all teachers give careful and critical consideration to the choice and use of incentives. The following statements are suggested as being of some value as criteria in the selection of incentives to be used in schools.

1. *An incentive should appeal and apply to all the pupils in a class.* The giving of prizes which can be won by only one or a few pupils would be a poor form of motivation. Providing for public recognition of all pupils who make commendable progress during a period of time would be a much better way to stimulate learning and practice.

2. *An incentive should build permanent interests and motivate activity which leads to further activity and broader interests.* Encouraging pupils to keep graphs to show their progress in learning activities is a device that can be used to good advantage in the motivation of learning. This plan enables each pupil to see the improvement he is making but does not drive him to attempt to do as well as other individuals who might be much better endowed with native ability. Working for a sweater, a gold football, a holiday from school, or for other extrinsic awards or prizes as an end in themselves is a short-sighted form of motivation and probably will not result in any permanent recreational interests or other desirable results.

3. *An incentive should stimulate pupils to strive for worthy objectives.* Undesirable attitudes and viewpoints are likely to result from the use of incentives such as giving a holiday from school to all pupils who have their teeth cleaned by a dentist. Having clean teeth is not a particularly worthy objective in and of itself, but living hygienically in order that one may have more energy and enthusiasm for doing interesting and valuable things is an objective that might well challenge the efforts of anyone. An incentive that would stimulate pupils to win games by any "hook or crook" would be highly objectionable and should not be used in schools.

The learning process. Learning is a process of change and modification of ways of reacting, and involves activity of the learner. A

[103]

summary of some of the generally accepted principles of learning is given in the following paragraphs.

1. *Human beings learn through experience which consists of inter-actions between the organism and its environment.* Experiences are necessary to learning and in most instances the ones which involve the greatest amount of self-directed activity on the part of the learner are of the most educational value. Human beings can learn many things through reading, seeing pictures, and other forms of vicarious experience but it is highly desirable for everyone to have as many complete, interesting, first-hand experiences as possible. This idea has been expressed in slang by the witticism which states that "most monkeys learn to monkey by monkeying, not by aping."

2. *New experiences have meaning to us in terms of past experiences.* After each experience one is the person that he was previously *plus* the new experience. This is the reason why a broadly and liberally educated person gets many meanings from almost all new experiences in a broad range of situations. The illustration which is frequently used to describe the fact that we interpret new experiences in terms of past experiences is the case of a group of individuals walking through a forest each of whom saw the situation in a different light. The biologist thought of the different forms of plant and animal life that lived in the forest; the lumberman thought mainly of the sawmill timber that could be obtained from the trees; the sportsman saw the possibility of wild game; and the artist was impressed primarily with the beauty of the situation. Each of these persons interpreted the same experience in a different way. This was due to the fact that their backgrounds and interests were different. In order for a person to be well-educated and to continue to grow, he must continuously have many new experiences and constantly increase the range of meanings of his past experiences.

One's philosophy and outlook on life are likewise determined largely by his past experiences and the meanings that he has associated with them. Some individuals have had experiences that cause them to be optimists who see opportunities in every difficulty, while others have become pessimists who see difficulties in every opportunity.

3. *Individuals learn "ways of reacting" or "responding" to situations and stimuli.* Some behavior is in the nature of a direct response to an immediate stimulus, whereas other forms of behavior are in the nature of complicated reaction patterns which arise from a series of simultaneous stimuli. Nearly all the responses that are made by pupils in

physical education are the result of relatively complex situations that cause many impulses to be carried to the central nervous system at the same time from a large number of receptors. Teaching pupils to perform these complex reactions in a well-coordinated and smoothly timed way is one of the main responsibilities of physical education teachers. Performance of this kind is an important goal of physical education.

4. *Some ways of reacting are natural and innate, such as reflexes and instinctive behavior; other ways of reacting are learned, such as habits and consciously directed behavior.* Physical education provides many opportunities for the wholesome expression of instinctive tendencies and emotions, and for the development of desirable habits. Good results depend largely on the quality of the leadership available for physical education. When there are available leaders who are intelligent, conscientious, and well prepared there is an excellent chance of pupils developing worthwhile traits of character and personality through experiences in physical education.

5. *The learning curves for most physical education activities are usually of the same general shape.* Most of these typical curves show an "initial spurt," "plateaux," a continuous general approach toward what appears to be a "physiological limit," and finally the "end spurt." These characteristics are not all present in every learning curve but they are common enough to be considered typical.

6. *Drill plays an important part in making skills in physical education habitual and automatic.* Most skills in athletics, games, sports, dancing and other physical education activities must be overlearned so thoroughly that they can be performed speedily and accurately without thought by the pupil. If one attempts to think about the execution of a complicated skill he becomes awkward, slow, and inefficient in performance of the activity. Most physical education skills must be made mechanical and automatic in their execution in order to secure excellent performance. Drill on each skill must be motivated well and carried on correctly in imitation of a good model.

Principles of learning. It has already been pointed out that there are several theories which attempt to explain learning and that most of these theories have advanced statements of principles to guide teachers and pupils in carrying on the learning process. The principles of this kind which seem to be most widely accepted among educators are the statements usually referred to as the "laws of learning." These laws are often called the Thorndike laws of learning because Thorndike's statement of them is generally known and commonly quoted. They are based on the *connectionist* theory of learning.

The laws of learning are usually stated as the laws of readiness, exercise and effect. The law of readiness points out that when an organism is in a state of readiness or "set" to do anything or to act in a certain way, to do that thing or to act in that way gives satisfaction, and not to act in that way provides annoyance. If, for example, a person is hungry he is in a state of readiness to eat and eating provides satisfaction, but to be kept from eating provides annoyance. The law of exercise expresses the generally known fact that, other things being equal, if a reaction is exercised often it becomes more firmly established and can be executed more rapidly and efficiently. In connection with a discussion of the law of exercise it should be emphasized, however, that the adage "practice makes perfect" is not a strictly accurate statement. A more acceptable statement would be that correct practice tends to make perfect.

The law of effect relates to the choice of reactions that will be retained. It is sometimes referred to as the law of satisfaction and annoyance. It points out that if a reaction provides satisfaction, one will tend to repeat and retain that way-of-reacting, but if a reaction results in annoyance one will seek to avoid and not to repeat it.

In order to secure efficient and effective learning the principles included in all the laws of learning must be applied in all learning situations. This means that in all cases the organism must be in a state of readiness and must practice the reactions in a way to bring satisfaction.

Transfer of training. Claims are often made in a general indefinite way that participation in physical education activities helps to develop desirable traits of character and personality. Many of these claims cannot be substantiated in light of the facts concerning the transfer of training. Most psychologists believe that specific learnings do not, in general, transfer readily from one situation to another. If, for example, a boy is required to be courteous and fair in basketball games there is no assurance that he will act courteously and fairly in his home, at school, in business, or in other situations. There is ample evidence, however, to justify one in believing that general learnings such as attitudes, ideals, and generalizations have a much wider applicability and that they will function in a wide range of situations. It is believed that a person can develop traits and characteristics such as these by having many experiences in a large number of situations in which he gets satisfaction by acting in the desired ways. If a person has developed a general ideal of fair-play, for example, it is highly probable that he will act fairly in sports and most other situations. Since physical education offers a large number of well-motivated opportunities for teaching desirable behavior, many teachers believe that the lessons learned in these situations are more lasting and significant than the ones learned in other situations at school.

Teachers of physical education, therefore, should take advantage of all opportunities to help their pupils see the broader social implications of their behavior and to develop generalizations concerning principles of conduct which may be applied in most of the situations that confront them in their daily living.

Summary. Human beings are able to use past experiences in meeting new situations and solving novel problems. The data which explain how they do this are contained in the science of psychology. Teachers of physical education should be familiar with the more important of these data in order that they may understand how children learn and behave. The topics in educational psychology which are most important in teaching physical education deal with (1) the original nature of man, (2) the physical basis of behavior, (3) the motivation of behavior, (4) the learning process, (5) the principles of learning, and (6) transfer of training.

The innate or inborn characteristics of man have been grouped by psychologists as (1) reflexes, (2) instincts, (3) emotions, and (4) capacities. Most reflexes should not be modified in their expression, but successful adjustment demands that many other natural tendencies be sublimated or changed in some way. The instincts and emotions play an important part in shaping the kind of society in which we live and in determining human behavior.

The known facts concerning the emergence and maturation of fundamental human reactions and other characteristics indicate that premature training of children in complex skills is at least a waste of time and may be definitely harmful.

Each experience of a human being involves the entire organism. The physical basis of behavior depends largely on the nervous system, the sense organs, the endocrine glands, and the muscles. One widely accepted theory of learning states that stimuli on the receptors cause impulses to be sent to the central nervous system, which in turn directs impulses to glands and muscles. The central nervous system is believed to serve a very important function in coordinating the large number of

[107]

simultaneous stimuli that reach the brain and spinal cord from many different receptors.

The use of wholesome motives is of fundamental importance in learning. This makes it necessary that incentives be selected in light of sound criteria. Learning is an active process and involves primarily the activity of the learner in modifying and changing his ways of reacting. The laws of learning are generally accepted as guides to efficient learning. It is believed that specific learning will not transfer to other situations that are entirely different. The available evidence indicates, however, that general learnings such as attitudes, ideals, and generalizations have a wide applicability in many different situations.

QUESTIONS

1. What topics in educational psychology supply data that are particularly significant in physical education?
2. Of what significance in education and the learning process are the innate characteristics of man?
3. What relation do the emotions have to learning in physical education?
4. What are the physiological processes underlying the emotions?
5. What are some of the ways by which the original characteristics of man can be modified?
6. What are some of the data that give support to the maturation hypothesis?
7. Of what significance to physical education are this hypothesis and its supporting data?
8. What is one widely accepted theory concerning the physical basis of behavior?
9. What is the basis of motives and how should they be used in teaching?
10. What are some of the generally accepted principles underlying the learning process?

REFERENCES

Benson, Charles E.; Lough, James E.; Skinner, Charles E.; and West, Paul V. *Psychology for Teachers.* Boston: Ginn and Company, 1933 (revised).

Davis, Robert A. *Psychology of Learning.* New York: McGraw-Hill Book Company, Inc., 1933.

Griffith, Coleman R. *An Introduction to Educational Psychology.* New York: Farrar and Rinehart, Inc., 1935.

Pintner, Rudolf. *Educational Psychology.* New York: Henry Holt and Company, 1929.

CHAPTER VII

Educational and Philosophical Foundations of Physical Education

Principles of education. The various fields of human knowledge such as biology, sociology, and psychology contribute many significant guides to the building of a sound statement of the principles of physical education. The interpretation and application of these principles, however, depends on an understanding of the educational and philosophical foundations of this subject. There is provided in this chapter, therefore, a brief discussion of pertinent doctrines from education and philosophy. The items include (1) the responsibility of the school to society, (2) education as a state function, (3) the function of philosophy in physical education, (4) principles of a pragmatic philosophy of education, (5) modern philosophical emphases, (6) philosophy of physical education, (7) social purposes of education, (8) the meaning and use of interest in teaching, (9) teaching social and moral behavior, (10) the influence of inherited abilities, (11) required participation in physical education, (12) the most suitable physical education program, (13) the development of leadership, and (14) emphases in teaching.

Responsibility of the school to society. Different kinds of societies throughout the time covered by recorded history have set up and supported schools for the purpose of perpetuating, improving, and re-creating themselves. At present the school is recognized in the United States as being one of the most important and costly social institutions. In a democratic society the general purposes of the school are (1) to pass on to each succeeding generation the most important and essential parts of the social inheritance which has been built and accumulated as the result of the experiences of the race during past centuries, (2) to help in the formulation and proposal of a clear and usable statement of social ideals, (3) to provide the leadership for a re-definition of social ideals as changes in society take place, and (4) to guide the individual and social group experiences of boys and girls in a way that will help them make successful individual and social adjustments.

In order to accomplish these purposes the school and its program must be dynamic, flexible, and subject to change. To insure the progress of civilization it is essential that experiences of past generations be transmitted effectively to younger generations. The school is the most efficient agent for accomplishing this. It is *not* the direct responsibility of the school to set up a plan for a model society and attempt to change our social order to conform to that model, but the school should be delicately sensitive to social changes and trends and should attempt to help the members of each generation to meet successfully the problems of living which confront them. It is inevitable, of course, that the school will have much influence on the development of society through its activities in working with other institutions of society in an effort to propose a clear and useful statement of social ideals.

The school should guide boys and girls in recognizing and defining clearly desirable social ideals, and should provide them with a background of experience which will qualify them to restate and define anew worthy social ideals when changes in industry, economic conditions, population, and other aspects of society indicate the need for such a revised statement. One of the main weaknesses and shortcomings of education in America has been its failure to state clearly its social ideals. This has been due in part to the abstract ideals, such as liberty, freedom, and equality, on which our democratic society is based. But it is also due to the failure of educators to grasp the importance and significance of their responsibility in this matter. The statement of the Commission on the Social Studies of the American Historical Association is one of the recent publications which has made a significant contribution toward the solution of this problem.[1] The proposal of social-economic goals of America by a committee of the National Education Association is another important effort to state the social ideals of American education.[2] These goals are discussed in this book in the chapter on "Functions of Physical Education in a Democratic Society."

The schools in a democratic society such as ours have a more uncertain and difficult responsibility in the preparation of boys and girls for life than do the schools in an autocracy. In a country that is ruled by a dictator there is no question in anyone's mind concerning the kind of society that is wanted because the government states definitely and specifically the desired social ideals. But in a democracy this dubious service is not rendered to the schools, and it devolves on the teachers and pupils

[1] Charles A. Beard, *A Charter for the Social Sciences in the Schools.* New York: Charles Scribner's Sons, 1932.

[2] "What Are Desirable Social-Economic Goals for America?" *Journal of the National Education Association,* XXIII (January, 1934), 6–12.

in cooperation with other social institutions to propose a descriptive statement of the desired kind of society. After the nature of society is determined the schools still have the responsibility of choosing and applying
subject matter and methods that will prepare young people most successfully for recognizing, analyzing, and solving the problems which confront them as individuals and as members of the social group.

Education as a state function. It is an accepted fact of governmental organization in this country that "education is the function of
the state." This was implied in the tenth amendment to the Constitution of the United States when it stated that "all powers not delegated
to the United States by the Constitution, nor prohibited by it to the
states, are reserved to the states respectively, or to the people." This does
not mean that the federal government has never aided public education;
since the beginning of the nation numerous subsidies to education in
the states have been made in money and land. Most of the grants for
education made before the Civil War were for the aid of education in
general and carried with them no administrative restrictions. The Morrill Act passed by Congress in 1862 to establish the Land Grant Colleges,
and the Smith-Hughes vocational education act of 1917 are two outstanding instances in which the national government has contributed to
the support of specialized forms of education and has set up certain
regulations concerning the program of education for which the money
may be expended. It is no doubt true that these federal appropriations
with their accompanying regulations have helped greatly the forms of
education which they were intended to encourage. There is a widespread feeling, however, that they have worked in a way to restrict local
initiative and freedom.

Emphasis on decentralization. The National Advisory Committee on Education in 1931 stated in their report [1] to President Hoover
that all federal appropriations to the various states for education should
be granted without any qualifications as to the curriculum or form of
organization and administration in the schools. This committee also
emphasized the importance of not centralizing in the federal government
the administration of the educational system of the country. It was
pointed out that the centralization of administrative authority would permit the national government to determine the social purposes of education for the entire nation; that such a plan would violate the traditions

[1] National Advisory Committee on Education, *Federal Relations to Education.* Part I,
pp. 29-30. Washington: American Council on Education, 1933.

of American school management which have been found to fit best with our democratic ideals; that it would result in a school program of relative inflexibility and unresponsiveness to local conditions and sympathies; and that it would make possible partisan or class propaganda designed to indoctrinate the young in a way to cause them to support a form of government that would not be conducive to the best interests of all the people.

The report of the National Advisory Committee on Education sets forth the ways in which the federal government could aid in the improvement of public education. The most fundamental recommendation provides for the establishment of a Department of Education with a secretary in the President's Cabinet. The main function of such a Department to the schools of the nation would be to collect and disseminate important data and facts bearing on education. It has not been proposed that this Department should have any administrative authority over education in the different states.

The delegation of responsibility for education by states. In addition to the implied statement of state responsibility for education included in the federal Constitution, many of the state constitutions provide for a state system of public schools and specify that the state legislatures must make provision for the support of the schools.[1] Most states have been lavish in delegating the responsibility for the operation of schools to the school districts, counties, cities, and other political units in the states. As a result, practically all the schools of the country are administered locally. While this local autonomy has many advantages in a democratic society, the educational opportunities of the school children are likely to be harmfully restricted if the unit of administration is so small and poor that it cannot provide adequate financial support and professional leadership.

It is generally agreed by students of education that each state should maintain control over the professional preparation and certification of teachers, standards for plans and specifications of school buildings, methods of accounting for funds, and procedures of child accounting and attendance. The state should also guarantee financial support for a minimum fundamental educational opportunity for all the children of the state. The state should not, however, attempt to standardize the finer

---

[1] John M. Matzen, *State Constitutional Provisions for Education.* Teachers College Contributions to Education, No. 462. New York: Teachers College, Columbia University, 1931.

details of the school curriculum, methods of teaching, and
of schools.

The function of philosophy. There has been a great deal writt
on the history of physical education and about the influences that various
political and social developments have had. This type of information
has value in helping teachers understand the different forces that have
helped shape physical education, but the most important and immediately
useful discussion for teachers relates to the philosophy of physical education and its application to a school program in a democratic society. Teachers are interested in securing practical help in planning their programs.

As already pointed out, many important and significant principles
can be derived from the data available in biology, sociology, and psychology; but it remains for philosophy to integrate these principles and to
focus them on the problems of physical education in the public schools.
The solution of many problems can be greatly facilitated in this way
and large numbers of new and unsolved problems can be more clearly
recognized and specifically defined for future solution.

Principles of pragmatic philosophy of education. The beliefs
and viewpoints on which rest the best known and most widely accepted
principles of education have been summarized by Rugg as follows:

First: Human experience is unified and continuous; there are no separate
instincts; ends and means, character and conduct, motive and act, will and deed
—all are continuous; hence all dualistic interpretations of experience are
fallacious.

Second: Knowing comes only through active response; meaning arises only
through reaction; a concept is synonymous with corresponding operations.

Third: Knowing arises through testing consequences. This is Dewey's
concept of "the experimental method of knowing" and the contemporary
physicists' "operational" definition of thinking.

Fourth: Experience consists primarily in the adjustment and interaction of
individuals; both individual and group understanding and behavior are the
product of the social human environment; the social environment "consists of
all the activities of fellow beings that are bound up in the carrying on of the
activities of any one of its members."

Fifth: Society is conceived as a democracy, built on the foregoing principles; that is, on the experimental method of knowing, the unity and con-
tinuity of experience, "numerous and varied points of shared common interest."

Sixth: An educational system, also based on the foregoing concepts, which
will give "individuals a personal interest in social relationships and control

[113]

...n secure social changes without introducing

...al emphasis. The contemporary emphasis in
...insists that there be provided for all children at
...nich will prepare them for life in a democratic
..., among other things, that the pupils must actually
...ities that will provide practice in democratic behavior.
...and talking about good citizenship, cooperation, and
...ons will not enable all boys and girls to adjust successfully
to ... in which they live. It is essential that they have a large
number ... meaningful experiences in democratic situations. This emphasis indicates, therefore, that the organization, content, and instructional methods of the school must be a significant part of the lives of the pupils. Schooling should not be thought of as preparation for life at some uncertain time in the future, but should be a meaningful and valuable part of the lives of children at the present time.

This viewpoint has initiated and brought into prominence several plans of school management, procedures for the organization of subject matter, and instructional devices. Among the descriptive catch-phrases that have become well known are "the child-centered school," "teaching children instead of subject-matter," and "self-directed pupil activity." Expressions such as these point to the fact that modern education should be primarily concerned with bringing about desirable changes in boys and girls and not with requiring them to learn subject matter as an end in itself. There are no doubt large numbers of teachers who are familiar with these contemporary emphases but who in practice do very little about it. In fact, there are relatively few private and experimental schools and still fewer public schools that definitely attempt to make a practical application of these philosophical beliefs to real teaching situations.

Serious and critical consideration leads one to realize that the educational philosophy which emphasizes the centering of interest on the experiences and activities of children is eminently suited to schools in a democracy. It is important, therefore, that teachers of physical education choose activities and use teaching methods which will tend to develop in pupils the ability to practice self-control and self-direction, and to make conscious choices and decisions intelligently. Autocratic, dogmatic,

[1] Harold Rugg, *Culture and Education in America,* pp. 123–24. New York: Harcourt, Brace and Company, 1931.

[114]

domineering, or "slave-driving" methods are clearly inconsistent with this philosophy of education and with the social ideals of democracy.

A philosophy of physical education. The first consideration in arriving at a philosophy of physical education is an understanding of the basic social philosophy of our people. The social philosophy which seems to be accepted by the great majority of American people indicates that they want a democratic form of social organization. There are no doubt aggressive minorities which would prefer a communistic, or other kind of society; but there seems to be no doubt that the great majority of citizens still have much faith in a democratic society. Two of the fundamental principles of democracy as accepted in this country are *freedom* and *equality*. The Declaration of Independence expresses the ideals of *equality* as interpreted by Jefferson. The Constitution of the United States emphasizes the principle of *freedom*. The two ideals were linked in the Gettysburg Address by Lincoln's statement that "fourscore and seven years ago our fathers brought forth on this continent a new nation, conceived in liberty, and dedicated to the proposition that all men are created equal."

Actually, however, *freedom* and *equality* are not the same thing; and in many respects they are exact opposites. Their application results in many conflicts. Most Americans want both. But present-day society has become so complex that it is not possible for all individuals to have complete freedom and also complete equality. It has become necessary to try to operate our society so as to maintain a balance in the application of these two ideals. At no one time, of course, will there ever be complete equilibrium between them. When some individuals or groups practice their freedom to such an extent as to interfere greatly with the rights of large numbers of people for equality of opportunity, we usually attempt to enact legislation to restrict freedom and promote equality. Likewise, when the ideal of equality is carried to such an extreme as to smother individuality and to hamper self-expression and initiative unduly, the pendulum of public opinion swings back and we pass laws to guarantee a greater degree of freedom. The support by public taxation of a system of free public schools open to all the children of all the people is probably the largest and most important thing that the American people have done in the interest of both freedom and equality.

This conflict between *freedom* and *equality* has existed ever since the beginning of this nation. During some periods in our history we have emphasized one more than the other. The tendency has always been, however, to maintain an approximate equilibrium between these two viewpoints. It seems evident, therefore, that in the maintenance of our society we must reach the best workable compromise of these two ideals.

In adapting a program of physical education to our society, similar compromises must be made in order to guarantee certain forms of freedom for the individual and at the same time insure equality for all. This means that activities and methods of presentation should be chosen in terms of their inherent citizenship values. Particular attention should be given to teaching boys and girls to play games that can be played by small groups or by individuals as recreational activities throughout the greater part of their lives. It is likewise essential to emphasize in connection with physical education activities the importance of courteous consideration for the rights of other people; it may limit freedom, but it fosters equality. General applications should be developed of the ideals of "abiding by the rules of the game," "fair play," "team play," and "playing the game." Here, again, is a judicious restraint of undue freedom in the interests of just equality. Prospective teachers of physical education should recognize these principles of social philosophy which underlie the program of the American public schools. They should also prepare themselves to teach activities and to use methods of teaching which conform to these principles.

The philosophy of physical education is, furthermore, a special application of a general philosophy of education. The philosophy of education which is most widely accepted by American educators emphasizes the importance of learning through self-directed pupil activity. Socialized participation in group activities is widely recommended, and it is generally advocated that a maximum of responsibility for leadership be placed on pupils. Modern educators believe that wholehearted and intelligent interest is fundamental to successful and efficient learning. The importance of having pupils understand the meaning and significance of the activities that they practice is also emphasized. Teachers believe that this causes pupils to have a clearly defined purpose for the drill on basic essentials in which they participate.

This viewpoint indicates that the use by teachers of coercive methods must be avoided. The application of this philosophy to physical education is significant in the choice of curriculum content and instructional methods. In the organization of squads, classes, and teams, every opportunity should be taken to provide experiences in leadership to the maximum number of boys and girls. The activities of the curriculum should be selected in light of the measured interests, needs, and abilities of the pupils. The methods used in teaching should stimulate the children to participate enthusiastically and intelligently in a rational program of activities. Teachers-in-training should have ample instruction and practice in the application of this educational philosophy to the specific problems of teaching physical education.[1]

Social purposes of education. Schooling and education are not necessarily the same thing. The school is the agency that society has set up to carry the major responsibility of organized education, but education should be thought of as being much broader than schooling.

The general function of education is to help individuals make an adequate adjustment to the problems of life. Knowledge and skills are valuable in education only to the extent that they facilitate human activity and make the adjustment of the organism to its environment more flexible. The procedures of education should serve to stimulate creative activity on the part of learners so that they will constantly reconstruct their beliefs, ideals, habits, and viewpoints. Education in a democracy should not attempt to set a pattern of mold to which this continual reconstruction of experience should conform, but should be interested primarily in providing the stimuli and guidance for creative activity by pupils. "Real education humanizes men. It does so, however, not by moulding them into unthinking acceptance of preestablished patterns, but by stimulating them to a continuous reconstruction of their outlook on life."[2]

Moral autonomy. It is the dream of nearly every free and intelligent human being to have the power and right to govern himself, to take his purposes in life from within and not to be ruled by any form of external authority. To this end a democratic society and democratic education should seek to emphasize the cooperative experiences and to lessen the competitive spirit which seems to motivate almost entirely the activities of large numbers of people.

Individuals grow in ability to govern themselves through experiences which broaden their vision and increase the range of meanings which they are capable of securing from a large number of different situations. Many persons in their thinking and conversation frequently group

[1] The discussion above is from: Jackson R. Sharman, "Preparation for the Profession of Physical Education," *Journal of Health and Physical Education*, VI (December, 1935), 11–13, 58.

[2] William H. Kilpatrick (Editor), *The Educational Frontier*, p. 31. New York: The Century Company, 1933.

together experiences of this kind and designate them collectively as a liberal education. A broadly and liberally educated person can truly be said to be relatively free from superstition, ignorance, prejudice, arrogance, and intolerance. President Butler has described a liberal education and a liberally educated person as follows:

There are comparatively few men and women alive in the world, although there are hundreds of millions of living human beings. The gap between a living human being and the man who is alive is far wider than the gap between the human being and the other primates, although it is much more easily and quickly bridged by one who truly understands the arts of design and construction. The bridge which is to be so designed and constructed is conventionally described as a liberal education. It is the most beautiful and the most capacious bridge in the world, and it could carry a far heavier traffic than it has ever yet been called upon to bear. . . .

The bridge which a liberal education is to build provides the only possible passageway from the insulated life where no currents of force, of vitality or of imagination can possibly reach, to that true and genuine life for which the spirit of man is meant. All our colossal expenditure, all our magnificent buildings, all our years of training for teachers are useless, unless this great and beautiful bridge can steadily be built for a growing number of men and women who are able and willing to be free. The insulated life is the selfish, the self-centered, the narrow, and sooner or later, the embittered life. Yet despite all this, it is the only life which millions upon millions of human beings ever know, as it is the only life toward which the footsteps of millions upon millions of innocent children are ever directed. . . .

Insulation is even worse than isolation, for it effectively stops the flow of that vitalizing current of spiritual and intellectual force which turns living into life. . . .

Narrowness of knowledge, narrowness of sympathy, narrowness of understanding, narrowness of conviction are the marks of that insulated life from which there is no escape save over the bridge which liberal education builds. That bridge leads to those fields of perennial wisdom which are the coveted resting place of the thoughtful in every age. It leaves behind that world of illusions which the insulated man calls facts, while so often entirely and blissfully unconscious of that world of realities which he derides as ideas.[1]

Integration of social experience and individual activity.

Modern educational theory attaches much importance to the recognition of individual differences and the planning of a school program to meet

---

[1] Nicholas Murray Butler, *The Insulated Life*. Address delivered at the 176th Commencement of Columbia University, June 3, 1930.

the needs and abilities of each pupil. It also emphasizes group activity and the value of experiences which are gained through cooperative participation with other people. If either of these viewpoints is applied to the exclusion of the other it is evident that undesirable results would be secured. Maintaining an equilibrium between these emphases so as to get for each person the optimal growth of individual traits and social consciousness provides one of the main problems that confront teachers. The successful solution of this problem offers a great challenge.

It seems, however, that physical education lends itself more readily than other school subjects to the successful solution of this problem. A consideration of methods of procedure makes it evident that one of the most practical and useful techniques for the integration of social experience and individual activity is to plan a program which includes: (1) a series of units the completion of which requires proficiency in several fundamental skills; and (2) a series of practice problems that the pupils could practice individually and which would help them achieve the aims set by the large units.

The program for seventh grade boys, for example, might include a series of several units such as: (a) to learn to play speedball, (b) to learn to swim the free style well, and (c) to learn to tap dance.

The practice problems in connection with speedball might include (1) dribbling, (2) kicking, (3) heading, (4) passing, (5) tackling, and (6) trapping. Levels of achievements and tests should be provided in connection with each practice problem so that each pupil could direct his own drill intelligently and appraise his progress and achievement.

Courtis has pointed out that the essential features of practice tests are: (1) unit tasks, each dealing with one new element, (2) standards of achievement for each task, (3) provision for self-directed study, (4) provision for self-appraisal of achievement and growth, and (5) individual progress from task to task instead of term to term.[1]

Importance of creative experience. Experiences gained through individual activity and through group participation are both essential in the all-round development of a person. Experiences of each type vary, however, in the quality of the contribution which they make to the education of boys and girls. Contemporary educational philosophy emphasizes the values and importance of creative, free, and meaningful experi-

[1] Stuart A. Courtis, "The Development of Individualized Instruction at Detroit," p. 111 in *Adapting the Schools to Individual Differences.* Twenty-fourth Yearbook of the National Society for the Study of Education, Part II. Bloomington, Illinois: Public School Publishing Company, 1925.

ences and the need for avoiding a rigid routine in guiding the activities of pupils.

A physical education program which is prescribed and dominated by the teacher restricts the opportunities of pupils to express themselves in the selection of activities, and to make conscious intelligent choices in light of the available data and the possible consequences of their acts. If we expect pupils to grow in consequence of their school experiences we must plan and guide their activities in a way to insure the maximum freedom and initiative of the largest number. Participation in creative activities develops the ability to plan, assume responsibility, and carry through to successful completion significant undertakings. But autocratic class procedures tend to develop docile, subservient, unimaginative individuals who are lacking in initiative and enthusiasm.

The meaning of interest in education. Teachers hear and read a great deal about interest and its place in education. It appears, however, that many individuals in the teaching profession and among laymen do not understand clearly what is meant by the writers and lecturers who have been aggressive in advocating the general application of the principle of interest to all teaching situations. Some persons believe that when interest is emphasized, all pupils should be permitted to do the things that happen to occur to them or catch their attention, and that the immediate interests of children should determine entirely the choice of subject matter to be included in the curriculum.

It is evident that children learn more effectively and efficiently when they are motivated by a keen interest. When they are not interested and coercion is used to obtain a semblance of attention and to secure participation in drill the skills, knowledge, or other materials which are learned are retained for only a short time and the teaching efforts appear to be almost entirely futile.

On the other hand children must learn many things regardless of their state of interest. There is clearly much material that is necessary for one to know in order to make satisfactorily the necessary social adjustments and to acquire the mental understandings that are essential to living successfully as a member of a group. The social aim of education and the importance of a common core of subject matter in the curriculum for all children are widely emphasized as being desirable irrespective of the interest of the pupils. It may be seen, therefore, that apparently there is a conflict between the doctrine of interest and the social emphasis in education. Interest is essential to efficient learning, but other viewpoints must be considered in choosing the activities and other materials which make up the curriculum.

This dilemma between interest and socialization does not exist, however, when one understands the meaning of interest and its rational application to educational procedures. Individuals are not born with interests, they build them through experience; and it is the responsibility of teachers to help pupils create and discover the things which are most interesting.

Interest, as used in education, means that the motivation for work, study, or practice comes from the activity which is being learned. That is, the activity is intrinsically interesting and meaningful. It is interesting and worthwhile in and of itself because it is closely related to real life in and outside of school and does not have to be made interesting by some form of extrinsic motive such as credits, marks, sweaters, gold footballs, or other forms of artificial award.

The use of interest in teaching. In order to make effective and intelligent use of interest as a motivation of learning it is necessary that the pupils concur and help in the choice of the activities and other subject matter to be taught. The content of the curriculum must be selected because of its value and importance, and the pupils must be helped to see that it is worth learning. This does not mean, however, that the curriculum for each child should consist of free electives and that the pupils should be left with the responsibility of deciding what the school should teach. Curriculum construction is one of the most difficult problems that confront educators, and the school authorities should not attempt to dodge their responsibilities in this regard by expecting the pupils to choose subject matter and arrange it in a desirable sequence.

It is important that teachers should avoid confusing the use of interest with "sugar coating," which is an effort to coax or fool children into learning things in which they are not interested and which have no meaning for them. The use of interest in teaching does not mean making everything easy and soft, so that pupils can go through the movements of securing an education without exerting any effort. An illustration of this "sugar-coating" procedure in the teaching of academic subjects is the use of arithmetic games and English games which are attempts to use extrinsic motives to secure learning easily. The practice of giving a holiday from school to all pupils who have their teeth cleaned by a dentist or giving a prize to the pupils who make a team or accomplish other achievements in skills are examples of the efforts that some teachers make to "sugar-coat" activities that do not seem important enough to boys and girls to be intrinsically interesting and to challenge their best efforts.

Interest and effort in education. Many teachers and laymen have the conviction that interest and effort cannot go together. This group of people seem to believe that sustained effort and hard work cannot be found associated with interesting activity. In reality nothing could be further from the actual facts. To disprove this assumption one needs only to observe the behavior of scientists engaged in research, artists participating in their creative work, or skilled craftsmen engaged in planning and making some beautiful and useful object, or an athlete attempting to improve his form and skill. Such persons are motivated by a strong and meaningful interest in the things they are doing. No amount or form of coercion from extrinsic sources could secure the willing and enthusiastic effort that results from the interest these people have in their respective activities.

Interest that arises from a real need, which is recognized by the learner as being of great importance, provides the kind of motivation that causes one to undertake unusually difficult tasks and to work at them persistently until they are completed. When children have a real interest in an activity which is part of a true-to-life situation, the problem of getting them to complete the things they undertake is solved almost completely.

The difference between the efforts of most varsity athletes and the members of some classes in physical education illustrates the difference between interest in activities that are accepted as being important and activities which the students consider of relatively small worth and importance. The members of varsity squads usually work diligently and willingly several hours each day, but in many instances some of the members of physical education classes try to avoid the classes as much as possible and others display a lack of enthusiasm while they are present in class.

In order to get boys and girls to put forth willing, intelligent, and enthusiastic effort in learning physical education activities, the use of each fundamental skill must be made to appear to each individual as being necessary for him to do successfully the games, sports, dances or other activities which he holds to be important. The practice of skills in the form of relays and simple games or compelling the pupils to drill on fundamental skills will not prove adequate to get real effort and efficient learning. The pupils must be brought face to face with the real situation in which the skills are needed, and must be helped to realize that improved skills will help them do better the things which they believe to be of much importance.

Social and moral behavior. Guiding children in the development of desirable social and moral ways of behaving is one of the most important opportunities and responsibilities of teachers. This type of behavior comes as the result of experience in the same way as all other learnings. It requires, however, a broad range of experiences which involve moral choices and decisions for one to develop the ability to decide and act in a morally desirable way in the innumerable situations that arise in our complex highly industrialized society. In a simple form of society the teaching of morality to children consisted merely of instructing them in the mores, customs, and approved standards of conduct which the social group believed to be necessary. But the great social changes which have occurred during the past several decades have made this form of moral education entirely inadequate for the preparation of boys and girls to meet the ethical problems which confront them in their lives. Many of the old standards and mores, still handed down to children, help them to guide their behavior; but boys and girls are placed in a large number of situations in which the traditional standardized code of behavior does not serve as a satisfactory guide.

If one asks the members of a group how they decide what is right and wrong he will receive a variety of replies. Some individuals will state that "their conscience is their guide"; others affirm that their parents taught them what was right and what was wrong; many state that the Ten Commandments tell them the difference between right and wrong; and still others believe that conduct is right if it meets the approval or avoids the severe condemnation of the immediate social group. These sources probably provide satisfactory guides for behavior in connection with many problems but there are a large number that cannot be solved in terms of these standards. Some problems from physical education that illustrate this fact are: (1) Should schools and colleges have eligibility rules for participation in athletics? (2) Are sound ethical principles reflected by the present amateur rules, which are based on whether a person has ever earned any money in connection with sports? (3) Is it right for girls to play basketball by boys' rules? (4) Should pupils serve as officials for games in which their classmates are participating? (5)

[123]

Should scores be used exclusively in determining the winners of games, or should sportsmanship be given some weight in choosing the winner? (6) Should state commissioners of high school athletics be paid out of gate receipts from basketball tournaments and other games of school children? (7) Should a tennis player intentionally hit a ball into the net, thereby giving his opponent a point, in order to compensate for a mistake of the official? (8) Should players attempt to confuse or "rattle" their opponents? (9) Are players justified in taking advantage of technicalities in the rules about which their opponents do not know? (10) Should social pressure of the school group be applied to big, strong boys in high school in order to make them try out for the football team? Many other problems of this nature could be mentioned.

It is clearly evident that problems such as these cannot be solved by reference to any standardized codes of behavior or fixed set of rules. Behavior is good or bad in terms of its social consequence. It is a mistake to conclude that acts, in and of themselves, are right or wrong. A statement of this viewpoint which has gained wide acceptance is that anything is right which works for the greatest good of the greatest number over the longest period of time. The application and interpretation of this principle will vary according to the background of experience of different individuals but it serves, nevertheless, to describe the fact that the social implications of behavior determine whether it is morally desirable.

Teaching morality. There are a large number of situations in connection with physical education that involve morally important decisions and behavior. Teachers should take advantage of the opportunities presented by these situations to guide pupils intelligently and sympathetically in their self-direction in social situations. Preaching at children, prescribing a rigid set of rules, and advocating the acceptance of a standardized code of behavior is an ineffective method of securing desirable moral conduct on the part of boys and girls. It has been clearly demonstrated that knowledge of right ways of acting is not adequate to cause people to act in the desired manner. It is no doubt true that nearly everyone who does anything immoral or antisocial knows that his conduct is wrong. Teachers should help pupils to realize that the possible consequences of one's behavior on himself, other individuals, and the social group are of fundamental importance in determining what is right or wrong. One of the essential responsibilities of every teacher, therefore, is to guide the educational experiences of children in such a way that all of them will improve their ability to analyze the social consequences of their acts.

In order to have moral teachings apply in a wide variety of situations one must develop generalizations and attitudes concerning honesty, fairness, truthfulness, and other ideals. It is generally believed that specific learnings do not have a wide applicability. If, for example, one is required to be fair in basketball or in swimming, there is no assurance that he will be fair with the members of his family at home or with his associates in business. Generalizations and attitudes can be built by acting in the desired way in a large number of different situations and by analyzing the moral problems that exist in each situation. Teachers should be of inestimable help to pupils in aiding them to analyze their experiences and make application of their ways of reacting to other situations that they will meet in life. A person probably learns more efficiently and effectively as the result of first-hand experiences. That is, if a person actually participates in an activity and reacts in the desired way he will learn more easily and better than if some one tells him about an experience or if he reads about it. We should not overlook, however, the possibilities of learning many valuable lessons through vicarious experiences that may be gained through reading, visual education and discussion.

In striving to build moral ways of behaving in their pupils, teachers should be cautioned against attempting to teach by direct instruction ideals and social generalizations. These things are formulas which have been built up as the result of a broad range of social experience and they cannot be understood by individuals who have not had an adequate background of experience. The algebraic expression $(x + y) (x - y) = x^2 - y^2$ is a generalization that sums up much algebraic experience. In a similar way the expressions "men should cooperate" and "men should be honorable" are social generalizations that sum up much social experience. These formulas or generalizations cannot be understood or comprehended by persons who lack the necessary algebraic and social experiences. It is useless, therefore, to attempt to teach these things by merely talking about them. The school program of physical education can make a real contribution toward helping boys and girls learn many valuable moral lessons, but these lessons must be learned through participation in meaningful experiences.

Teaching social behavior through physical activities. It is generally agreed by most modern psychologists that transfer of training

[125]

of specific learnings takes place only when there are identical elements, or, in other words, much similarity between two situations. This means that a specific way of reacting in one situation will not be likely to transfer or carry over to another situation. It is almost universally agreed, however, as has already been pointed out, that general traits such as attitudes, appreciations, and generalizations have a wider applicability. Most educationists believe that if a person builds up a general concept or an ideal in regard to a way of behaving, he probably will be guided by this concept or ideal in most of his experiences in life. Assume, by way of illustration, that a person has developed an attitude of fair play by acting fairly in a wide variety of situations during his life. In such a case this person would be likely to act fairly in connection with most experiences where "fairness" was a problem.

Many teachers believe that physical education offers a large number of opportunities for helping boys and girls develop favorable social attitudes. Some educators insist that teachers of physical education and athletic coaches should take advantage of all incidental opportunities for teaching desirable behavior; and that they also should plan their teaching so as definitely to include instruction in social and moral ways of behaving. A large number of teachers and coaches, on the other hand, state that their job is primarily the teaching of skills and that if they spend time in trying to teach sportsmanship their pupils will fail to make adequate and satisfactory improvement in the performance of physical activities. They apparently are certain that one or the other must be taught and that any effort to teach either sportsmanship or skills must result in a total neglect of the other.

The available evidence indicates that emphasis on desirable forms of behavior in connection with physical education activities can influence the attitudes of the pupils. It also seems to be true that such emphasis does not interfere with the development of motor skills by the members of the class. In fact, in some instances the pupils made more progress in skills when sportsmanship was emphasized than they did when all the attention of the teacher was given to the development of skills. There are no data which prove that skills are sacrificed when more idealistic educational outcomes are sought. Clevett's study [1] shows, among other things, that definitely planned efforts to develop honest behavior in connection with physical activities are approximately three times as effective

[1] Melvin A. Clevett, "An Experiment in Physical Education Activities Related to the Teaching of Honesty and Motor Skills," *Research Quarterly* III (March, 1932), 121-27.

as when teachers depend on honesty being developed as a by-product of the activity.

In light of these facts it is recommended, therefore, that physical education activities be taught in a way to emphasize sportsmanlike behavior on all occasions. Such instruction should be definitely planned. It is also advisable for teachers to take advantage of all incidental opportunities to teach good forms of behavior to their pupils.

Inherited abilities. Many people are convinced that individuals possess as the result of their biological inheritance special traits in dancing, swimming, mathematics, music, and other subjects. There is no authenticated evidence to justify this belief, and one who attempts to investigate its origin will be led to conclude that it is largely superstition. It is very much the same kind of thing as the faculty theory of psychology which has been repudiated by reputable psychologists for many years. The organization of the school curriculum into subjects and fields is an administrative and instructional device of recent origin and has no relationship to the biological inheritance of human beings.

General ability and power to learn differs in individuals, but it seems to be definitely true that differences in ability to achieve in different subjects is the result of interest, background of experience, and quality of the teaching to which individuals are exposed. The available evidence justifies considerable doubt that there is such a thing as general motor ability, although it seems that there is probably such a thing as general athletic ability. A person may have, for example, excellent ability in threading a needle, playing the piano, or writing on a typewriter, and yet be unusually deficient in ability to swim or play basketball.

Required participation in physical education. The question is frequently raised concerning how long pupils should participate in physical education. Some teachers believe that all the physical activity of children should be in the form of unorganized, undirected play, while there are still a few people who insist that the superfluous energy of children should be used in productive labor. There are practically no accurate data which would guide one in answering this question. It becomes necessary, therefore, to answer it in terms of the values which one believes to be important and in terms of the accepted philosophy of education.

In general it seems to be accurate to state that children should continue to attend regular physical education classes until they can go on participating rationally, happily, and successfully in wholesome physical recreation without the help and stimulation which they are expected to secure through class participation.[1] In the case of some children in some schools under the guidance of some teachers this period of time might include only through the sixth grade, in other cases the end of the junior high school might be an appropriate time to discontinue required participation, and in some exceptional cases the requirement might be continued through two or more years of college.

The kind of physical education. Among teachers of physical education and also among school patrons there is frequently much discussion of the kind of physical education that should prove of the most benefit to children. Some individuals believe that calisthenics and other types of formal exercises are the best kinds; others are convinced that sports and games with their opportunities for socialization should receive greatest emphasis; many insist that dancing, expressive gymnastics, and training in relaxation meet more fully the needs of present-day children; and still others stress the importance of measuring in much detail and with great care the individual differences of each child and planning an individual program for each child.

There is probably much truth and value in the statements made by the advocates of all these viewpoints. The most suitable program of physical education could probably be arranged through a compromise of the various claims. In general, however, it can be said that the program should be suited to the individual needs of the pupils, and should also contain a common core of skills, interests, and appreciations which will enable the pupils to fit in American society satisfactorily.

The application of a democratic philosophy of education indicates that children should not be segregated for physical education on the basis of intelligence, motor ability, or in any other way. The similarities of different individuals are greater than their differences, and the school program should help to emphasize these similarities and to socialize all pupils. No procedures should be used which tend to emphasize the peculiarities and idiosyncrasies of boys and girls.

Development of leadership. One frequently hears the statement that education should definitely attempt to develop leaders, that the urgent need of society at the present time is capable, inspired, unselfish leadership. There is also much being said about the development of good followers. Some teachers state that it is true we need leaders but

[1] This problem is discussed well in: James L. Mursell *Principles of Education*, pp. 238–40. New York: W. W. Norton and Company, 1934.

everyone cannot be a leader and that we should stress the development of followers as well as leaders. These differences of opinion seem to raise an important question for educators. Should we attempt to train all children to be leaders, or should some be leaders and some followers?

In attempting to solve this problem we need first to define what is meant by a leader and a follower. The kind of follower we need in a democratic society is an intelligent cooperator, not a blind robot who docilely and submissively does what he is told to do. A good follower should also make equally as good a leader of the group. The same kind of preparation is needed to make good followers and good leaders.

In some schools leaders' corps and clubs are organized in which a selected group are given intensive instruction and experience in acting as leaders. These specially trained individuals are expected to function efficiently as leaders and the other pupils are expected to be docile followers. Under intelligent and well-informed guidance the leader corps device can probably be used to secure good educational results, but as it is used in many schools it cannot be justified in a democratic society.

Emphasis in teaching. The instructional efforts of teachers must be influenced by the principles of education and philosophy in order for these principles to have any effect on the experiences of school children. Merely the incorporation in textbooks of a discussion of these beliefs and ideals will not result in any significant experiences for boys and girls in schools. Teachers should make an intelligent and conscientious effort to conduct their teaching in the light of accepted principles. A summary and application of the viewpoints which have been discussed in this chapter indicate that physical education teachers in American schools should emphasize the following principles:

1. Pupils must be active in order for learning to take place.

2. The recognition of the interests and abilities of the pupils is fundamental to efficient teaching.

3. Group participation is basic to social growth and development of individual pupils.

4. Subject matter should be organized in terms of the maturity, ability, and interests of the pupils.

5. The ultimate outcomes that should be sought are the habits, knowledge, attitudes, and skills which would help the pupils to live successfully as members of a cooperative social group.

Summary. Some of the material which is supplied by education and philosophy seems essential to a clear understanding of the foundations of physical education. Some of the important items with which students should be familiar are: (1) the responsibility of the school to society, (2) education as a state function, (3) the function of philosophy in physical education, (4) principles of a pragmatic philosophy of education, (5) modern philosophical emphases, (6) philosophy of physical education, (7) social purposes of education, (8) the meaning and use of interest in teaching, (9) teaching social and moral behavior, (10) the influence of inherited abilities, (11) required participation in physical education, (12) the kind of physical education program, (13) the development of leadership, and (14) emphases in teaching.

The responsibilities of the school to society include (1) the passing on of the social inheritance, (2) the proposal of social ideals, (3) providing leadership for a re-definition of social ideals, and (4) guiding the educational experiences of boys and girls.

In the United States it is generally agreed that education is the function of the state, and much emphasis has been placed on the importance of the decentralization of educational authority.

It is the function of philosophy to integrate and tie together the contributions from other fields of human knowledge, such as biology, sociology, and psychology, and to focus these data on the problems of physical education. The current philosophical emphasis in education is on the guidance of children in self-directed democratic experiences. The generally accepted philosophy of physical education is based on a democratic social philosophy that maintains an equilibrium between *freedom* and *equality*, and on a general philosophy of education.

The social purposes of education are directed toward helping individuals make an adequate adjustment to the problems of life, a liberal education makes it possible for an individual to make adjustments successfully and efficiently. Interest is the most important motivation in learning. Guiding children in the development of desirable social and moral ways of behavior is one of the most important opportunities and responsibilities of teachers.

There are inadequate data to justify one in concluding that one's biological inheritance accounts for special traits and abilities in school subjects. It seems that differences in ability to achieve in different subjects is the result of interest, background of experience, and quality of teaching to which individuals are exposed. In regard to required participation in physical education it seems that children should continue to attend regular physical education classes until they can go on participating rationally, happily, and successfully in wholesome physical recreation without the help and stimulation that comes from class participation.

In physical education we should seek to develop intelligent cooperators and not train some individuals as docile followers and others as autocratic leaders. In a democratic society a person prepared to be a good follower should also be a good leader.

QUESTIONS

1. How do the responsibilities of schools in a democratic society differ from those of schools in an autocracy?
2. What is the historical background and contemporary emphasis in regard to the responsibilities of the state for education?
3. What is the important and immediately useful function of philosophy to teachers of physical education?
4. What are some of the items that are emphasized in most discussions of modern educational philosophy?
5. What are the bases of a justifiable philosophy of physical education?
6. How may the apparent conflict between "socialization" and "individual differences" be avoided in teaching physical education?
7. What is the meaning of "interest" and "effort" as used in education?
8. What principles should guide teachers in their efforts to help children develop desirable social and moral ways of behaving?
9. What principles should be followed in teaching morality?
10. What principles should guide teachers in their efforts to develop leadership qualities in their pupils?

REFERENCES

Hetherington, Clark W. *School Program in Physical Education.* Yonkers, New York: World Book Company, 1922.

Kilpatrick, William H. (Editor). *The Educational Frontier.* New York: The Century Company, 1933.

Mursell, James L. *Principles of Education.* New York: W. W. Norton and Company, 1934.

Rogers, Frederick Rand. *Educational Objectives of Physical Activity.* New York: A. S. Barnes and Company, 1929.

Rugg, Harold. *Culture and Education in America.* New York: Harcourt, Brace and Company, 1931.

Williams, Jesse Feiring. *The Principles of Physical Education.* Philadelphia: W. B. Saunders Company, 1932. (Revised)

CHAPTER VIII

The Physical Education Curriculum

෨

Development of the curriculum. A school curriculum is ordinarily thought of as all the experiences which a child has at school as the result of the consciously planned efforts of teachers and other school authorities. The curriculum would include, therefore, the traditional types of courses which a child takes at school and also other activities which are provided. Similarly the physical education curriculum includes the experiences in connection with motor activities that the school provides for children.

In the development of the physical education curriculum there have been two radically different points of view. One has emphasized the traditional in subject matter and method, and the other has held that the preparation of a curriculum should begin with ideals, the statement of an educational philosophy, and principles. The dynamic nature of society is recognized and the needs of children for life in a changing world are emphasized. The first influence caused a program of formal gymnastics to be borrowed from some European countries and to be fastened on many schools in America for a period of approximately half a century. Only in the past two decades has the latter philosophy had a wide acceptance and influence in planning physical education curriculums.

A number of other influences, in addition to the point of view held by many of the early leaders in physical education, have affected the development of the physical education curriculum. Among these are European systems of physical education, including the German and Swedish systems of gymnastics and the English program of sports; the emphasis on military preparedness which has been quite strong at several different periods; state legislation which in most states has made physical education mandatory in the schools; college entrance requirements, especially in the states where the colleges give credit toward college entrance for physical education; the growth in school enrollments, and the change in type of organization (specifically, the growth of the junior high school movement and the rapid spread of the 6-3-3 type of school organization); the reports of national committees, particularly the committees of the National Education Association, the Department of Superintendence, and the White House Conference on Child Health and Protection; the emphasis on child health which has been especially strong since the World War; the emphasis on education for leisure; the widespread attention that has been given to the study of individual differences; the lack of respect for and faith in physical education that has been common among many prominent educators as well as among the lay public; and the relatively low level of professional preparation of physical education teachers until recently.

Bases of the curriculum. The physical education curriculum must be based on an expressed or implicit philosophy of life, social philosophy, philosophy of education, and statement of the objectives of physical education. This means that, to form an acceptable curriculum, there must be an agreement on the values of life; the kind of society we want; the types of ideals, characters and personalities we want to develop; and what we may reasonably expect to accomplish through physical education. In planning a curriculum for a school or a group of schools the statement of objectives is determined largely by the philosophy of education held by the curriculum planners. In turn one's philosophy of education is shaped by the kind of society he wants to develop or maintain, and by his philosophy of life. The first and most fundamental step, therefore, in setting up a curriculum in physical education is to make a searching and critical evaluation of the values of life which are approved by the majority of the people in the state, city, or other political unit for which the curriculum is being prepared. The second step consists of stating the principles of a social philosophy, thereby indicating the type of society which is desired. Social ideals must be accepted which can be used to integrate the thinking of the population in regard to physical education. Most of the people should hold similar views in regard to the values of physical education to society. On the basis of the statement of approved life values and of the desired type of society a philosophy of education should be proposed. In terms of the accepted philosophy of education the aim and objectives of physical education should be stated.

In constructing a physical education curriculum there must be maintained a broad perspective of school procedures and personnel, the needs of developing children, and the characteristics of American society. These facts indicate that the principles underlying the curriculum should be developed from the contributions that could be made by persons

[133]

engaged in many different occupations. Sociologists, economists, political scientists, industrialists, trade unionists, writers, biologists, and representatives of many other fields of work, ideally, should contribute to the development of the physical education curriculum. Ordinarily it is not feasible to have the benefit of help from such a cosmopolitan group; physical educators engaged in curriculum construction should therefore qualify themselves for an intelligent consideration of the child, the school, and the social trends in American life.

Social philosophy underlying the curriculum. Since our form of government is democratic and the preparation of the oncoming generation for successful living in a democracy is the accepted policy of American education, the schools should seek to develop and maintain that form of society. Emphasis on freedom of self-expression, the importance of individuality, and of respect for personality, and the responsibility of each individual for developing the ability of self-control and self-direction are some of the fundamental ideals of democracy. These ideals are in great contrast to those in an autocracy where the qualities of docility, unthinking obedience, and unquestioning loyalty to authority are emphasized. They also differ greatly from those in socialistic and communistic societies where much emphasis and force are used to achieve the submergence of the individual in the hope of securing a greater common good for society as a whole.

In planning a school curriculum in physical education for American schools the purposes and ideals of a democratic society must be kept constantly in mind. The philosophy of education, the aims and objectives of physical education, the subject matter, methods of teaching, and techniques of organization and administration must all conform to the accepted social philosophy.

Principles of educational philosophy. The next step in the preparation of a curriculum following the acceptance of a social philosophy is the statement of the principles of an education philosophy. The following statements are quoted as an acceptable summary of the principles of a progressive educational philosophy.

1. Self-activity is fundamental to learning.
2. While transfer of training may take place under certain conditions, it is neither automatic nor inevitable.
3. There is no desirable discipline in doing what is merely difficult and distasteful.
4. Education serves both proximate and ultimate ends.

5. The universal interdependence of man is basic for education.
6. The welfare of society demands the optimum development of the individual.
7. Public education represents an investment by society to promote the common welfare.
8. The school is only one of the educative agencies established by society, and the inevitable overlapping in duties and responsibilities necessitates mutual cooperation.
9. Schools serve two interests: those of the individual and those of society; wherever the two come into conflict that of society takes precedence.
10. It is the duty of the school to adjust itself to social progress.
11. The school should endeavor to give to all a common integrating body of functional knowledge, of habits, of ideals, and of appreciations.
12. It is the duty of the school to adapt the means of education to the needs of the individual, whatever may be the mental, physical, moral, or environmental conditions.
13. The need of the individual for two coordinate types of ability is recognized: unspecialized, to discharge common personal, domestic, and civic duties; specialized, to render expert service to society.
14. Widespread individual differences condition the results that may be expected from the educative process.
15. Education includes teaching the individual to do better the desirable things of life that he would do anyhow.
16. Culture as a desirable outcome of education consists in the all-round development of those capacities and ideals which make for human progress—it includes social service, many-sidedness, democracy, physical well-being, development of spiritual life, esthetic appreciations, well-mannered expression, insight, force, and idealism; it is altruistic, dynamic, and creative.[1]

Principles and assumptions underlying the physical education curriculum. Curriculum making is a highly technical job and should be carried on under the direction of a professionally prepared and experienced person. It is not practicable in a book on principles to discuss the techniques and methods of curriculum construction, but some consideration may be given here to the principles and philosophy that guide the development of the curriculum in physical education. This is important because a large number of administrative and teaching procedures are carried on for the purpose of helping to achieve the goals

[1] *General and Divisional Aims Program of Activities*, p. 7. Curriculum Bulletin No. 1. St. Louis, Missouri: Board of Education, 1926.

set by the curriculum. A discussion of some of the principles and assumptions which underlie the physical education curriculum follows.

1. *Participation in physical education activities is beneficial to most normal young persons.* Physical education makes a distinct and important contribution to the organic development, mental hygiene, and recreational life of young people. It should be recognized, however, that its activities are intended primarily for normal healthy people. Sick or handicapped people should participate in vigorous physical activity only on the advice of a physician.

2. *One of the main advantages of the long period of human infancy is that it provides a protracted play time for children.* The period between birth and the time when a child can successfully take care of himself is longer than is the case of any other animals. A number of reasons and theories have been stated explaining this relatively long period of human infancy. All of them accord to play an important place in the education and development of children. Some authorities hold that the protracted period of immaturity, in which children grow and develop through play, seems to develop a high intellectual, ethical, and social level.

3. *Physical education is primarily an educational and recreational procedure.* It is not the same thing as health education and does not have the same specific objectives and goals. In the minds of many laymen and of some teachers there has been some confusion as to the relationship of physical education and health education. Physical education is directly concerned with providing educational experiences for boys and girls. These experiences in many instances are connected with their recreational interests. Health education is primarily concerned with the development of habits and attitudes that will help individuals to live in a way which will be healthful to the individual and to the community. Physical education no doubt makes an important contribution to health, but so do a number of other fields such as music, art, science, literature, and dramatics. It is not accurate, therefore, to think of these fields as if they were the same. Educational administrators frequently have found it convenient to establish physical education and health education as a single department, but it has been found equally effective to place health education and science in one department. Health education and attendance supervision have also been satisfactorily combined.

4. *Physical education has definite contributions to make to the education of boys and girls.* It should not be incorporated in the curriculum

for the purpose of relieving the boredom or unhygienic procedures which result from poor organization or instruction in traditional academic subjects. It has frequently been advocated that physical education be included in the school curriculum for the purpose of relieving children from sitting at uncomfortable desks for long periods, and to provide relaxation from the monotony of studying uninteresting academic subjects. If these conditions exist in a school, the program should be reorganized so as to correct the evils. It is foolish to subject pupils to unhygienic procedures and then attempt to counteract the bad results by means of physical education. The activities which make up the physical education curriculum are intrinsically interesting and, if properly graded, appeal to most boys and girls. It is for their recreational, educational, and developmental values that the interesting physical education activities should be included in the school curriculum.

5. *The physical education curriculum must always be dynamic and easily subject to change so as to meet changing needs and conditions in society.* One of the main criticisms which has been made of physical education is that its curriculum has been static and has not grown and changed in compliance with changing social needs and conditions. It must be understood that a curriculum which might be suitable at one time will not necessarily be adequate ten years later. A satisfactory curriculum must be in a continual state of change and growth. American society has been extremely dynamic during the past half-century and the indications are that it will change much more rapidly in the next few years. One illustration of social change, which is of great import to physical education, is the rapid increase in the amount of leisure time that has come almost suddenly to large numbers of men and women in this country. The present social trends seem to show that this increased leisure will continue permanently and possibly become more widespread. Other social changes are taking place in the school, the home, the church, in industry, and in practically all other institutions of society. All of these social changes have some significance for the physical education curriculum.

6. *Physical education is based on principles of educational philosophy, physiology, anatomy, psychology, and sociology.* Data and material from several fields of human knowledge contribute to the fundamental bases of physical education. Its aims and purposes are dictated largely by educational philosophy and sociology. Methods of teaching, techniques of setting levels of achievement, procedures of measuring results, and

[137]

the planning of the physical education program to fit the individual needs of pupils are based largely on educational psychology, physiology, and anatomy. It is imperative that a person engaged in the preparation of a curriculum in physical education be familiar with the contributions that these different fields of knowledge make to physical education.

7. *The physical education curriculum must seek to create and develop broader, deeper, and more widely shared interests.* A person who has many wide interests in common with others will be likely to receive much stimulation to intellectual growth and to get the maximum of satisfactions from his social relationships. Physical education provides many opportunities for individuals to meet and associate with others in pleasant informal situations. Recreational and avocational interests which contribute greatly to the experiences that one shares with other people are frequently developed through physical education. The attitudes of others can be better understood through the freedom associated with play than in most other contacts.

8. *The physical education curriculum must develop ideals, attitudes, and habits that will help determine good and desirable behavior.* Most behavior is the result of ideals, attitudes, and habits associated with emotional reactions. We like to hope that most people act in many situations after an intelligent choice of a way to act, but the available facts do not indicate that this is the case in very many instances. It seems that most of us act largely on an emotional basis. It is recommended, therefore, that definite plans be made in the physical education curriculum to develop emotionalized attitudes, ideals, and habits, which should be conducive to behavior accepted by the most intelligent members of society as being good and desirable. The attitudes, ideals, and habits chosen for development should be clearly and definitely stated, and an intensive effort should be made to associate them with emotional responses. Since physical education involves many emotional reactions, it provides unusual opportunities for such development.

9. *The physical education curriculum must contribute to a liberal education.* A person with a liberal education is one for whom a wide range of experiences have much meaning. A liberally educated individual can get many meanings and secure many appreciations from reading newspapers, magazines, and books. He is also able to take part more satisfactorily in conversations and discussions with others whose interests, occupations, and experiences are different. The physical education curriculum should contribute to the liberal education of all pupils.

This can be accomplished by teaching physical activities and the appreciation of their values. The knowledge which is naturally a part of physical education activities should also be taught in connection with the activities. The historical and social background of dances is an illustration of knowledge which is inherent in physical education situations. The political and historical significance of marching and of formal gymnastics, and the nature study incident to outing activities are other examples of important knowledge that physical education can contribute to a liberal education.[1]

10. *The physical education curriculum must be functional in the present lives of the pupils.* The content of the physical education curriculum should have utilitarian value to the pupils in the present, during the ages in which it is being taught. The practice of teaching subject matter with the expectation that it will function in the lives of the learners at some remote time, cannot be justified. If we agree that education is a process of growth through the continuous reconstruction of experience, it is necessary that the content of the curriculum be such as to contribute to this growth. Growth, as conceived in this way, takes place through accretions to the whole child, not by the addition of compartments or blocks. If the curriculum is to make its proper contribution to the education of boys and girls it must be of use to them from day to day as they are maturing.

11. *Speed and accuracy of performance in physical education activities usually go together and help to secure greater satisfaction from participation.* The physical education curriculum should provide ample opportunities for drill so that most pupils may develop a reasonable degree of speed and accuracy. As a usual thing people like to do the things that they can do well. Therefore, if we hope to prepare our pupils in physical education activities to the extent that they will participate in them outside of the regular class periods it is essential that considerable skill be developed.

The meaning of aims and objectives. It is proposed here that *aims* be considered as the ultimate outcomes which might be secured through physical education. They are usually expressed in general terms and must be analyzed into more definite and specific statements of objectives in order to provide practical guides to teaching. *Objectives* are more specific statements of the things to be achieved through physical

[1] Jackson R. Sharman, "The Subject Matter Inherent in Physical Education Situations," *Journal of Health and Physical Education*, IV (February, 1933), 26.

education; the accomplishment of the objectives should lead up to and contribute to the achievement of the main general aim. In planning a curriculum it is common practice to state both general and specific objectives, the latter being more definite statements involving more detailed analysis. It is often desirable to break up these specific objectives into still smaller units, the immediate *goals*. The goals should, in most cases, be expressed in such a way that they can be measured in terms of success or failure, so that a pupil reaches them (does some specific thing) or fails to do so, thus removing the occasion for the subjective judgment of the teacher.

The achievement of the immediate goals should lead up to the achievement of the specific objectives which, in turn, should contribute to the accomplishment of the general objectives. Achieving the general objectives should culminate in an appreciable contribution toward accomplishing the main general aims of education and of physical education.

An illustration of these four levels of achievement follows: The general aim of education and of physical education may be, as proposed by Herbert Spencer, the preparation of individuals for "complete living." One of the general objectives might be "preparation for the worthy use of leisure time"; a specific objective may be to teach every high school boy and girl to play tennis well enough to get satisfaction and pleasure out of playing it; and a goal may be stated as "the ability on the part of every high school boy and girl to make at least three good serves out of five trials." The ability to serve well would help each pupil to play tennis successfully. Playing tennis well would make some contribution to the worthy use of leisure time, and being able to spend one's leisure time wholesomely would help one to achieve "complete living." The goals and objectives should serve as guide posts or, to change the figure, a compass to point the direction to the accomplishment of the general aim.

The aim of education and of physical education. The aim of education and of physical education that is accepted by a person or a group largely determines the kind of curriculum that will be proposed. If, for example, one believes the aim of education is to prepare children to do better the specific activities in which adults participate he will construct a different curriculum from that of one who believes the aim of education is to help pupils solve the problems of everyday life, or to grow and develop through experience.

A large number of statements of the aim of education and of physical education have been made by different writers. Many of these statements

are involved in technical and ambiguous language which makes it diffi
cult to understand just what they really mean. In order to function as
guides in the educational process aims must be stated so simply and
clearly that they cannot be misunderstood or misinterpreted. The fol
lowing statements are intended to meet this requirement.

*The aim of education is to help boys and girls do more successfully
the things which are useful to them in living.*

*The aim of physical education is to provide facilities, leadership, and
opportunities for participation in physical activities that will help boys
and girls do more successfully the things which are useful to them in
living.*

In this connection the word *useful* must be interpreted broadly. There
is sometimes a tendency to think of an activity as being of value only
if it contributes to vocational efficiency. An activity is really of use to a
person in living if it helps him to have better recreational interests, to get
broader and better satisfactions out of his social relationships, to enrich
his home life, or to live better and more fully in any way. The acceptance of these aims of education and of physical education indicates that
the curriculum should contain only subject matter and activities that
have utilitarian value either immediately or in the future; it implies
that the curriculum content occurs commonly in the lives of many people;
and that the content will help improve the quality of living of the pupils.

The choice of objectives. An objective is something that we
believe is desirable and seems possible of attainment. The way in which
an objective is stated frequently gives some indication of the methods
that might be used in its achievement. For instance, if "preparation for
the worthy use of leisure" is stated as an objective of education it may
be recognized immediately that one way to accomplish this end is to
teach all school boys and girls activities which can be used as recreations
during leisure time. In this sense an objective serves as a goal and also
as a guide post in arriving at the goal.

In determining objectives we must (1) make an analysis of the life
interests, needs, ideals, and activities of humans in contemporary society;
(2) classify and interpret the results of this analysis in terms of their
relative importance and desirability in life as it is lived in different communities; and (3) compare the classifications of activities with those
proposed by recognized educational philosophers as being desirable. It is
proposed that emphasis be placed on an analysis of activities because
attitudes and skills are important only when they function in directing

action. As curriculums and school procedures are now organized and conducted the objectives of physical education can be best determined by combining the results of an analysis of life activities with a list of activities that are desired; even though these desired activities might not be found in the lives of persons who are recognized as good citizens. It is for this reason that it is essential to consider the results of an activity analysis in terms of life in different communities and to supplement the list of activities with some proposed as being desirable by speculative philosophers.

Uhl [1] has pointed out that at different times in the history of civilization different methods have been used to derive the objectives of education. These include listing the characteristics of a citizen in an ideal society, as Plato did in his *Republic;* stating the qualities of successful men in one social class, as Castiglione did in *The Courtier;* setting up objectives in terms of the nature of children rather than in terms of the nature of society, as was proposed by Rousseau in his *Émile;* deriving objectives by analyzing the values of some one field of human knowledge, as many classicists claim Herbert Spencer did in his essay "What Knowledge Is of Most Worth?"; and determining objectives by an analysis of society to find the values which should be of the most sociological worth, as was done by Small. [2] Each of these methods has made some contribution to the development of the newer and more generally used contemporary techniques of analyzing social activities of children and adults as they are living at the present time.

Methods of activity analysis. It has been proposed by Bobbitt [3] that the first step in making an activity analysis is to analyze the whole field of human experience into major fields. He submitted the following classification of activities as one that has been found serviceable.

1. Language activities; social intercommunication.
2. Health activities.
3. Citizenship activities.
4. General social activities—meeting and mingling with others.
5. Spare-time activities, amusements, recreations.

[1] Willis L. Uhl, *Secondary School Curricula,* pp. 294-301. New York: The Macmillan Company, 1927.

[2] Albion W. Small in the *Report of the Committee of the National Council of Education on Economy of Time in Education.* United States Bureau of Education Bulletin, 1913, No. 38.

[3] Franklin Bobbitt, *How to Make a Curriculum,* pp. 8-9. Boston: Houghton Mifflin Company, 1924.

6. Keeping one's self mentally fit—analogous to the health activities of keeping one's self physically fit.
7. Religious activities.
8. Parental activities, the upbringing of children, the maintenance of a proper home life.
9. Unspecialized or non-vocational practical activities.
10. The labors of one's calling.

The second step in this activity-analysis technique is to break up each of the major fields of human activity into the more specific activities. This process of analysis and division is continued until specific activities are listed which can be performed.

Charters [1] emphasizes the technique of job analysis as a desirable method of making an analysis of the activities of the members of society. He points out that there are at least four methods of making a job analysis: introspection, interviewing, working on the job, and the questionnaire.

Other methods of determining objectives. It should not be concluded, however, that these methods of choosing objectives by means of an analysis of contemporary society and of the activities of people exhaust the fruitful possibilities. Harap [2] has stated that there are five principal methods of deriving objectives. A summary of his statements follows:

1. *Direct analysis of the natural activities of children.* (*a*) Quantitative analyses of questions most frequently asked by pupils. Oberteuffer's study in connection with hygiene for college freshmen is an example of this type of analysis.[3] (*b*) Informal analyses. This type is illustrated by the informal courses of study that have been published as project curriculums. (*c*) Analyses made by observation and by reports of children. Schwendener's study [4] of the games preferred by fourth grade children and studies reported by Lehman and Witty [5] illustrate analyses of this kind.

2. *Direct analysis of the social needs of the learner.* (*a*) Analysis of life

---

[1] W. W. Charters, *Curriculum Construction,* pp. 38–39. New York: The Macmillan Company, 1923.

[2] Henry Harap, *The Technique of Curriculum Making,* pp. 38–39. New York: The Macmillan Company, 1928.

[3] Delbert Oberteuffer, *Personal Hygiene for College Students.* New York: Teachers College, Columbia University, 1930.

[4] Norma Schwendener, *Game Preferences of Fourth Grade Children.* New York: Teachers College, Columbia University, 1933.

[5] Lehman, Harvey C., and Witty, Paul A., *Psychology of Play Activities.* New York: A. S. Barnes and Company, 1927.

needs. (*b*) Analysis of the needs of a homogeneous group (case group). (*c*) Analysis of industrial jobs.

3. *Secondary analysis of the needs of the learner.* (*a*) Analysis of newspapers and magazines. This type of analysis is illustrated in a study[1] by Bobbitt. (*b*) Analysis of social surveys, social statistics, and other social documents. A study[2] by Lerrigo illustrates this type.

4. *Analysis of the needs of the learner in the opinion of competent persons.*

5. *Analysis of existing objectives as found in, or inferred from, curriculum studies, courses of study, and textbooks.* Studies[3] by Patty and by Meier illustrate this type.

The difficulty of choosing objectives. The difficulty of making an adequate sociological analysis, on which to base a statement of objectives, must be recognized. Society is so complex and individuals are so much opposed to revealing their thoughts, interests, and emotional reactions that many obstacles arise to interfere with obtaining reliable results. The rapidity with which social changes take place makes many of the results of such studies only temporary in value. The tremendous cost involved in a sociological analysis of a geographical or political unit as large as a county or state or the nation makes it almost impossible to finance a complete and continuing study. In order for this job to be done adequately and correctly there should be created and maintained a permanent commission to work at the problem continuously. The personnel of this commission should be made up of highly skilled and experienced technical experts.

The social philosophy needed to guide the development of physical education in our rapidly changing and complex society cannot be formulated successfully by any one man or by any small group of persons who are engaged in full-time jobs at the same time. What is really needed, therefore, is a commission, composed of the best minds in sociology, philosophy, economics, political science, education, and physical education, to give their entire time over an indefinite period to a study of

[1] Franklin Bobbitt, "Discovering Objectives of Health Education," Elementary School Journal, XXV (June, 1925), 755–62.

[2] Marion Lerrigo, *Health Problem Sources.* New York: Teachers College, Columbia University, 1926.

[3] Willard Walter Patty, "The Teaching of Health Education in Elementary Schools," *Journal of Health and Physical Education,* V (January, 1934), 3–7, 60; "Outcomes of Health Education," *ibid.,* V (February, 1934), 34–37, 62; and "Health Supervisory Activities of the Teacher in Elementary Schools," *ibid.,* V (March, 1934), 50–51, 65.

Lois Meier, *Health Material in Science Textbooks.* New York: Teachers College, Columbia University, 1927.

social conditions and developments. Out of this study by these superior persons should be proposed a social philosophy for the guidance of physical education. After this clearly stated social philosophy has been submitted, discussed, and accepted, the schools should aggressively—with the spirit of evangelism—help to secure a general understanding and acceptance of it.

It is not practicable, however, to wait until such an ideal basis for physical education is provided. Boys and girls are growing up, and the best program that can now be provided must be planned for them. It is essential, therefore, that the objectives of each physical education curriculum be based on the best immediately feasible and practical analysis of the life activities of the social group involved. At the same time the desirability and importance of a more comprehensive sociological analysis should be kept in mind, and efforts should be made to bring about the organization and support of a commission which could do this important work properly.

Motivation of objectives. Economic, physical, psychological, and moral forces lead one to action in attempting to achieve a value or ideal that is consciously accepted as being desirable of attainment. Merely the acceptance of an ideal, such as universal participation in physical education or the preparation of all pupils to spend a part of their leisure time in physical recreation, will not furnish the force necessary for the attainment. Persons frequently give lip service to an ideal and yet lack the drive that might cause them to strive to achieve it. A definite want or desire must exist in order that an individual may be motivated to obtain the value consciously recognized. Frequently the objectives proposed for education and physical education are merely names of recognized values and they do not serve as motivating forces to action. Health, citizenship, and ethical character are only abstractions and are not ordinarily attached to or associated with the activities in which boys and girls participate. In order to serve as motivating forces, these abstract ideas must be analyzed into definite ways of acting and a desire aroused for proficiency of performance in these ways of acting. The desire, in turn, must be allied with economic, physical, psychological, or moral forces in order to assure the socially desired action.

To illustrate this principle, assume that one of the social goals in teaching basketball to tenth grade boys is to teach them to be respectful to officials at all times. In order to cause these boys to act in this way it would be necessary to make them *want* to be respectful. A psycho-

[145]

logical motive to this desirable form of behavior might be to win the approval of the teacher or coach, or the approval of their social group. An economic motive might be the winning of a valuable prize offered for the team showing the best sportsmanship, although this motive should not be used by teachers or others interested in the education of boys and girls. Teachers must keep always in mind when planning their methods of teaching that a motive should be considered in relation to all goals.

Integration of objectives and curriculum. The failure to carry the objectives of physical education into the planning of the curriculum is an error that is made by many curriculum builders in physical education. Some curriculums have consisted of general proposals of abstract values which have not been analyzed into specific statements that might be used in choosing subject matter or methods; other curriculums have been largely a mass of subject matter and activities which had no direct relationship to any definite objectives; and still other curriculums have attempted to state objectives, subject matter, and activities without any consideration of the social needs and interests of the pupils.

Objectives should be derived as has been proposed, by a sociological analysis of the needs and activities of the social group to which the pupils belong. Each objective proposed should carry with it a statement of the subject matter, pupil activities, and methods that may be used in the achievement of the objectives. Techniques for measuring results and suggested references for wider reading and study should also be suggested. Arranging these items in five or six parallel columns in tabular form is a device that has been found useful in making simpler and clearer the mechanics of curriculum organization.

The objectives of education. A number of analytical methods and other techniques have been used in arriving at statements of the objectives of education. These have been set forth in many different forms. Educational philosophers, curriculum experts, and committees of professional educational organizations have been the source of most of the proposed statements of the objectives of education. The North Central Association of Colleges and Secondary Schools in 1918 appointed a Committee on Standards for Use in the Reorganization of Secondary School Curricula. This committee has continued in existence and among its contributions has been a good statement of the objectives of education. It has been stated that the primary and most fundamental thing in making a curriculum is a clear and definite statement of objectives.

These objectives must serve two functions: (1) to serve as criteria for the evaluation of present curriculums, and (2) to be guides for the selection of new curriculum content.[1] The statements of the committee have been made with the curriculum of the high school in mind, but the ultimate objectives of education are in terms of dispositions and abilities equally as applicable to all other school levels.

Their ultimate objectives of education are selected and modified from the Cardinal Principles report and are "to produce in boys and girls the dispositions and abilities needed: (1) to maintain health and physical fitness; (2) to use leisure in right ways; (3) to sustain successfully certain definite social relationships, civic, domestic, community, and the like; and (4) to engage in exploratory-vocational and vocational activities."[2] The health, leisure-time, social, and vocational objectives of education, with the dispositions and abilities needed by pupils to achieve these ultimate objectives, are summarized in the table on page 148.

General objectives of physical education. The general objectives of physical education have been set forth by the author in another book.[3] These statements indicate that physical education has the responsibility for guiding the experiences of boys and girls in such a way that they will be helped to spend their leisure happily, to develop the organic systems of their bodies, and to develop wholesome personalities and good traits of character.

The following statements of the general objectives of physical education are proposed as satisfactory and practical.

1. *To develop skills in activities and favorable attitudes toward play that will carry over and function during leisure time.* Physical education should help individuals to spend their leisure time successfully as children and also as adults. Many persons emphasize the development of skill in activities such as tennis, golf, handball, squash, and swimming, which may be valuable as leisure-time activities during adulthood. This is a desirable and important emphasis, but at the same time the recreational interests and needs of boys and girls must be provided for. There are a number of activities which are interesting to boys and girls at different ages but are not particularly valuable as direct preparation for adult life. Just as playing in a sand pile and playing with blocks are valuable

[1] *High School Curriculum Reorganization,* p. 12. Ann Arbor, Michigan: The North Central Association of Colleges and Secondary Schools, 1933.

[2] *Ibid.,* p. 13.

[3] Jackson R. Sharman, *Introduction to Physical Education,* pp. 66–68. New York: A. S. Barnes and Company, 1934.

[147]

A CONDENSED SURVEY OF THE ULTIMATE OBJECTIVES [1]

AMPLIFIED IN TERMS OF DISPOSITIONS AND ABILITIES

Health: *To secure and maintain a condition of personal good health and physical fitness.*

1. To develop in individuals correct health practices, and daily habits of indoor and outdoor exercise, and of relaxation, which assist in the maintenance of bodily vigor and vitality.

2. To develop a lifelong desire for participation in wholesome activities, and to develop wholesome and intelligent attitudes toward the necessity for recreation and systematic exercise, in case of all individuals and all kinds of activities sponsored in community centers.

3. To prevent and correct ill-health and bodily defects, and to maintain freedom from bodily handicaps in individuals.

Social: *To sustain successfully certain definite social relationships; civic, domestic, community, and the like.*

1. To have due personal regard for the rights of others in all personal contacts and relationships, and a proper sense of social obligations.

2. To recognize the proper relationships of individuals within a single group.

3. To recognize the proper relationship of one group to another.

4. To be socially efficient through participation in varied modes of group activities.

Leisure-Time: *To use leisure time in right ways.*

1. To express in leisure-time activities the nobler emotions, such as courage, altruism, esthetic feeling, reverence, and loyalty to one's home, community, and country.

2. To secure wholesome recreation and relaxation through games, sports, travel, good literature, the fine arts, conversation, and hobbies.

3. To be socially helpful through avocational activities in the home, church, and community.

Vocational: *To engage successfully in exploratory-vocational and vocational activities.*

1. To secure satisfaction in skillful performance and to have pride in the rendering of service through one's vocation.

2. To provide adequately life's necessities for oneself and one's dependents.

3. To save a financial reserve for the emergencies of the unproductive period of life.

4. To contribute from one's surplus for one's own leisure, and from one's wealth and energy toward the advancement of community life.

5. To cooperate in industry or profession on a basis of common ideals and interests.

[1] *High School Curriculum Reorganization*, p. 28.   Ann Arbor, Michigan: The North Central Association of Colleges and Secondary Schools, 1933.

activities for small children, so there are other more highly organized games which appeal to boys and girls of high school and college age. Physical education should contribute to the worthy use of leisure by individuals at all ages from early childhood through adulthood.

2. *To develop the organic systems of the body to the end that each individual may live at the highest possible level.* There is much evidence from the field of physiology and from clinical observations to substantiate the belief that participation in vigorous physical activities contributes to organic development. It seems clear also that rational participation in physical activities helps to maintain the normal functioning of the metabolic and nutritive processes. It can be expected, therefore, that physical education will make a definite and valuable contribution, through organic development, to helping boys and girls live a full and abundant life.

3. *To provide opportunities for controlled participation in physical activities that will result in educative experiences.* Physical education offers many excellent opportunities for guiding the experiences of pupils in ways that will contribute to the development of desirable traits of character. The opportunities that arise in connection with the expression of instructive or innate tendencies are particularly valuable. The development of desirable emotionalized attitudes and sportsmanlike ways of behaving are other educational outcomes that should be achieved through physical education. The ideals of team play, social cooperation, and playing according to the rules of the game may also be developed.

Experts in the field of mental hygiene point to the responsibilities that physical education has for developing good mental habits and main· taining mental health. It is believed that the objectiveness of the experiences in physical education makes them especially valuable in this connection. The habit of facing the realities and problems of life squarely, without sidestepping them or running away from them, is one of the important mental traits that can be developed through physical education.

Adapting the curriculum to individual differences. In a consideration of how to adapt the school curriculum in physical education to the individual needs of the pupils there emerge differences of opinion concerning the procedures to be used. One of the questions which must be answered is whether pupils of different degrees of ability should be expected to learn different amounts of the same thing or whether some pupils should be taught entirely different subject matter from others.

[149]

Some teachers assume that all pupils can learn the same thing. The available evidence indicates that there is wide range of native ability among children and that some of them find great difficulty in mastering activities which require a high degree of coordination or rhythmical ability.

A number of ways have been used to adapt the curriculum to the individual needs of the pupils. These methods have included: (1) the organization of pupils in homogeneous groups on the basis of the results of a medical examination, native motor ability, strength, or skill; (2) the use of an elective program which permits each pupil to choose any activity he wishes; (3) the organization of the content of the curriculum into "contracts" or assignments which individual pupils may complete as rapidly as their interests and ability permit; and (4) provision for individual instruction and practice.

In order to adapt the curriculum to the individual differences of pupils a teacher must know the individual status of each child; must organize his instructional materials so that assignments can be made which are suited to the different levels of ability of the pupils; and must adopt a technique of teaching which will permit him to give much of his time to individual instruction. The status of each child can be most accurately determined by the use of a number of tests and examinations.

Criteria for selection of curriculum content. After the objectives of physical education have been stated the next step in the organization of a curriculum is the selection of subject matter and methods of instruction which will be instrumental in achieving these objectives. In order to choose the content of the curriculum intelligently it is desirable to have some detailed criteria to use as a guide. The following statements are proposed as suitable criteria for this purpose.

1. The activities should be interesting to the pupils.
2. The activities should have some meaning to the pupils in terms of past experiences which they have had.
3. The activities should be within the range of the abilities of the pupils so that each child may have opportunities for achieving a reasonable degree of success.
4. Activities should be provided to meet the needs, interests, and abilities of each individual pupil.
5. Activities should be chosen which will carry over and function during adult life as leisure-time recreational activities.
6. The activities included in the curriculum should have intrinsic worth.

No content should be included in the curriculum merely to provide variety, or with the hope that some vague intangible values may transfer to the real experiences of life.

7. Activities which can be taught with a minimum amount of equipment and supplies are preferable.

8. The activities included in the curriculum should be such that they can be used often by most of the pupils. For example, it would not be wise to try to teach ice hockey to boys in the senior high schools located in the southern part of Florida.

9. The activities included in the curriculum should be ones that are not provided satisfactorily by any other agency in the community.

10. The activities of the curriculum should be physiologically wholesome and should contribute to the developmental needs of the pupils.

The influence of social conditions on the curriculum. The school curriculum is influenced in all schools by local conditions—more in some than in others, but the local influence is always present. This is probably desirable in that it may help the school curriculum to be more flexible in meeting the needs of individual pupils and in conforming to peculiar needs of geographical sections and communities. Many conditions in all communities are similar. Much of the curriculum content which is suitable in one community is suitable in many other communities. Many of the basic activities such as team games and rhythmic activities should be taught in all communities, but the method of approach and types of illustrations and explanations may vary in different communities.

The school plant determines the content of the physical education curriculum to a considerable extent. If there is no swimming pool in a school it is usually not feasible to teach water activities. If a school has no locker and shower facilities it would probably be inadvisable to conduct activities during class periods which would cause pupils to become hot and dirty. If there are no tennis courts or handball courts it would be difficult to teach these games effectively. The supplies and equipment for physical education help determine the content of the curriculum. If there were no musical instrument such as a piano or phonograph in a school the deficiency would be a real handicap to the teaching of dancing. If no volley balls or volley ball nets were available, the sport would probably have to be omitted from the curriculum.

The type of school—whether it is a city, rural, or consolidated school—also influences the kind of physical education program and the content of

[151]

the curriculum. For example, in a consolidated school where most of the pupils are transported to school in busses the pupils must leave for home immediately after the dismissal of school in the afternoon in order that they may ride home on the busses. This makes it difficult in these schools to carry on a satisfactory after-school program of athletics or recreational activities. In rural schools frequently the number of pupils is so small that some activities cannot be taught.

Climatic and topographical conditions also influence the content of the curriculum. Ice skating and hockey would not be suitable for curriculum content in Florida schools, and golf cannot be played during most of the school year in Minnesota. Schools located on the side of mountains or in the congested districts of large cities probably should not attempt to emphasize football, soccer, and other games that require large playgrounds.

The size and qualification of the teaching staff is an important factor in determining the curriculum content. In a high school, for example, where all the physical education for boys is taught by a man whose sole qualification for the job is previous membership on a college football team the curriculum content for boys cannot be extended much beyond the range of team games. It is clearly evident that if the pupils are to be taught gymnastics, dancing, swimming, sports, and other activities there must be some member of the staff who is qualified to teach them.

The prevailing attitudes and prejudices in a community frequently influence the curriculum. In a few situations there is definite opposition to teaching dancing in the schools. In other places much emphasis is placed on swimming, and in some communities certain nationality groups have much enthusiasm for gymnastics.

State laws and the regulations of state boards of education sometimes influence the organization and the content of the curriculum. It is common practice for state courses of study to set up minimum requirements of things that must be taught.

The things which have been mentioned are only some of the local conditions and influences that help determine the physical education curriculum. There are many others. A person concerned with the construction of a curriculum should be thoroughly familiar with the ones peculiar to his local community and take them into consideration when he is planning the curriculum.

The influence of administrative factors. The administrative policies and practices of a school influence the curriculum to a considerable extent. If, for instance, physical education is required throughout all years the curriculum which would need to be planned would be longer, more complete, and arranged in more orderly sequence than if it were required in some years and elective in others. The degree of flexibility permitted in pupils' schedules would likewise influence the curriculum. If a prescribed program is laid down for all pupils the physical education instruction must be incorporated in this prescription. Whether credit is allowed for physical education toward high school graduation and college entrance is another administrative factor which has an important bearing on the curriculum, its methods of organization, methods of teaching, and of keeping records.

The type of school organization, that is, whether it is organized on a 6-3-3; 8-4; 6-2-4; or some other basis, determines the set-up and content of the curriculum to a considerable extent. Whether an elementary school is a platoon school, Dalton Plan school, traditional type school, or some other kind of school is similarly of much significance in planning the curriculum. The time allotment for physical education in the daily schedule for the school helps to shape the curriculum. If only two periods a week are allowed, the curriculum must be more restricted than if five periods are assigned. The way in which pupils are assigned to physical education classes has a bearing on the curriculum. It is believed to be the best practice for the individual needs of each pupil to be determined by a battery of tests and examinations, including a medical examination, and for the pupils to be placed in homogeneous groups for physical education on the basis of the results of these tests. If pupils are classified on some such basis the curriculum can be better planned than if the pupils were assigned to classes regardless of sizes, ages, interests, and abilities.

These are some illustrations of how administrative policies and practices influence the curriculum. Nearly all such policies and practices have some influence either directly or indirectly on the curriculum. It is also true that the objectives accepted for physical education and the curriculum set up to achieve these objectives determine many administrative practices. It can be seen, therefore, that the curriculum and the administration of physical education are interrelated and interdependent.

Applying the curriculum. In teaching the content and striving to achieve the objectives of the curriculum the efforts of each individual teacher are of fundamental importance. The efforts are directed specifically toward bringing about desirable changes in the pupils. Every experience one has brings about at least some small change in him. Every time a boy picks up a basketball from the floor and shoots at the basket he is different to some extent from what he was before he shot at the basket. The outcomes of our teaching with which we are primarily concerned, therefore, are modifications of the knowledge, attitudes, ideals, appreciations, and skills of the boys and girls we teach. We must seek to secure these desired outcomes by means which are most effective and economical of time and effort and at the same time hold the least possibility of harm to the pupils. In order to do this, we must (1) know definitely and clearly the goals sought; (2) know the materials or subject matter which can be used to the best advantage in securing the desired outcomes; (3) be familiar with the mental, physical, and emotional characteristics of children at different ages; (4) know something of the way in which people learn; (5) be familiar with the techniques of school organization and administration; (6) have command of the better methods of presenting material and helping people to learn; (7) know the best methods of class procedure; (8) know the fundamentals of motivation of learning; (9) have command of the techniques of class control; and (10) know how to test results of teaching by use and interpretation of the best measuring instruments.

Summary. The development of the physical education curriculum has been affected by a large number of influences. These include European systems of physical education; military preparedness; reports of prominent committees; the emphasis on child health; the increase in leisure time; and the widespread attention given to individual differences.

An expressed or implicit philosophy of life, social philosophy, philosophy of education, and statement of the objectives of education should be basic to the curriculum. An evaluation of the values of life which are approved by the majority of citizens is the first step in planning a curriculum. Our form of government is democratic and the schools, therefore, should educate boys and girls for life in a democratic society. The accepted principles of a progressive educational philosophy emphasize learning through self-directed pupil activity.

A knowledge of the principles and assumptions underlying physical education is important to persons engaged in curriculum construction.

In stating the desired outcomes of physical education the general aims must be analyzed into specific statements of objectives and goals in order that teachers and pupils may strive definitely for their achievement. The steps used in the choice of objectives should be (1) to make an analysis of the activities of people in contemporary society, (2) to classify and interpret the results of this analysis in terms of their relative importance, and (3) to compare this classification with the ones proposed by recognized educational philosophers.

Bobbitt, Harap, and Charters have each proposed methods of making analyses and determining objectives. The achievement of objectives must be motivated by some economic, physical, psychological, or moral force. Merely the acceptance of an ideal will not furnish the force necessary for the attainment.

The general objectives of physical education are usually stated to include its educational, developmental, and recreational values. The curriculum should be adapted to the individual differences of the pupils. In order to choose the content of the curriculum intelligently it is necessary to have some definite criteria to use as a guide.

Other factors which influence the curriculum are the social conditions of the community; the school plant; type of school organization; climatic and topographical conditions; the size and qualifications of the teaching staff; state laws and regulations; and the administrative policies of the school.

QUESTIONS

1. What influences have affected the development of the physical education curriculum in American schools?
2. What social philosophy should underlie the curriculum?
3. What are some of the principles of modern educational philosophy?
4. What are some principles and assumptions that are basic to the physical education curriculum?
5. What steps should be followed in determining objectives?
6. What methods have been proposed by Bobbitt for making an activity analysis?
7. What other methods of determining objectives have been proposed by Harap?
8. What are some of the difficulties involved in choosing objectives?
9. How may objectives be motivated?
10. What are the general objectives of physical education?
11. What criteria might be used for the selection of curriculum content?
12. What are some extrinsic conditions and factors that influence the curriculum?

REFERENCES

Bobbitt, Franklin. *How to Make a Curriculum*. Boston: Houghton Mifflin Company, 1924.

Caswell, Hollis L., and Campbell, Doak S. *Curriculum Development*. New York: American Book Company, 1935.

Charters, W. W. *Curriculum Construction*. New York: The Macmillan Company, 1923.

Harap, Henry. *The Technique of Curriculum Making*. New York: The Macmillan Company, 1928.

Staley, Seward C. *Curriculum in Sports Education*. Philadelphia: W. B. Saunders Company, 1935.

Uhl, Willis L. *Secondary School Curricula*. New York: The Macmillan Company, 1927.

CHAPTER IX

Leadership in Physical Education

∾

The development of teaching as a profession. Teaching has arrived at the point where it can be said to have at least semi-professional status. This marks a point in professional progress which has been continuous for the last two hundred years and quite rapid during the past fifty years. In ancient times teachers were slaves, in most instances, and at a later time, although they were free men, they occupied an inferior social, political, and economic level. The widespread acceptance of the principle of universal education has resulted in the recognition of the important professional service that teachers render.

The dependence of democratic government on universal education. It is only through the education of the masses of the people that democratic government can be successful. Early in our history the importance and significance of the common man were emphasized to the extent that it was believed the decisions of the masses of the people, as indicated by their votes, could not be wrong. The participation of a large part of the population in determining the affairs of government makes it essential for every one to have at least the fundamentals of an education. The work of the teacher has been recognized not only as of great importance in establishing and maintaining a democratic government but, with the rapid increase in scientific knowledge, as the essential means of perpetuating accumulated experiences of mankind and handing them on from one generation to the next. There is reason to believe, furthermore, that the happiness and success of each individual is determined to a considerable extent by the opportunities which he has had for education under the guidance of teachers.

The need for well prepared teachers. The faith that the American people have in education to benefit the individual and society, and the opportunities that education has to influence the progress of civilization and the lives of the people of the country, place on the teachers a great and challenging responsibility. In order that they may be qualified to assume this responsibility they must be selected carefully, prepared well, and skillfully guided in their work. Every teacher should be a superior individual who has been well educated.

[157]

The beginnings of professional training. The development of professional training in all professions has followed very much the same route. The early procedure was for a person who wished to prepare for professional service in a given field to serve a period of apprenticeship under the guidance of an experienced practitioner. In the field of medicine, for example, until not many decades ago it was customary for a prospective physician to go into the office of a practicing physician for the purpose of reading medicine. The older and more experienced man would direct the reading of the student and frequently take him on professional calls to sick people which provided clinical experience along with his theoretical studies. Up to comparatively recent times similar procedures were followed in law, dentistry, pharmacy, and the ministry. This, in general, was an apprenticeship method of professional training.

As the need and demand for broader preparation developed in each professional field, proprietary schools were organized to supplement and take the place of the apprenticeship type of training. These schools were operated as private enterprises for the purpose of making money for the proprietors, and many of them had low standards of admission and achievement. For instance, in 1906 there were 162 medical schools with an enrollment of 25,204 students. There were no hospitals available to 94 of these schools; in 57 of them the professors examined patients in the presence of students in hospital amphitheaters, and in only 11 schools were opportunities provided for students to examine patients and write case histories.[1] Since that time medical education has made rapid progress so that nearly all medical students are now assured of an opportunity for sound professional training. In other professions the proprietary school situation was probably worse than it was in the case of medical education, and comparable improvement has not yet been made. The proprietary schools were an improvement over earlier methods.

Professional training in universities. The growth of professional schools in connection with universities has had more influence on the improvement of professional preparation than any other one thing. The ability of universities to provide adequate facilities and staffs and to require a protracted period of pre-professional and professional training has served to establish and maintain standards that many proprietary schools could not reach. Consequently the weaker and poorer of these schools have gone out of existence and most of the stronger and

---

[1] N. P. Colwell, *Medical Education, 1924–1926,* p. 6. Bureau of Education Bulletin, 1927, No. 9. Washington: Government Printing Office, 1927.

better ones have affiliated with universities. Meanwhile there is a continual up-grading of professional schools in all fields which seems to indicate that within a few years nearly all proprietary professional schools will have served their period of usefulness.

The development and recognition of professional "levels" in the various fields has taken place during the process of expansion and organization of the different professions. It is important that these "levels" be given consideration in planning and directing a program of professional preparation. In the field of medicine there are the levels represented by the nurse and the technician, the general practitioner, the practicing specialist, and the research specialist. In dentistry the professional levels are occupied by the dental nurse, the dental mechanic, the practicing dentist, and the research specialist. In law there are the law clerk, the practicing attorney, and the research specialist. In other professions there are, or seem to be developing, corresponding levels of professional service. Similar trends are evident in physical education.

The development of professional preparation in physical education. The development of professional preparation in physical education has followed and is now following much the same path which marks the growth of professional training in other professions. The periods of apprenticeship training and of proprietary schools have been experienced. The affiliation with universities within the past few years of some of the stronger private professional schools of physical education indicates that professional preparation in physical education is following the usual pattern of development set by older professions. The higher certification standards set by state departments of education and the increasing requirements for graduation from teacher-training institutions shows that a continual upgrading is taking place in physical education. Physical education is rapidly coming to the point where it will require two years of pre-professional training on the college level for admission to professional study on the higher levels. The content of these two years will be largely prescribed in somewhat the same way as pre-medical and pre-law courses are now prescribed. When this plan is adopted it will take a minimum of three years of professional preparation to meet the requirements for a professional degree, making a total of at least five years of college work. Under such a plan the student, at the end of two years of pre-professional training, would be required to have, in addition to basic training in science and liberal arts subjects, satisfactory motor skill in the different physical education activities. The beginnings of this trend are evident in the requirement in California of five years of preparation for the higher type of certificate and the requirement by some colleges of five years of preparation for the professional degree.

Professional levels in physical education. Clearly differentiated levels of professional service in physical education which correspond to the professional levels in other professions are clearly and rapidly taking form. This differentiation must be recognized if the development of professional preparation is to be directed intelligently. These levels are occupied by: (1) the physical education technician, represented by such workers as physio-therapy aids, athletic trainers, and by technicians in such activity fields as swimming, boxing, wrestling, fencing, dancing, and football; (2) the physical education teacher who is qualified to teach a comprehensive program of physical education at the various school levels such as elementary school, high school, or college; (3) the director or supervisor of physical education who is qualified to act as a city or state supervisor of physical education or as head of a department of physical education in a college; and (4) the research specialist in physical education.

The professional preparation of persons for the three upper levels should be the responsibility of the better universities of the country. The preparation of technicians for the lower professional level could be carried on successfully in the better private schools of physical education and in normal schools.

The morale and economic welfare of teachers. The relationship between the number of teachers needed to fill the available positions and the number who would like to fill the positions is an important problem which influences the morale and economic welfare of teachers at all times, particularly during periods of deflation and retrenchment. This relationship is frequently spoken of as "teacher supply and demand," which is an expression borrowed from the field of economics, where it is used to describe market conditions.

The demand for teachers. The demand for teachers is said to be relatively easy to determine, because the number of new positions due to the increase in school population, the number of replacements, and the number of unfilled vacancies can be accurately predicted. If this is true, each state department of education and the Federal Office of Education, by carrying on continuous and extensive studies of teacher demand and supply, could know definitely at any time the demand for teachers of physical education and of all other subjects. If each state knew definitely

[160]

the number of teachers needed, the problem of regulating the supply could be attacked more intelligently.

The supply of teachers varies. The supply of teachers varies more and is harder to predict. Some of the factors which influence the supply of teachers of physical education are stated in the following paragraphs:

1. The number of persons with teachers' certificates who are engaged in other kinds of work influence the supply of teachers. It is almost impossible to predict the number of these people who will be added to the supply of teachers during any one year. This is particularly true when positions in business and industry are scarce. During these periods of economic depression many who have left educational work in prosperous times for more lucrative employment return to teaching. The practice in some states of issuing certificates good for life without any requirements of experience or renewal adds greatly to the difficulty of determining the number of teachers who may be added to the supply from this source.

2. The rapid increase in the number of institutions engaged in the preparation of physical education teachers has a definite influence on the supply of teachers. And since no progress has been made in establishing standards for such institutions many of these more than 400 schools now training physical education teachers are certain to have unsatisfactory staffs, facilities, and standards of achievement. This is likely to result in a large number of persons being graduated who are poorly prepared and are devoid of professional ideals and ethics. The Society of State Directors of Physical Education, in cooperation with several other professional organizations, is sponsoring a movement for the organization of some kind of standardizing agency for professional schools of physical education.

3. The lack of centralized certification authority in some states makes it difficult to predict the supply of physical education teachers. In some states the counties and other local units still have the authority to issue certificates to teachers, and in others the graduates of teacher-training institutions are given life certificates by the institutions from which they are graduated. The state department of education in each state should be the only agency for issuing certificates.

4. Students who begin teaching before completing their preparation form a part of the supply of teachers of physical education. There are always quite a few students who, after two or three years of study, drop

out of college and seek teaching positions for which they can secure certificates in a number of states. There are no statistics to show how many of these people are seeking positions each year, but no doubt they make up quite a large group.

5. The number of graduates in physical education who go into work other than teaching influences the supply of teachers. Each year many who prepare to teach physical education go into recreation work, physiotherapy, private gymnasiums, and studios, and into other vocations; many women marry and retire from professional work or never enter it. At present there is no way of finding out how many withdraw from the teaching profession for these reasons.

The importance of a state program of teacher training. In order that the supply of teachers may be regulated to fit the demand and that the quality of teachers may be continuously improved it is essential that each state have an effective program of teacher training. In most states it would be preferable to have a single state program of teacher training including physical education teachers and all other kinds of teachers. This program should be organized and carried out under the leadership of the state department of education. Where the professional leadership in the state department of education is unprepared to set up and administer a state program of teacher training, the institutions engaged in the work should have a state teacher-training conference to organize the efforts of the colleges and universities of the state into a unified plan.

The principles of a state program of teacher training. The state program of teacher training should make provision for carrying out the following principles:

1. The control of all teacher-training agencies should be placed under one unified board. In situations where each institution has a separate board of trustees it is practically impossible to set up and carry out a unified program for the selection, preparation, certification, and placement of teachers for the schools of the state.

2. In each state where it is impossible to place the control of all teacher-training agencies under one unified board there should be created a state council of education made up of representatives from the public schools of the state, the state department of education, and the colleges and normal schools of the state. Part of the responsibilities of this council should be to hold state teacher-training conferences, conduct studies of the status and needs in the field of teacher-training, set up a desirable

state program of teacher-training; and attempt through the weight of its influence to put the program into operation.

3. The control of the teacher-training budget procedures should be under the same unified board, usually the state board of education, which controls the institutions. This is necessary in order that the efforts of each institution may be effectively directed along the lines that will make the best contribution toward achieving the goals of the general state program.

4. The state department of education should be made the only agency for issuing certificates to teachers. It is only through such a plan that it will be practicable to make a reliable estimate at any time of the supply of teachers, to guarantee that every child will be taught by a teacher with at least a reasonable minimum preparation, to raise the level of preparation required for certification during periods when there is an oversupply of teachers, and to have a uniform certification plan throughout the state on which can be based an agreement of reciprocity with other states.

5. There should be state stimulation and encouragement of guidance programs for high school students to the end that a desirable and superior type of person may be directed into teaching.

6. Definite standards for teacher-training institutions should be formulated and after being approved, they should be strictly enforced. These standards should relate to such matters as the number, preparation, experience, and teaching load of faculty members; the training schools and critic teachers; directed teaching; the buildings and equipment; the library; the requirements for admission and graduation; and the curriculum.

7. There should be established in each state department of education the means of carrying on at all times continuing research in the field of teacher-training. It will be by means of scientific study of this kind that facts can be obtained on which to base a program for the professional preparation of teachers. It will be most difficult to plan a satisfactory program as long as accurate data are lacking concerning such things as supply and demand of teachers; subject combinations of teachers in schools of various sizes; and the annual replacement or turnover of teachers. The most important and fundamental problem facing persons interested in the preparation of physical education teachers is that of how to secure accurate data on which to base a program.

Factors in the selection of prospective teachers. There have been a great many studies made on how to predict the future teaching success of college students. Such studies are important and worthwhile, but what is needed is to find some accurate method of selecting persons to be trained as teachers who will be reasonably sure to make successful teachers. The methods that have been suggested for predicting the teaching success of college students have not been very successful but even if they were, much money, time, and effort could be saved by choosing the desirable prospective teachers at the time they entered college rather than wait until they reached the junior or senior year in college.

The State Department of Education in California [1] has made the following statement concerning the selection of students to be trained for physical education teachers:

> Students may be able to meet high school graduation requirements, college entrance requirements, complete the curriculum necessary for state certification for teaching and still not be successful as physical education teachers because of being inferior in one or more fundamental personal traits. Expert opinion seems to indicate the qualities listed below have high predictive value for success in physical education teaching: (1) high intelligence, (2) excellent character, (3) good personality, (4) good social qualities, (5) excellent physical fitness, (6) average or better than average scholarship in academic subjects, (7) high ability and accomplishment in physical education activities, and (8) evidences of leadership in extra-class student activities.

Ashbrook [2] suggests the following list of qualifications by which students applying for admission to undergraduate study in physical education might be judged: (1) scholarship, (2) medical examination, (3) personnel examination, (4) achievement examination, (5) consultation, and (6) evaluation.

Temple University has prepared the following list of standards for admission to their freshmen physical education class:

1. *Health:* Present a physician's certificate stating that upon a complete and thorough examination given within a period of two weeks before entering college, you are in good health and capable of participating in the activities of this department. He must also present a Vaccination Certificate, as required by the laws of the State of Pennsylvania.

---

[1] State Department of Education, *A Curriculum for the Professional Preparation of Physical Education Teachers for Secondary Schools.* Bulletin E–1. Sacramento: California State Printing Office, 1930, p. 103.

Willard P. Ashbrook, "A Selective Student Examination Prior to Training in Physical Education," *Journal of Health and Physical Education,* III (February, 1932), 18.

[164]

2. *Physical:* The applicant must be free from any deformities and not deviate too much from the normal in height and weight.

3. *Scholarship:* It is highly desirable to be ranked in at least the upper half but preferable in the upper quarter of your graduating class from either high school or preparatory school.

4. *Activity:* A previous interest and some participation in the severa. phases of physical activity is essential for the student entering this department.

5. *Personality:* Good character, qualities for leadership, high ideals and determination to achieve will enhance the student's progress.

6. *Professional Reference:* At least two references should be presented from men or women in the field of Physical Education whose conviction is that you give promise of success in this particular branch of Education.

7. *Examination:* Qualifying tests, to determine physical condition and natural ability in physical education must be completed before the candidate will be permitted to register.

A review of these statements and others in the literature indicates a preponderance of opinion to the effect that institutions engaged in the professional preparation of physical education teachers should admit only those students who were in the upper half of their high school graduating class, who took a "stiff" course in high school including such subjects as mathematics and science, who had an interest while in high school in preparation to be a teacher of physical education, who have good health and character, and who have motor skill and ability above the average.

Standards of fitness for entering the profession. An unimpeachable example of acceptable conduct, competency as a teacher both in the classroom and on the athletic field, and a thorough willingness to cooperate with the policies of the school administration, have been listed by Weidemann [1] as the three most important factors in the success of men teachers of physical education. The table on page 166 from Weidemann's study shows reasons given by replies from 130 schools why high school athletic coaches are dismissed.

Monroe [2] reports the opinions of 841 men engaged as teachers of physical education and coaches of athletics in high schools concerning the conditions which these men considered most important for retaining their positions. The table on page 167 gives a summary of the opinions of these men.

[1] C. C. Weidemann. "Why do Physical Education Instructors Fail and Why Do They Succeed?" *Educational Research Record,* I (October, 1928), 3.
[2] Monroe, Walter S.—*The Duties of Men Engaged as Physical Directors or Athletic Coaches in High Schools.* Bulletin No. 30, Bureau of Educational Research, College of Education, University of Illinois, Urbana, Illinois, 1926, p. 15.

TABLE II

WHY HIGH SCHOOL ATHLETIC COACHES ARE DISMISSED

REASONS	Frequency of Occurrence	
	As stated by board members	As stated by super-intendents
1. Undesirable personal habits (profanity, smoking, drinking, gambling, social indiscretions, too sporty)............	25	25
2. Unable to discipline, control, or hold respect of the boys...	11	14
3. Bad influence on the boys (poor example to exemplify)....	8	14
4. Incompetent as a teacher in the classroom...............	8	15
5. Incompetent as a teacher of athletics....................	8	12
6. Lack of cooperation with the administration and its policies (little consideration for scholarship).................	7	10
7. Easy going, loafer, slovenly in dress, lack of interest in work	5	7
8. Poor sportsmanship (win by means, foul or fair).........	5	8
9. Failed to produce a "winning team"....................	3	7
10. Unable to win boys and get their cooperation............	3	6
11. Not square in money matters (careless, not economical)..	2	5
12. Tried to center school activities about athletics (too aggressive, coach tried to "star" himself)..................	4	4
13. The "fans" wanted a new coach........................	2	5
14. Undue familiarity with students out of school hours......	2	0
15. Lack of judgment, understanding, tact..................	2	1
16. Too formal ("hard boiled") in discipline...............	1	1
17. Poor health	2	0
18. Lack of interest in development of community interest in school affairs	0	2
19. Salary of coach out of proportion to that of the other teachers	0	1
20. Did not possess a teacher's certificate..................	1	1

It may be seen by referring to Table III that "Personal Character" was named by slightly more than two-fifths (43 per cent) and "Teaching Ability" by a slightly smaller proportion (39 per cent). Only five men checked "Political Influence," and "Winning Teams" was indicated by only 91 (11 per cent). "Popularity in the Community" was checked by only 32, but 17 of these are in the fifth group of cities (population 2,500–4,999) which suggests that this is a more important factor in small communities.

It seems safe to conclude that any teacher of physical education who hopes to succeed must exhibit excellent traits of character in all his behavior and must have teaching ability which will be considered satisfactory by school authorities. There are other items which determine the success of physical education teachers but these two appear to be the most important. Teacher training institutions should make sure to the best

TABLE III

CONDITIONS CONSIDERED MOST IMPORTANT FOR RETAINING PRESENT POSITION

CONDITIONS	SIZE OF CITY					TOTAL	PER CENT
	I over 100,000	II 30,000 to 100,000	III 10,000 to 30,000	IV 5,000 to 10,000	V 2,500 to 5,000		
Personal Character	97	35	53	70	108	363	43.0
Political Influence	—	—	2	1	2	5	.6
Winning Teams	9	9	14	20	39	91	11.0
Placating Superior School Officers	7	1	2	3	5	18	2.2
Teaching Ability	150	22	45	48	67	332	39.4
Popularity in Community ...	1	5	3	6	17	32	3.8
TOTAL QUESTIONNAIRES	264	72	119	148	238	841	100.0

of their ability that no person is graduated or sent into the field as a teacher who does not show every indication of the very highest type of character, professional ideals, and teaching ability.

Recruiting superior persons for teaching. If physical education is to attract and hold superior persons in the profession definite efforts should be made to recruit individuals of unusual ability for professional training. On both the undergraduate and graduate levels, scholarships and loan funds should be established to help superior students complete their preparation. This suggestion must not be confused with scholarships and subsidies for athletes who are material for varsity teams.

Efforts at recruiting should be directed especially at exceptional individuals on the graduate level who show promise of making some worthwhile contribution to physical education through research. Promising students of physical education should be encouraged to take a major part of their work in chemistry, physics, physiology, or psychology and to continue their graduate work and research in the aspects of one of these subjects which apply to physical education. Exceptional persons who have majored in some of these scientific fields should be encouraged to do their graduate research in the applications of these sciences to the problems of physical education. It no doubt would prove helpful if such scientifically trained persons had a background of preparation and experience in physical education, but unquestionably they could make valuable contributions without such preparation and experience. Observe, for example, the contributions that have been made and are continuing to be made to such a well established profession as medicine by persons who were not prepared as physicians: Pasteur was a chemist; MacLeod, one of the leaders in the production and use of insulin, is a physiologist; E. V. McCollum is a professor of biochemistry; and there are many scientists teaching and carrying on research in medical schools who do not have medical degrees. If physical education is to become firmly established on solid foundations it is essential that a body of accurate and well authenticated data be developed and organized as a basis for the development of sound programs. The most effective way to accumulate and organize these data is to attract into physical education a large number of superior individuals who have the interest and ability to carry on continuous programs of research.

The length of period of professional preparation. The period of professional preparation for teachers of physical education should cover at least four full academic years beyond high school graduation. Persons who wish to prepare for positions of greater responsibility in administration, supervision, or research should have five or more years of preparation. Williams[1] (himself an M. D.) states that:

Professional training in physical education for the higher levels (supervisorships, directorships, professorships) should be through the doctorate in education (Ph.D) with a major in physical education rather than through the doctor of medicine (M.D.)

a. The problems in physical education 20 years ago were considered to be essentially corrective; the problems today are essentially educational.

b. The older organization required the professor of physical education to serve also as college physician; today the health service in the college is increasingly assigned to a staff of physicians giving full time to health service.

c. The demands of modern medicine are so great, and the educational problems of physical education so pressing that it is inadvisable to have a combined position.

d. The feasibility of the Ph.D. for the higher positions in the field is indicated by numerous instances where this training is considered acceptable.

e. The doctor of medicine who knows neither physical education nor education is greatly handicapped. Numerous false steps in physical education can

[1] Jesse F. Williams, "Development of Professional Leadership in Physical Education," *The Pentathlon,* II (October, 1929), 6.

be attributed to those who thought that an M.D. gave them the right to speak concerning matters of which they were really quite uninformed.

McCurdy in a recent article emphasized the same facts.[1]

The 1928 Yearbook of the Department of Superintendence, of the National Education Association states that physical education teachers in junior and senior high schools should have four years of preparation, and the certification requirements of most states specify that teachers of physical education should have at least four years of preparation. Studies made by the National Education Association indicate that city school systems have increased the amount of preparation required of a teacher for initial appointment since 1928. This increase has been particularly rapid in respect to requiring four or more years of college work for appointment in junior high schools.

Summary. Teaching as a profession has made much progress during the past fifty years and has arrived at the point where it can be said to have at least semi-professional status. The success of a democratic form of government, which provides for universal suffrage, depends on the education of the masses of the people. In order to carry on successfully a public school system, equal to the responsibilities imposed on it, every teacher should be a superior individual who has been well educated.

Professional training in physical education has followed much the same path of development as the older professions of medicine and law. The apprenticeship and proprietary school periods have been passed. Most of the recognized professional training is now carried on in the universities and colleges.

Definite professional levels are developing in physical education which correspond to the professional levels in other professions. These levels are occupied by: (1) the physical education technician; (2) the teacher; (3) the director or supervisor; and (4) the research specialist.

Data concerning the demand for and supply of teachers are inadequate. It is highly desirable that continuing studies be carried on which will furnish the information needed to control more intelligently and accurately the supply of teachers.

In each state there should be an effective state program of teacher training. This program should provide for (1) the control of teacher-training agencies; (2) control of teacher-training budget; (3) centraliza-

---

[1] J. H. McCurdy, "Recent Trends in Physical Education Leadership," *Journal of Health and Physical Education*, VI (December, 1935), 19.

tion of authority for issuing certificates; (4) definite standards for teacher-training institutions; and (5) continuing research on the problems of teacher-training.

Institutions engaged in the preparation of teachers should select their students instead of admitting all who apply. A definite organized effort should be made to recruit superior persons for teaching. The minimum period of college preparation for teachers of physical education should be four years. Persons who wish to prepare for positions of greater responsibility should have five or more years of preparation.

QUESTIONS

1. Why is universal education of great importance in a democratic society?
2. Professional training in physical education has passed through what steps in its development?
3. What professional levels are represented in physical education?
4. What conditions cause the supply of teachers to be extremely variable?
5. Why is it important to have a state program of teacher training?
6. What principles should guide a state program of teacher training?
7. What criteria should be used in the selection of prospective teachers?
8. What characteristics are associated with successful teaching?
9. What desirable outcomes might be expected from recruiting superior persons for teaching and research in physical education?
10. What should be the extent of professional preparation for persons occupying the different professional levels in physical education?

REFERENCES

Nash, Jay B. (Editor). *Professional Preparation.* New York: A. S. Barnes and Company, 1935.

State Department of Education. *A Curriculum for the Professional Preparation of Physical Education Teachers for Secondary Schools.* Bulletin E-1. Sacramento: California State Printing Office, 1930.

Teacher Demand and Supply. Research Bulletin No. 5, Vol. IX, November, 1931. Washington: National Education Association, 1931.

Williams, Jesse Feiring. "Development of Professional Leadership in Physical Education," *The Pentathlon,* II (October, 1929) 6.

CHAPTER X

Principles Underlying Method

Sources of principles. The common sources of principles of method are (1) the observation and experience of practitioners in the schools, (2) the philosophy of education which one accepts, and the aims and objectives that are developed from this philosophy, (3) the psychology of education, and (4) the field of biology, particularly physiology and anatomy.

In formulating a statement of fundamental principles the possible contributions from these sources should be critically examined and evaluated. The ones should be sought which seem to be most nearly objective and which are based on what seems to be valid and reliable evidence. In organizing the statements of principles which are set forth on the following pages an effort has been made to use sound evidence from the various sources listed above, and to state the principles definitely and clearly.

Statement of principles. The principles underlying method are proposed in the following statements. Each of these statements will be discussed in more detail in the succeeding paragraphs of this chapter.

1. Organic development and desirable health habits and attitudes can be secured through healthful physical activity if it is carried on in a hygienic environment.

2. Every person is different from every other individual in a large number of different traits and characteristics.

3. Learning can be facilitated by a teacher who points out faults and errors to pupils and helps them to overcome weaknesses and remove their deficiencies.

4. Correct drill or skills helps to make the execution of these skills faster, more accurate, and automatic.

5. The wants, needs, and interests of a person provide the initiative and basic motivation for most of the activities in which one participates.

6. Contemporary social conditions indicate that educational activities should emphasize the socialization of individuals and of groups.

7. New experiences and learnings are interpreted and based on the previous experiences of an individual.

8. Interested and willing persons learn much more quickly and retain the learnings longer than individuals who are bored or who act in response to coercion.

9. Awareness by the learner of the objectives to be sought contributes to efficient learning.

10. Opportunities to put into actual use the things which are learned contribute to efficient learning.

11. Participation in physical activities that provide satisfaction in connection with desirable behavior, contributes to personality and character development.

12. Methods of management and control are intrinsically part of educational experiences in school.

13. Individuals develop the ability to assume responsibility by having experiences in which they serve as leaders.

14. Individuals learn many things at the same time and often the incidental learnings are of greater importance than the learnings which are primarily sought.

15. All learning takes place as the result of the activity of the learner. Self-directed activity on the part of children is much more valuable than activity directed and dominated by the teacher.

16. The growth and development of children takes place according to natural laws.

Developmental values of activity. *Organic development, and desirable health habits and attitudes can be secured through healthful physical activity if it is carried on in a hygienic environment.* This means that the activities themselves should be such as to contribute to the organic development of boys and girls, and that instructional methods should be used and an environment provided which will insure that no harm or hurt will happen to any of the pupils. One rarely hears nowadays of a physical education program in which boys and girls are encouraged to participate in events that are likely to cause prolonged effort or extreme fatigue.

But it is equally important that the methods of conducting activities, and the conditions under which they are carried on, shall contribute to the health of the pupils. The ventilation and cleanliness of the gymnasiums, locker rooms, and shower rooms must be as nearly perfect as it is possible to make them. The clothing worn by the pupils must be clean and provide adequate protection. The mats, horse, buck, and other pieces of apparatus must be clean. The floors of the gymnasiums,

[172]

corridors, stairs, locker and shower rooms must be maintained in a condition that will reduce to a minimum the danger of falling. The surfaces of outdoor play courts and fields must also be in excellent condition so as to avoid accidents and the annoyance of dust. Ropes, bars, ladders, and all other pieces of apparatus must be in perfect condition so that there will be no possibility of injuries attributable to defective apparatus. The facilities for drinking water must be maintained in an absolutely sanitary manner. The swimming pool and its environment must be maintained under conditions that reduce the danger of infection to a minimum. The supply of towels, soap, and bathing facilities must be managed so as to insure the highest possible degree of cleanliness.

The esthetic impression one gets from the surroundings in which physical education is carried on is believed by many teachers to have a health significance. This is believed to be true particularly in regard to mental health. In all situations it is incumbent on physical education teachers to arrange and maintain the physical education facilities in an attractive and pleasing manner. Even if the buildings themselves are relatively ugly, much can be done to improve their appearance. Important details include such things as having brightly varnished floors instead of dark oil-treated floors, appropriate wall plaques, statuary, mural designs, shields, posters, wall charts, and attractive bulletin boards. It is also important to emphasize the teaching of esthetic appreciations in class work, demonstrations, and pageants.[1]

Individual differences. *Every person is different from every other individual in a large number of different traits and characteristics.* It is a well established fact that every individual differs from every other individual in a large number of different traits and characteristics. In the seventh grade in a school, for example, there may be a 14-year-old boy who has matured early and has achieved the muscular strength and bodily size of most boys who are 18 years old. In the same grade there may be another boy of 14 years of age who has matured slowly and is only as big and strong as many other boys of 12 years. There may also be in a class some children who habitually maintain good posture and others who have poor and unattractive types of body carriage. The results of a medical examination may show that some are deficient in organic development or have some abnormality in organic functioning. Achievement tests in different physical activities will reveal a wide distribution

---

[1] For a discussion of this point see editorial by E. D. Mitchell, "An Esthetic Ideal for Physical Education," *Journal of Health and Physical Education*, V (December, 1934), 20.

of accomplishment in any unselected group. In like manner, the interests of pupils in the various activities of physical education are certain to differ widely.

There has not been a great deal done, however, toward finding the interests of pupils in physical education. It seems that teachers of physical education should be much more active in determining the interests of their pupils in order that teaching methods and activities may be selected in light of these interests. There have been spasmodic efforts of individual teachers to find the interests of their pupils by the use of informal questionnaires, and this procedure probably gives a teacher a general idea as to some of the decided preferences of his pupils. But there is a need for a more reputable, well-organized, scientific technique. Physical educators in their conversations and writings state rather glibly that the methods and content should be adapted to the interests of the pupils; yet very few of these teachers in actual practice make any effort to do anything about it.

Many leaders in education believe that the interests of individual pupils are of the greatest significance. They insist that it is on the basis of individual interests that new experiences with widened meanings can be built most effectively. The interests that pupils have in motor activities can be used successfully not only in teaching physical education more successfully but also as a means of leading on to further and broader activities. In many cases, for example, high school boys who were not interested in anything that the school had to offer became interested in some curricular offering after they had become established as successful athletes. The following quotation emphasizes the opportunities and responsibilities of a school to find and develop the interests of each pupil.

Every coach knows that many a star athlete who is down as a "flunker" would also be a star in some other field besides athletics if only the school were capable of arousing his interest in something else. The school is slowly coming around to a realization of this value in education, and would go much farther and faster were it not for the conservative cry of "frills" and "fads."

It is well recognized that not every student, athlete or no, of low mental development and sluggish interest in worth-while activity can be aroused to an active and sincere participation in some accepted phase of school work and life. It is the school's task to do its utmost, with the aid of the best knowledge of the day, to direct these sub-normal or one-sided pupils into better balance. Few cases are ever hopelessly beyond improvement.[1]

[1] Clarence Hines, "Scholarship among High School Athletes," *Scholastic Coach*, IV (October, 1934), 12.

Weedon [1] has proposed a technique for determining interest which appears to be valid and reliable. The work of Sonquist is also important in this connection, and forms of his Interest Finder are available for use with physical education classes. [2] All teachers of physical education could very profitably familiarize themselves with the work of these two writers.

Remedial teaching. *Learning can be facilitated by a teacher who points out faults and errors to pupils and helps them to overcome weaknesses and remove their deficiencies.*

One of the purposes in having classes in physical education under the leadership of teachers is to help pupils learn more quickly and efficiently. It is probably true that practically all individuals could learn to perform motor skills reasonably well if they were interested enough to keep trying and would continue practicing long enough. By the process of trial and error they no doubt would be able to achieve a rather high degree of skill. The assumption is, however, that a teacher can help pupils to discover their faults quickly and can suggest methods of practice which will result in the maximum degree of skill with the expenditure of the least amount of time and effort. Some teachers of physical education are not much more than clerks or custodians in charge of the facilities and supplies. They serve a very useful function as supervisors of the locker rooms, playgrounds, and gymnasiums, but do practically no real teaching. Every teacher of physical education should take seriously his responsibility to teach.

In many cases a pupil makes an error in only one part of a skill, with the result that the form and execution of the entire skill are poor and ineffective. In punting a football, for example, a boy may take the necessary steps, swing his leg and foot in good form, and follow through in the approved style, and yet his kick may be an absolute failure because the ball is too far out on the toe of his foot at the time of the impact. In such a case the teacher should correct this item in form immediately and show the pupil how to place the ball in the correct position on his foot. This explanation and demonstration should be followed by practice under the direction of the teacher.

In connection with many skills it is often possible to give tests which will help a teacher to diagnose the difficulties of his pupils more quickly

---

[1] Vivian Weedon, "A Technique for Determining Interest," *Educational Research Bulletin*, XIII (November 14 and December 12, 1934), 191–97, 231–34.

[2] David E. Sonquist, *Interests of Young Men*. New York: Association Press, 1931.

than would be possible by watching each individual in a large class. It is relatively easy to test large groups expeditiously in such skills as throwing, passing, and kicking for accuracy and distance; pivoting, scuffling, and dribbling; and most track and field events. Much can be learned concerning the ability of pupils in physical activities through the use of written tests of the informal and objective type such as true-false, completion, or multiple-choice.

In diagnosing the difficulties of pupils teachers should seek to help them analyze their performances so as to discover and recognize their own faults. This will help the pupils to know more clearly the difficulty which confronts them in each instance. After the problem has been recognized and described by the pupils they should suggest ways in which the execution of the skill might be improved, or how any other pertinent problem might be solved. The different proposals for the solution of the problem should be discussed and evaluated. Then the solutions which seem to be the best should be tried out in actual practice and finally a solution of the problem should be chosen in light of the tests which have been made.

These steps in the solution of a problem do not necessarily follow each other in the sequence described here. Two or more of these processes may take place simultaneously. It is important in good teaching, however, that the *activity* involved in taking each of these steps should be done to the greatest possible extent by the pupils.

Proper use of drill. *Correct drill on skills helps to make the execution of these skills faster, more accurate, and automatic.* The solution of many learning difficulties involves drill on fundamental skills. In motor learning, if one has to stop and think how to perform a skill the speed and expertness of execution will be greatly decreased. When a boy bats a baseball, his step and swing all form one smoothly coordinated skill. If it were necessary for him consciously to plan and execute the movements of all the different muscles involved in batting he would never hit the ball. All a batter thinks about is hitting the ball. He gives no thought to his feet, his elbow, the muscles in his abdomen, or the muscles in his shoulders.

Drill should be carried on for the purpose of perfecting skills after the pupils have had experiences which cause them to understand the need for and meaning of the drill. The pupils must realize the necessity of drill if it is to have maximum educational value. To illustrate this fact an example might be taken from basketball. Assume that you are teaching a class of junior high school boys who have had no previous experiences with the game. If they were placed in lines and required to practice the pivot, the activity would have very little meaning to them and it would be only a short time before the boys would be bored with the exercise. If, however, the game is explained and the pupils are permitted to play for a short time, they see the need of being able to pivot well and to develop other fundamental skills. After they realize the importance of a relatively high degree of expertness in these skills they participate in the drill on fundamentals much more intelligently and with much better results.

Motivation of activities. *The wants, needs, and interests of a person provide the initiative and basic motivation for most of the activities in which one participates.* Teachers should strive to stimulate and develop in their pupils the initiative for educational activity. In order to accomplish this it is essential that boys and girls participate in purposeful activities out of which will arise clearly recognized wants and interests. Some human wants and interests come from inborn tendencies but most are apparently the result of experiences an individual has. A person who has many broad and varied experiences will increase the number and variety of his shared interests and wants. He will also be better qualified to satisfy his wants. Teachers should seek to improve the quality and increase the number of interests and wants of their pupils. Physical education is particularly rich in opportunities for increasing and enriching the recreational and social interests of boys and girls.

There are often pupils in physical education classes whose experiences in connection with physical education have been unusually limited and restricted. Sometimes they are children who have come from rural districts but frequently they are city children whose home, school, or social background has been such as to restrict the normal expression of their play interests. These pupils in many instances have no knowledge or appreciation of the spirit or rules of games and are markedly deficient in skill. A few physically retarded children of this kind in a class can offer teaching problems that may become annoying if not a serious handicap to efficient teaching.

Some teachers state that if they had the authority to reorganize school classifications they would group all pupils homogeneously on the basis of achievement in motor activities. This procedure would place the children who are handicapped by inadequate skills in classes with children

[177]

much younger, smaller, and more childish. It would be highly objectionable, furthermore, because it would interfere with the wholesome development of personality both in the retarded pupils and in the normal group of younger children. It would not contribute to the best educational results in either group.

The solution of this problem in most cases should consist of making every reasonable effort to broaden the interests and enrich the experiences of these pupils. Some of the techniques of doing this include (1) encouraging the children to read interesting stories of sports and games; (2) using stories, anecdotes, and pictures by the teacher in an effort to develop a broader appreciation and understanding of the spirit and traditions of games; (3) providing in the daily programs some simple and easy activities that all the pupils are able to do well; (4) outlining certain practice exercises for the retarded pupils that will help them to improve their fundamental skills; and (5) giving as much individual help and instruction for these pupils as the teacher can possibly give without neglecting the instruction of the other members of the class.

Socialization through physical education. *Contemporary social conditions indicate that educational activities should emphasize the socialization of individuals and of groups.* Physical education should be organized and taught in a way that will emphasize the social experiences that are inherent in a large number of physical education situations. Although the hygienic and developmental values of physical education are important, the opportunities for social training are the most significant of the contributions that are made to the education of children by physical education. The emphasis on playing together, abiding by the rules, putting forth one's best efforts, carrying through to completion a worthwhile undertaking, taking the bumps and punishments of games without whining, and other forms of social behavior are eminently worthwhile.

It has been pointed out that the objectiveness of experiences in physical education cause them to be of particular value in the socialization of boys and girls. The ability of individuals to comprehend the meanings and personal significance of the experiences gained in physical education is another thing which accentuates its socializing values.

It should be kept in mind, however, in teaching physical education that there are no private virtues. All forms of reactions are of, about, from, or toward persons or things. A person cannot be honest, fair, cooperative, or loyal entirely divorced from other people and other aspects

[178]

of his environment. All behavior of an individual in modern society has a social significance. There are practically no situations in civilized society in which a person should feel free to do entirely as he pleases without any consideration of the effect of his behavior on others.

Teachers of physical education, therefore, should definitely plan to develop desirable social habits and attitudes in their pupils. They should also be on the alert to take advantage of all incidental opportunities which arise to help boys and girls make good ways of behaving habitual. In order to do this most efficiently and effectively it is essential that teachers be familiar with the nature of children and how they grow and learn.

The meaning of experience. *New experiences and learnings are interpreted and based on the previous experiences of an individual.* A person thinks and learns in terms of the meanings which he has accumulated through experience. Persons who use an expression such as "that does not make sense to me" are attempting to convey the idea that they have never had any experiences which enable them to comprehend the new idea or experience. If, for example, a teacher suggests playground baseball to a group of boys who had never heard of playground baseball, the suggestion has very few meanings to them. But they would understand something about the game if he told them that the game is played something like the regular game of baseball, that the bases are forty-five feet apart, the ball is about twelve inches in circumference, and that the pitcher must toss the ball to the batter in an underhand fashion. In such a case the new game would begin to take on meanings as the result of previous experiences of the boys in regular baseball.

In order for a generation or an individual to profit most from the experiences of generations and individuals who have gone before it is necessary that they accept the results of the experiences of others without actually repeating the experiences. It should not be necessary for a boy to be run over by an automobile or to jump off an office building in order to learn the hazard and pain of such activities. If we insisted that all educational experiences must be first-hand it would be necessary for each generation to begin where the human race began and practically all progress of civilization would stop. It is impossible to state definitely, of course, the number, variety, and proportion of educational experiences which should be first-hand.

First-hand experiences are usually more vital and innately meaningful than second-hand experiences. If, for instance, a teacher introduced

[179]

speedball to a class by telling them it is played with a round inflated ball and combined some of the characteristics of basketball, football, and soccer the new game might take on some meaning for them if they were familiar with the other games.

In teaching practically all physical education activities the pupils should be permitted to begin participation as quickly as possible with the minimum amount of time spent in explanation. After gaining first-hand experience in this way they should be introduced to the finer and more technical aspects of the games. They will then be more ready for practicing some of the highly developed fundamentals and techniques which have been perfected over long periods of time by generations of expert players in the same and related sports.

The place of subject matter in physical education. *The fact has been emphasized that an organism and its environment are so closely related that practically they cannot be differentiated.* Personality is the result of the combination of one's biological inheritance and of his experiences since birth. Experience comes from the interaction of an organism and its environment. The more limited and restricted is one's environment, the fewer and more barren will be his experiences. Experience consists of activity. When one has an experience, some form of behavior takes place. It is not necessarily motor activity; it may be mental or emotional, but some modification in ways of behaving has occurred. These facts indicate, therefore, that the subject matter taught in physical education must be such as to provide the largest possible number of first-hand experiences.

When a person has an experience he has learned a new way of reacting or of behaving to the stimuli in a situation. If one reads or hears about the knowledge that has been accumulated by the human race during the past he becomes familiar with the ways of reacting or of behaving that were learned by other individuals who have gone before. In either case, whether one is learning through first-hand experience or second-hand experience, he is learning "ways of behaving." In physical education, therefore, as in all other phases of education, the things that should be taught primarily are ways of behaving. These may be reactions that are conducive to the wholesome exercise of the impulsive and emotional responses, the establishment of social ideals or standards, the development of organic power and health, the promotion of safety, or the protection of health. In any event it is a way of reacting or of behaving which has been learned. It is indicated, therefore, that in teaching physical education emphasis should be placed on behavior that will actually function in the lives of the pupils.

Interest as motivation of learning. *Interested and willing persons learn much more quickly and retain the learnings longer than individuals who are bored or who act in response to coercion.* Activities which thoroughly call forth the powers of an individual are interesting to him. A person is interested in an activity when the material or subject matter to be learned is compatible with his innate tendencies, his habits, and his previous experiences. Interest which is real and sound furnishes the most desirable and highest type of motive for learning. Most of the natural, informal, play activities taught in physical education are activities in which there is inherently a motivating interest. The motive is *in* the activity itself and therefore it is not necessary to stimulate or create a motive *for* the activity. They do not have to be *made* interesting; they are in most instances activities which are naturally and inherently interesting to boys and girls.

In many cases the main problem in physical education is not so much to arouse interest as it is to keep from killing the interest children already have. Frequently, as the result of poor leadership, the use of unwise methods, or the choice of unsuitable subject matter, pupils are caused to dislike activities in which they normally would be interested. If very many boys or girls dislike physical education and seek to avoid taking part in it, there is a strong probability that there is something wrong with the curriculum or the teacher. Often teachers conclude that pupils who do not like to participate in the physical education program are stubborn, obstinate, contrary, or relatively unintelligent. Before the blame is placed on the pupils a teacher should make a critical evaluation of himself, the methods he uses, and the content of the program.

The period over which an individual can keep a sustained purpose is usually spoken of as his interest span. As a person increases and broadens his experiences, he broadens the meanings each new experience has for him. An individual who has had only a few experiences of narrow scope is not able to see much significance or meaning in any new experiences he might have.

The length of the interest span is determined to a considerable extent by the breadth of meaning one is able to get from the activities in which he is taking part. If they are meaningful and purposeful to him he is likely to be interested for a relatively long period. Most normal children increase and broaden their experiences as they grow older and thereby increase their interest span. The interest span of young children is usually quite short and becomes progressively longer as they become older. A child in the first grade, for example, may be interested in playing the game of *cat and rat* for only about ten minutes, whereas boys in senior high school may be eager to practice football for two hours each afternoon for five afternoons each week.

In teaching physical education, teachers should present new ideas, problems, and skills that are within the interest span of the pupils, but they should also be striving continuously to stimulate and develop new, broader, and more sustained interests.

Importance of specific objectives. *Awareness by the learner of the objectives to be sought contributes to efficient learning.* Definite and specific goals to be accomplished during each semester or term should be clearly understood by all pupils. A statement of these goals should be given ample publicity, so there will be no question as to whether all pupils are familiar with them. The teacher should discuss the goals with the pupils in class, and copies should be posted on the school bulletin boards and published in the school paper. It is also advisable to send a copy of the goals to the parents of all children in school.

Specific goals should be set up for each activity included in the physical education program. Most programs in junior high schools, for example, include stunts, games, track and field athletics, water activities, athletic sports, rhythms, outing activities, and individual gymnastics. To illustrate, the goals to be achieved in stunts might be set forth by preparing a list of twenty-five stunts arranged in five groups according to type of stunts. Each pupil might be expected to select and learn well at least seven new stunts during a semester, at least one of which should be chosen from each of the five groups. In all other forms of activity the pupils should know clearly the specific goals for which they are striving.

It is also important that the instruction be organized and planned in a way that will enable each pupil to know frequently what progress he is making toward the achievement of the goals. The common practice of track coaches in having "time trials" each Friday afternoon is an example of the techniques that might be used to help pupils know the progress that they are making. The use of achievement norms and scales based on the performances of large numbers of children has also proved to be an interesting and valuable device in connection with this problem. Such devices as bar graphs, profile graphs, and charts have been of much help to many teachers. Showing the percentile rank of test scores of pupils in a given grade or group is another method of helping pupils evaluate their progress.

Use of things learned. *Opportunities to put into actual use the things which are learned contribute to efficient learning.* Putting into actual use the skills which have been learned in physical education classes is one of the most effective means of associating satisfaction with the learning of motor skills. In teaching physical education it is important that many opportunities be provided for pupils to play games in which they can actually use the fundamental skills they have learned. Intramural leagues, carried on in the afternoon after school is dismissed, and during the long noon period in some schools, provide occasions for the demonstration by pupils of the things they have learned. Many other opportunities for boys and girls to use the activities learned in physical education may be found in field days, play days, athletic carnivals, tournaments, meets, and play festivals. The use of achievement tests also provides a means for children to demonstrate the things they have learned.

Character and personality development. *Participation in physical activities that provide satisfaction in connection with desirable behavior contributes to personality and character development.* This belief is based on the theory that motor expression is of fundamental importance in growth and learning. The proponents of this theory emphasize group participation in all forms of educational experiences, including physical education. Merely listening to someone tell about the desirable ways of behaving or reading about social cooperation are not effective ways of habituating the desired behavior. It is on this principle that the modern activities curriculum is largely based.

Appropriate control in classes. *Methods of management and control are intrinsically part of educational experiences in school.* In any teaching situation it is necessary to have enough organization and discipline to make it possible for the class to be conducted efficiently and for learning to take place. There are some activities such as certain exercises on apparatus that require a routinized form of management and procedure in order that each individual may take his turn promptly in good form. Other activities, such as marching and calisthenics, following tradition, have always used a formal type of discipline and control. There are other kinds of activities which include dancing, sports, athletics, and swimming which ordinarily are conducted in an informal and natural

[183]

way. It is highly desirable that these natural play activities be taught in a way that will emphasize self-control and self-direction on the part of the pupils. The players should be encouraged to make conscious choices between conflicting lines of action, and to attempt the intelligent solution of problems which arise.

Direction of activities by pupils. *Individuals develop the ability to assume responsibility by having experiences in which they serve as leaders.* Every effort should be made to plan and teach physical education in a way that will make the maximum use of pupil leadership. It is probably much easier to conduct teacher-dominated classes than it is to provide opportunities for pupils to assume responsibilities in the direction of these activities. It is essential, however, that pupils be encouraged to assume responsibility and assert themselves in situations that require leadership.

One of the more common ways of providing experiences for boys and girls to act as leaders is to let them serve as captains, squad leaders, scorers, and officials. Experiences of this kind can be easily provided in connection with the regular classes in physical education and in special events such as tournaments, meets, and play days.

Beginning in the first grade and continuing throughout the entire school emphasis should be placed on activities directed by the pupils. Many teachers apparently do not believe that children have sufficient maturity and ability to act as squad leaders and in other positions of responsibility. Experiences covering several years of experimentation in Detroit, Michigan, in Montclair, New Jersey, and in other places have shown that even first grade children can receive much benefit by serving as squad leaders.

It is evident, of course, that unlimited freedom and responsibility cannot be given to pupils who have never had any opportunity to direct their own actions and control their own behavior. Children who have always been repressed and subordinated by parents and teachers should be permitted to have a limited amount of responsibility and restrained freedom at the beginning of the school year. As they increase in ability to practice self-direction and self-control they should gradually be encouraged to assume responsibility for the direction of class activities. LaSalle [1] outlines a series of steps that might be followed in sequence in physical education classes for the development of leadership qualities.

[1] Dorothy LaSalle, *Play Activities for Elementary Schools,* pp. 11–13. New York: A. S. Barnes and Company, 1926.

Attendant learnings. *Individuals learn many things at the same time and in a large number of instances the incidental learnings are of greater importance than the learnings which are primarily sought.* A teacher is likely to assume that the only things a pupil learns during a class period or during the participation periods are the skills and knowledge of the activities that are being taught. In reality it is no doubt true in many situations that the other things learned by pupils are more numerous and important than the primary things being taught by the teacher.

A group of boys would no doubt improve their skill in basketball during the practice periods of two hours in the afternoons during a semester. They would also develop some habits, attitudes, and ideals that would probably be of more importance in shaping their personalities and characters than all the skills which they might learn.

Conscientious teachers must realize that these kinds of learnings are taking place all the time. In setting up teaching situations they must recognize their importance and attempt to direct the experiences of the pupils so that the simultaneous learnings will be of definite positive value. This is one of the reasons why it is imperative that teachers of physical education be individuals of excellent personality and high ideals.

Learning as an active process. *All learning takes place as the result of the activity of the learner. Self-directed activity on the part of children is much more valuable than activity directed and dominated by the teacher.* "We learn to do by doing" is a catch phrase that has been used for many years to emphasize the fact that efficient learning is dependent on the activity of the learner. Practically no learning takes place by absorption. Learning takes place most effectively when the learner is interested and actively trying to learn. It can be seen, therefore, that participation in interesting activities that permit conscious choices and decisions to be made by the players provides valuable educational experiences.

Teachers should be cognizant of these facts and attempt at all times to encourage their pupils to try actively and enthusiastically to learn the activities being taught. If boys and girls merely hear someone describe how to execute a dance or to swim they will not learn much about these activities. However, if they actively practice the correct forms in these events they will perfect the skills rapidly. Efficient learning depends on interested pupils participating in correct practice which results in satisfaction to them.

[185]

Laws of growth and maturation. *The growth and development of children take place according to natural laws.* There is a large body of literature on the growth of children. Some of this material has been discussed in Chapter III on the Biological Foundations of Physical Education. Efficient and ambitious teachers should seek to broaden their professional background by becoming familiar with this material. The laws which govern the growth of children are of much importance to all teachers but are of particular significance to teachers of physical education.

It is generally recognized that most human beings will achieve a certain anatomical, physiological, mental, emotional, and social maturity as the result of natural growth. This is true in regard to spelling ability, artistic talent, musical interests, organic development, and many other traits and characteristics. It is known also that one's environment and experiences have much to do with the retardation or acceleration of the growth of these traits. Sunshine, food, rest, freedom from disease, clothing, and exercise are some of the things that influence physical growth. Factors of the environment such as training, family interests, and frequent exposure to favorable and pleasing experiences likewise have much to do with the growth of mental and cultural characteristics. It is the function of physical education teachers, therefore, to guide and direct along wholesome lines the natural growth of children which takes place as the result of maturation. And also they should be especially concerned with helping their pupils achieve an organic, mental, and cultural development beyond that which might take place as the result of natural growth and maturation. In this way physical education should make a real contribution toward helping boys and girls develop in a way that they can live fuller, richer, happier lives and at the same time be of the maximum service to society.

The implications of the laws of growth. It may be seen, therefore, that an understanding of the laws of growth is of much significance in the teaching of physical education. Such knowledge would enable teachers to plan their programs in conformity with the characteristics of children at different levels of growth. The instruction and subject matter can be adapted to the interests and abilities of the pupils. Pupils of superior ability may be stimulated to reach a higher level of achievement.

The regularity and constancy of growth indicates that pupils should make regular progress throughout all age levels and that dependence should not be placed on spurts of learning at any one period of time.

The data on growth also point to the fact that habits, attitudes, ideals and the ability to reason and make judgments should be developed at all ages and need not be emphasized irregularly during different ages. Older and more mature children should be expected to learn more difficult things but the types of learnings are not necessarily different at various age levels.

A summary of the laws of growth. The following summary of the general laws of growth, by Burton, should prove helpful to teachers:

1. Growth is determined by both heredity and environment.
2. Growth is, in general, regular and even. It is not saltatory and irregular.
3. Growth in individuals, on the average, usually maintains the pace at which it starts.
4. Growth in a given individual may vary greatly from the average but will be in accord with the general laws.
5. Growth of various separate items is at different rates, maturity is achieved at different times, but these differentials are subordinate to the general laws.
6. Growth shows slight oscillations in rate at various times, varying with individuals and items. There are some sex and race differences.
7. Growth irregularities in the sense of serious variation from expectancy are usually caused by outside agencies.
8. Growth is rounded, the factors being correlated positively with one another, rather than uneven in amount and power.[1]

Summary. Principles of method are the fundamental concepts on which the development of methods can be based. The principles underlying methods are not so exact and objective as are the laws and principles in physics and engineering, but they are established well enough to justify their use. The common sources of data on which to base principles of method are: (1) the observation and experience of practitioners in the schools; (2) the philosophy and objectives of education; (3) educational psychology; and (4) biology, particularly physiology and anatomy.

The principles underlying method are proposed in the following statements.

1. Organic development and desirable health habits and attitudes can be secured through healthful physical activity if it is carried on in a hygienic environment.

2. Every person is different from every other individual in a large number of different traits and characteristics.

[1] William H. Burton, *Introduction to Education,* pp. 485–86. New York: D. Appleton-Century Company, 1934.

3. Learning can be facilitated by a teacher who points out faults and errors to pupils and helps them to overcome weaknesses and remove their deficiencies.

4. Correct drill on skills helps to make the execution of these skills faster, more accurate, and automatic.

5. The wants, needs, and interests of a person provide the initiative and basic motivation for most of the activities in which one participates.

6. Contemporary social conditions indicate that educational activities should emphasize the socialization of individuals and of groups.

7. New experiences and learnings are interpreted and based on the previous experiences of an individual.

8. Interested and willing persons learn much more quickly and retain the learnings longer than individuals who are bored or who learn as the result of coercion.

9. Awareness by the learner of the objectives to be sought contributes to efficient learning.

10. Opportunities to put into actual use the things which are learned contribute to efficient learning.

11. Participation in physical activities, that provide satisfaction in connection with desirable behavior, contributes to personality and character development.

12. Methods of management and control are intrinsically part of educational experiences in school.

13. Individuals develop the ability to assume responsibility by having experiences in which they serve as leaders.

14. Individuals learn many things at the same time and in a large number of instances the incidental learnings are of greater importance than the learnings which are primarily sought.

15. All learning takes place as the result of the activity of the learner. Self-directed activity on the part of children is much more valuable than activity directed and dominated by the teachers.

16. The growth and development of children takes place according to natural laws.

QUESTIONS

1. What are principles of methods and how may they be of help to teachers of physical education?
2. How do the principles underlying method compare in objectivity and accuracy with principles in physics and engineering?

3. What are the more common sources of data on which to base principles of method?

4. What methods of organization and instruction should be used in order to help pupils secure desirable developmental values through participation in physical education?

5. In what ways should the individual differences of children influence methods?

6. In what ways may drill be used to overcome learning difficulties?

7. What are some of the methods of motivation that might be used to broaden the interests and enrich the experiences in physical education of retarded children?

8. In what ways are many situations in physical education particularly rich in opportunities for the socialization of children?

9. What are some of the reasons why a clear statement of specific objectives is of great importance in teaching physical education?

10. The principle of "learning by doing" should influence in what ways the methods used by teachers?

REFERENCES

Burton, William H. *Introduction to Education.* New York: D. Appleton-Century Company, 1934.

Caswell, Hollis L., and Campbell, Doak S. *Curriculum Development.* New York: American Book Company, 1935.

Sharman, Jackson R. *The Teaching of Physical Education.* New York: A. S. Barnes and Company, 1936.

Williams, Jesse Feiring, Dambach, John I., and Schwendener, Norma. *Methods in Physical Education.* Philadelphia: W. B. Saunders Company, 1932.

CHAPTER XI

Principles of Administration

❧

Definition of administration. Administration is frequently thought of as being synonymous with management, regulation, execution, or dispensation. In connection with school work, however, the word *administration* is accepted as the broader and more inclusive term; the functions implied by the other terms are considered as part of administration and subordinate to it. Administration in physical education involves the integration of activities which are concerned specifically with providing educational experiences for pupils. This includes problems of the curriculum, teaching staff, equipment and facilities. It involves also problems of a business and financial nature. It is convenient at times to consider these different kinds of problems separately but in practice they cannot be separated. The educational and business aspects of administration are interdependent and interrelated. Each is tied to the other in the practical administration of the physical education program.

One of the main jobs of administration in physical education is to integrate the objectives of the program, the activities of the teachers and pupils, and the materials that are used. The success of the efforts should be judged by the smoothness and effectiveness with which the organism works in achieving the objectives. Merely placing the objectives, personnel, and materials in proximity to each other will not automatically result in an efficiently functioning organism. Administration must fuse these parts into an integrated unit.

The administration of school physical education may be defined as that part of the school program which is concerned with the organization, management, regulation, and control of personnel and materials so that they will function smoothly, efficiently, and effectively as an integrated whole in achieving the desired goals.

General function of administration. The general function of administration is to manage matters in such a way as to facilitate the effective teaching and guiding of pupils. The provision of effective opportunities for children to learn is the main function of the school and all school activities should be directed to that end. Historically, the position of educational administrator developed in this country as schools grew beyond the size where the head teacher could satisfactorily handle all the details involved in running a school or a group of schools. Administrators should seek to smooth the path for teachers so that they may teach and be free to the greatest possible degree from outside duties and responsibilities in connection with the operation of the school.

Unfortunately this point of view is not dominant with all persons engaged in the administration of physical education. Some individuals who occupy administrative positions are of the opinion, apparently, that a big part of their job is to check up on teachers, to be an inspector or boss. There are a large number of others, however, who really function as helpers to teachers and make it much easier for the real work of teaching physical education to be carried on.

Types of administration. The administration of physical education in schools is concerned primarily with the management of human beings in their various relationships which occur in connection with participation in physical activities. The management of persons in situations of this kind implies a definition and statement of the function of the school program of physical education; the objectives of the program; the size, qualifications, and duties of the teaching staff; the money, supplies, equipment, and facilities available for use in physical education; the curriculum to be taught; and the cooperative relationships that must be maintained in regard to all these items.

There are at least three distinct types of administration, or management of persons, that are used in physical education. One type follows the path of least resistance, develops much skill in evading issues, formulates no definite program, sets up no objectives to be achieved, and is primarily concerned with maintaining the status quo. A second type of administration is personified in the individual of the "go-getter" and "efficiency expert" type. This form of administration usually has for its motivating force a person of dominating personality who prescribes the program and the objectives and arbitrarily directs the activities of the staff. Frequently results are achieved promptly under this type of administration. The interests and originality of the other members of the staff are likely to be suppressed, however, with the result that the progress and development which come from the cooperative pooling and discussion of interests and ideas are stifled. The third type of administration places much emphasis on cooperative effort. The program, objectives, and procedures are determined in a democratic manner by the persons involved. The distinction between professional superiors and inferiors tends to disappear. The conscientious and original efforts of individuals are recognized and encouraged. This type of administration is believed to be best in practically all school situations, and throughout this chapter administrative practices will be recommended which conform to this policy of administration.

Administration a functional process. The integration and fusing of the objectives, personnel, and materials into a functioning organism should be the goal of administration in physical education. Administrative procedures should be recognized as means of accomplishing the objectives of physical education and not as ends in themselves. This calls for the organization of the program within the school to be on a functional basis. Legislation, execution, and appraisement must all go together. A true analogy cannot be made between teaching and manufacturing as is often attempted by some writers and speakers. The functions of a teacher naturally include duties which involve planning the program, carrying it out, and measuring the achievements. It is a mistake, therefore, to set up a plan of organization and administration of physical education which provides for some persons to prepare the program, others to do the teaching, and still others to measure the results. The entire process should be unified in order that the accepted objectives may be achieved successfully.

The techniques of administration which are recommended in this chapter are based on the conception of administration as a functional process and not as a separate series of procedures, each organized into different units or compartments.

Types of school organization. The administrative relationship of the physical education department to the rest of the school organization is another aspect of physical education which is significant in any consideration of principles of administration. There are two types of administrative organization of schools which are fairly common. These may be designated as the *empirical* and *functional* types. The *empirical* type of organization is guided by observation and experience rather than by principles. The *functional* type of organization is based on the principle that school activities should be grouped according to the functions they perform.

Under an empirical type of administrative organization the things which appear to be related are placed under the same administrative head. Expediency also often plays an important part in this kind of organization. In a school system organized on this basis there is usually a department of physical and health education, which includes health service and supervision, health instruction, and physical education. The division having to do with physical education in most schools is responsible for inter-institutional athletic competition, including the financial and business matters. Under this kind of organization the business affairs, the supervision of instruction, the medical service, the supervision of part of the school plant, and the instruction of pupils are all placed in the same department. It is easy to see what an administrative hodgepodge would result if all, or even several, departments in the school were charged with many different types of functions such as these.

A large number of city school systems and colleges have organized their programs of physical and health education on an empirical basis. In many, the organization has held together as the result of the strength of the personalities involved or because the administrative officers and school boards have exerted an unusual and artificial pressure to make the organization succeed. In many other institutions such an organization has broken down completely. Numerous thoughtful school administrators doubt that an empirical organization of physical and health education will operate with reasonable efficiency along its various lines of responsibility in any case.

With a functional type of administrative organization the school activities would be organized in departments according to function. For example, all instructional activities would be in one department, business matters in another, child accounting and attendance in still another, and public relations in a fourth department. In a large city school system each of these different functional departments would be under the immediate direction of an assistant superintendent. In a small school system all of these departments would be directed by the superintendent of schools. Under an organization of this kind all instruction, including the instruction in physical and health education, would be in the same department; all business matters, such as purchases and payment of salaries, would be in the same department; and all public relations activities would be handled by the same department.

Under a functional type of administration there should be two service units which are directly responsible to the superintendent of schools. They should be known as the "Psychological Service" and the "Health Service." The psychological service should be under the charge of a psychologist. The health service should be under the charge of a physician. Neither of these persons should have any administrative responsibilities. As the names imply, the units should be strictly service organizations. If the principal and faculty of a school, for example, wished to have a medical examination of all the pupils in the school they would call on the health service to make the examination and to furnish the teachers with a detailed report of the results of the medical examination. The teachers could then use the results of the medical examination as a guide in planning the educational program of the children.

Teachers of physical education should be familiar with both types of organization in order that they will be qualified to render the best professional service possible under either plan of administration. The author believes, however, that it will be only a relatively short time until the better school systems are organized on a functional basis. When that time comes, teachers and supervisors of physical education can give their undivided attention to the important job of teaching children, and will not be required to spend a large part of their interest and energy in serving as business agents, publicity directors, or school physicians.

Principles of administration. The fundamental concepts, which are believed to be true, that underlie the administration of physical education are summarized in the following statements. They relate to philosophy, aims, policies, curriculum experiences, facilities, evaluation, personnel, and public relations. Generalizations such as these should have a wide applicability to many specific administrative problems in physical education. It is clearly impractical and unwise for anyone to attempt to state the specific administrative techniques which should be used in connection with the innumerable situations which arise in managing and directing a program. Basic principles, however, should provide a sound foundation on which to build. Each of the statements proposed in this paragraph will be discussed in more detail later.

1. Administrative procedures must be consistent with a sound social philosophy and philosophy of education.

2. Administration must propose and support a definite statement of policies and aims.

3. Administration must be the means of making it possible for children to have experiences which will help accomplish the objectives of education. Administration should not be an end within itself.

4. Administration must provide and maintain adequate facilities and equipment for the physical education program.

5. The means, procedures, and routine which are set up by administration should be based largely on tested knowledge.

[194]

6. Administration must set up a plan of organization which provides clear and direct lines of control and responsibility.

7. The means of appraisal and evaluation of the results of accepted policies and practices must be provided by administration.

8. Administration must expedite changes in policies and procedures when such changes are indicated by adequate evidence.

9. Administration must provide for adaptations, changes, and experimentation in the adopted policies, and for the evaluation of the results of these adaptations, changes, and experiments.

10. Administration must provide for the cooperative efforts and growth of all persons engaged in carrying out the school program.

11. Administration should bring about the coordination and integration of the activities of teachers, pupils, and other individuals and organizations in the community.

12. The interpretation of physical education to the general public and to the members of the teaching body must be accomplished by administration.

Philosophy underlying administration. *Administrative procedures must be consistent with a sound social philosophy and philosophy of education.* Teachers are often heard to state that it does not do them any good to study, read, and get progressive ideas because their principals or superintendents operate the schools in such a dogmatic and autocratic manner that it is almost impossible for individual teachers to apply a sound philosophy. Comments such as this illustrate only one of the serious evils which result from administrative procedures that are not in line with sound social and educational principles. The direct and indirect effects on the pupils of poorly conceived administration are bad.

Democracy as a form of social and political organization is accepted as being desirable by the majority of teachers and other citizens. Since this is true all school activities should be conducted so as to provide experiences in democratic living and behavior for the teachers and pupils. Autocratic "cracking-the-whip" methods may appear for a limited period of time to get results effectively, but more lasting outcomes can be secured through intelligent and willing cooperation.

Support of policies. *Administration must propose and support a definite statement of policies and aims.* A clear understanding of the aims of the program and of the policies to be used in achieving these aims is essential in order that all members of a staff may work together smoothly and effectively. In many situations there is a certain degree of indifference and friction which is due to the ignorance of different individuals and groups in the department concerning the aims that are held by other staff members. In nearly all cases where there is a lack of cohesion and cooperation in a department it is caused in part by the failure of administration to secure a common understanding of the aims and policies.

After the aims and policies are adopted by the staff it is the duty of the administrative officers to support and carry them out. In nearly all situations the stated aims will be criticized and objections to the policies will be raised, but the persons charged with the responsibility of administration should consistently and tactfully hold to them until careful consideration indicates that they should be modified.

In a large number of schools the policies are not defined clearly enough for teachers to become familiar with them easily. In such cases the policies emerge and become evident from time to time throughout the school year. This procedure reveals a lack of organization and planning, and should be avoided in sound administrative practice.

Educational experiences. *Administration must be the means of making it possible for children to have experiences which will help accomplish the objectives of education. Administration should not be an end within itself.* Cynical teachers sometimes say that administrators and the machinery of administration are the greatest handicaps to successful teaching which they confront. It is also probably true that in some cases attending useless meetings, filling out meaningless reports, and performing other nonessential functions consumes an undue amount of the time and energy of teachers. All administrative procedures should be directed toward making it easier for teachers to plan and guide the educational experiences of children. It can easily be understood how a school or department which provides an excellent form of education might not operate as mechanically and automatically as some administrators desire. Quietness and the lack of problems are not the best criteria for judging educational efficiency and effectiveness.

Administration should be guided by the modern viewpoints that education is a process of growth through experience and that the most valuable educational experiences are gained through the self-directed activity of the learner. Unless the school situations are planned with this concept in mind it is very difficult for pupil initiative and leadership to be developed as successfully as they otherwise might be.

Adequate facilities and equipment. *Administration must pro-*

vide and maintain adequate facilities and equipment for the physical education program. Many valuable and interesting physical education activities can be carried on with a very minimum of facilities and equipment. And no teacher should give up hope and fail to put forth his best efforts because of the lack of an elaborate physical lay-out. It is highly desirable, however, to have adequate facilities and equipment to carry on a broad program of activities suited to the needs of the pupils. There are a large number of activities which are highly desirable that cannot be undertaken unless the facilities are available for them. Swimming, for example, requires a pool or some other body of water; a piano or phonograph is necessary for dancing; balls, bats, and nets are essential for many games; a relatively large plot of level ground is required for most of the highly organized team games; and several items of equipment are necessary for remedial exercises.

Successful execution of a comprehensive program depends almost as much on adequate expendable supplies as it does on more permanent facilities such as gymnasiums and swimming pools. If, for example, a teacher and a class were engaged in drill on shooting baskets, dribbling, or passing it would be necessary that a large enough number of good basketballs be available to enable each pupil to practice the skill correctly many times during each period. If each player has an opportunity to practice with a ball only five or six times during a class period he will make practically no improvement. Some school administrators seem to think, at times, that a very limited number of balls, bats, nets, mats. and other kinds of supplies are adequate for large classes in physical education. The same individuals will agree that every child must have a pencil and paper in learning to write and that each pupil must have the use of a typewriter in practicing typing. It must be recognized that in learning skills in physical education frequent and continued repetition plays an important part just as it does in perfecting other types of motor skills, and that adequate supplies are essential to successful teaching and practice.

Scientific basis of administration. *The means, procedures, and routine which are set up by administration should be based largely on tested knowledge.* Rule-of-thumb procedures and untried methods are entirely inappropriate in the administration of physical education when scientifically established data are available as a foundation on which to base procedures. There remain many problems in physical education, the solution of which must be attempted without recourse to adequate scientific data, but there is still a widespread failure on the part of physical educators to use the methods that have been accurately authenticated.

The neglect of techniques available for the classification of pupils in physical education illustrates how scientifically established procedures have failed to get into common practice. The majority of schools use no method at all for the classification of pupils or they use some outworn and unjustifiable technique.

Establishing objectives and levels of achievement, and the evaluation of accomplishments are some other problems that have been studied scientifically, but which are met in a large number of schools in a haphazard and inaccurate manner. Many other administrative problems can be solved in light of the proved data and tested knowledge that are available. It is the responsibility of teachers and administrators to become familiar with the scientifically established procedures in physical education and to use these methods in the solution of important problems.

Lines of responsibility. *Administration must set up a plan of organization which provides clear and direct lines of control and responsibility.* In public school systems and in colleges the entire program should be organized in a way to provide clearly defined lines of responsibility for administration and instruction. In each individual school or department this same plan should be followed. This would make it possible for the accepted aims and policies to be carried out efficiently with a minimum of friction and misunderstanding.

In a preceding paragraph of this chapter the different types of organization were described, and a *functional* form of organization was recommended as being sound in principle. This viewpoint stresses the fact that physical education should be primarily an educational and recreational activity and *not* a therapeutic, orthopedic, or public health procedure. This principle is emphasized in the following statement by Dr. J. H. McCurdy, formerly medical director, and dean of graduate courses at Springfield College.

The problems in health education, physical education, and athletics are largely outside the field of medical preparation and are not included generally in the real interests of those practicing in this field. The average physician desires to practice medicine rather than occupy his time in teaching and in varied administrative problems. If he gives his time to administration, health, physical education, and athletics, it unfits him for the medical service.

The ideal plan in the university and large college is an independent unit in medical service and another in health education, physical education, and athletics. A joint college committee on coordination of policies is desirable. In the small college the medical service is better handled by a regular practitioner who gives part time to college medical service.

The physical education field includes health education, physical activity, and competitive athletics. Health instruction requires a broad preparation in physiology and hygiene. Physical education assumes: (a) a thorough mastery of body mechanics including corrective exercise; (b) thorough preparation in teaching of physical activity and recreation skills; (c) coaching ability in some varsity sports. Athletic management requires large administrative ability. These three general fields, health, physical activity direction, and athletic management, are almost entirely outside the field of medical practice. *The combination of medical practice and physical education has proved impractical after a trial of forty years in the average college field.*[1]

The application of this principle to situations in public schools indicates that the principal of each school should be responsible for all activities which are carried on in his school. Directors of instruction or supervisors should function in the capacity of expert helpers to the principal and teachers, and should not assume any administrative authority. The line of administration extends from the board of education to the superintendent, principals, and teachers, and does not include the persons who are members of the supervisory staff.

Evaluation of results. *The means of appraisal and evaluation of the results of accepted policies and practices must be provided by administration.* Assume, for example, that a senior high school required all pupils to attend physical education classes for one hour, five days each week, during grades ten, eleven, and twelve. Another high school might require the pupils to take physical education only two days each week. Most physical education teachers would probably agree that the pupils who participated for five days each week would be benefited more than the ones who took part only two days each week. The unsupported opinion of the teachers is not an adequate means of evaluating the results of the instructional programs. To arrive at reasonably sound conclusions it would be necessary to measure the results of each program by means of valid and reliable measuring instruments. Snap-judgments, opinions based on isolated cases, and the biased or prejudiced reactions of individuals should not be used as means of appraising the success or failure of physical education programs.

It is the job of administration to make it possible for teachers to set

[1] J. H. McCurdy, "Recent Trends in Physical Education Leadership," *Journal of Health and Physical Education*, VI (December, 1935), 19.

up the machinery, and direct its operation, for the appraisal and evaluation by scientific techniques of the results secured through physical education.

Changes in policies and procedures. *Administration must expedite changes in policies and procedures when such changes are indicated by adequate evidence.* It happens sometimes that certain policies and procedures become entrenched and established so firmly that it is extremely difficult to change them. This often handicaps progress and improvement to a harmful extent. Good administrative technique should free educational policies and procedures from the impediment of unintelligent tradition and the influence of vested institutional interests.

The content and methods of the school curriculum should not remain fixed and static merely because they have been a certain way for a long time. Neither should they be changed just for the sake of change. We should always avoid confusing *change* or *speed* with *progress*. But if the available evidence indicates after careful consideration that changes are desirable, such changes should be made.

The long period of time during which the school program of physical education was composed almost entirely of formal gymnastics is an illustration of the tendency for policies and procedures to remain static. The insistence of teachers of athletics on emphasizing showmanship and intense competition in face of the apparent social need for emphasis on cooperation and social living is another example of the influence of vested interests in the schools.

Physical education has made much progress in philosophy and practice during the past two decades, but we still have a long professional climb to make. Sound administration should prevent physical education from becoming stagnant and fixed, and should make certain that the program and form of organization are flexible enough to encourage change and growth.

Adaptation and experimentation. *Administration must provide for adaptations, changes, and experimentation in the adopted policies and procedures and for the evaluation of the results of these adaptations, changes, and experiments.* One of the most effective means of insuring growth in physical education is to encourage experimentation and adaptation in regard to the accepted policies and procedures. Experimentation does not mean merely "trying out" something in an informal uncontrolled way. In order to determine the effect of an experimental factor, definite procedures must be planned and carried out under controlled conditions. It is also necessary that the results of the experiment be accurately measured.

Some people are opposed definitely to anything that appears to be an experiment or a change. In fact, in some cases the very idea of experimentation apparently arouses strong opposition to the suggested procedures. Attitudes such as these are in direct opposition to the ideals of intellectual curiosity, freedom of investigation, and growth through experience.

One of the main responsibilities of administration in physical education is to manage personnel and programs so that they will not get in a rut and that continual growth will be maintained. Being in a rut is the same thing as being in a grave with the ends knocked out, and an individual in such a situation may scramble along within the narrow confines of his walls but will never rise to any height of service or living unless he climbs out. Administration should help teachers and pupils to avoid this pitfall and should also help those who have become intellectually and professionally static to escape from their impediments and continue to grow.

Staff Cooperation. *Administration must provide for cooperative efforts and growth of all persons engaged in carrying out the school program.* Pulling at cross purposes, professional jealousies, and failure by different individuals to comprehend the importance of the entire program and the work of the whole department are some of the chief handicaps in many schools to close cooperation among members of the staff in carrying out the school program of physical education. Many teachers apparently fail to realize that if the entire school and department is a success, it will work to the advantage of all the individual staff members. Anything which hurts the reputation or standing of the department, or of any of the members of the staff, will also prove to be a disadvantage to every member of the faculty.

It devolves on administration, therefore, to secure the willing, conscious, and intelligent cooperation of all persons concerned in carrying out the physical education program. This involves mainly the members of the faculty; but it includes also business agents, stock room employees, bath attendants, caretakers, and other employees. Providing the means for all members of the organization to become familiar with all phases of the work of the department, and stimulating the staff to carry on professional study and growth while in service are two effective ways of helping to build a cooperative spirit.

[201]

Community relationships. *Administration should bring about the coordination and integration of the activities of teachers, pupils, and other individuals and organizations in the community.* Securing the enthusiastic cooperation of all members of the staff is of fundamental importance in the successful operation of the physical education program, but one's efforts at integration and coordination should extend beyond this point. It is of almost as much importance to coordinate the activities of the school and of certain groups in the community as it is to organize the work of the staff.

In most communities there are many individuals and organizations whose interests and programs touch in some way the school program of physical education. Among these are often public health authorities, Red Cross, playgrounds, recreation associations, sports writers, Tuberculosis Association, Congress of Parents and Teachers, Federation of Women's Clubs, Women's Christian Temperance Union, and various other philanthropic, health, and recreational groups.

In some places groups of this kind can make worthwhile contributions to the physical education program if their activities are guided wisely. It is clearly evident, of course, that they could also be the source of much friction and annoyance. To integrate and coordinate the activities of these groups so far as they apply to the school program is one of the significant problems in the administration of physical education. Intelligent effort should be directed toward their solution.

Interpretation of physical education. *The interpretation of physical education to the general public and to the members of the teaching body must be accomplished by administration.* Every individual assigns meanings to new experiences in terms of his past experiences. For this reason, physical education to some people means a football team, to others gymnastics and apparatus exercises, and to still others playground activities. Everyone has a background of experience that is unique and different from that of every other person. No two individuals have had exactly the same experiences or been influenced alike by their similar experiences.

In a democracy the schools must provide the kind of physical education programs that the majority of citizens in a community want. But it is the responsibility of the physical education teachers to make the citizens more intelligent about physical education and to make them want a better program. This process of raising the standards and appreciations of excellence among the population can be carried on most effectively by

[202]

means of an organized program of public relations designed to interpret and explain physical education.

One of the important functions of administration in public school systems and in colleges is to provide for the interpretation of physical education to the public and the teachers. There is probably no one administrative activity that will prove more helpful and beneficial in the long run to teachers and pupils. There is a well organized body of printed material on this problem with which teachers and administrators of physical education should be familiar.

Summary. Administration in physical education involves the integration of activities which are concerned specifically with providing educational experiences for pupils. This includes problems of the curriculum, teaching staff, equipment, and facilities. One of the main responsibilities of administration in physical education is to integrate the objectives of the program, the activities of the teachers and pupils, and the materials that are used.

The conception of administration as a functional process and *not* as a separate series of procedures, each organized into different units or compartments is recommended in this chapter.

The following principles are proposed as a foundation for administrative practice:

1. Administrative procedures must be consistent with a sound social philosophy and philosophy of education.

2. Administration must propose and support a definite statement of policies and aims.

3. Administration must be the means of making it possible for children to have experiences which will help accomplish the objectives of education. Administration should not be an end within itself.

4. Administration must provide and maintain adequate facilities and equipment for the physical education program.

5. The means, procedures and routine which are set up by administration should be based largely on tested knowledge.

6. Administration must set up a plan of organization which provides clear and direct lines of control and responsibility.

7. The means of appraisal and evaluation of the results of accepted policies and practices must be provided by administration.

8. Administration must expedite changes in policies and procedures when such changes are indicated by adequate evidence.

9. Administration must provide for adaptations, changes, and experi-

[203]

mentation in the adopted policies, and for the evaluation of the results of these adaptations, changes, and experiments.

10. Administration must provide for the cooperative efforts and growth of all persons engaged in carrying out the school program.

11. Administration should bring about the coordination and integration of the activities of teachers, pupils, and other individuals and organizations in the community.

12. The interpretation of physical education to the general public and to the members of the teaching body must be accomplished by administration.

QUESTIONS

1. What is the main responsibility of administration in physical education?
2. In what ways do the administration of education and of manufacturing differ?
3. What are the differences between *empirical* and *functional* types of administration?
4. How should physical education be organized in a city school system under a functional type of administration?
5. What should be the responsibility of administration in regard to the proposal and support of policies and aims?
6. What facilities and equipment for physical education should be provided?
7. What direct lines of control and responsibility should be set up for physical education by administration?
8. What should be the responsibility of administration for the appraisal and evaluation of policies and practices?
9. What viewpoint should administration assume in regard to experimentation?
10. What should be the responsibility of administration in regard to the interpretation of physical education?

REFERENCES

Hughes, William Leonard. *Administration of Health and Physical Education in Colleges.* New York: A. S. Barnes and Company, 1935.

Nash, Jay B. *The Administration of Physical Education.* New York: A. S. Barnes and Company, 1930.

Williams, Jesse Feiring, and Brownell, Clifford Lee. *The Administration of Health and Physical Education.* Philadelphia: W. B. Saunders Company, 1934.

INDEX

~

Ability to learn, **60**
Academic credit for physical education, 29
Academy, contributions of, 5
 influence of Benjamin Franklin on, 6
Acceleration of bodily growth, 37
Acquired characteristics, 36
Activities, motivation of, 177
 direction of by pupils, 184
Activity analysis, methods of, 142
Activity, developmental values of, 172
Adjustment activities, 60
Adjustment, 12
Administration, definition of, 190
 general function of, 190
 types of, 191
 a functional process, 192
 principles of, 194
 philosophy underlying, 195
 scientific basis of, 197
Administrative factors, influence on the curriculum, 152
Age, chronological, 41
 of development, 41
 educational, 41
 mental, 41
 physiological, 41
Aim, the meaning of, 139
 of physical education, 139
 of education, 140
American civilization, nature of, 77
Anatomical age, 41
Application of evolution to physical education, 34
Athletics, contests, 9
 the place of inter-institutional, 30
 danger in, 37
Attendance laws, 8
 effect on schools, 8
Attendant learnings, 185

Basic capacities, 47
Behavior, physical basis of, **99**
 motivation of, 102
Body mechanics, 22
Body types, 52
 classification of, 53
Bone tissue, 38
Boston English High School, 7
Breathing exercises, 20
Butler, President Nicholas Murray, 118

Calorie, 50
Cardinal principles, 7
Carnett, John B., 22
Causes of development in physical education, 2

Changes, in American society, **2**
 in policies, 200
Character, development, 23
 and personality development, 183
Characteristics, of society, 58
 of current society, 77
Child development, 33
Chlorophyll, 49
Chronological age, 41
Community relationships, 202
Compulsory, education, 7
 physical education, 25
Conflicting views, 18
Conformity, 12
Connectors, 42
Constancy of development, **39**
Control in classes, 183
Cooperation of staff, 201
Creative, activity, 59
 experience, 119
Credit for physical education, 29
Culture, evolving, 79
Curriculum, in physical education, 2
 of the Latin Grammar School, 5
 differentiation in, 27
 development of, 132
 basis of, 133
 principles of, 134
 social philosophy underlying, 134
 principles of the physical education, 135
 criteria for selection of content, 150
 the influence of social conditions on, 151
 the influence of administrative factors on, 152
 applying, 153

Davenport, studies of, 36
Deaver, G. G., 22
Decentralization, emphasis on, 111
Defects, of school children, 54
Demand, for teachers, 160
Democracy, ideals of, 10
 meaning of, 77
Democratic society, 10
Development, of physical education, 1
 of public education, 3
 of character, 23
 child, 33
 of man's body, 33
 of human skeleton, 36
 mental and physical, 39
 unsynchronized, 40
 age of, 41
 of leadership, 128
 of the curriculum, 132

[205]

Index